THE LAW ENFORCEMENT HANDBOOK

THIRD EDITION

DESMOND ROWLAND
&
JAMES BAILEY

ITP Nelson

an International Thomson Publishing company

Toronto • Albany • Bonn • Boston • Cincinnati • Detroit • London
Madrid • Melbourne • Mexico City • New York • Pacific Grove
Paris • San Francisco • Singapore • Tokyo • Washington

International Thomson Publishing
The ITP logo is a trademark under licence
www.thomson.com

Published in 1999 by
I︎T︎P︎® Nelson

A division of Thomson Canada Limited
1120 Birchmount Road
Scarborough, Ontario M1K 5G4

Canadian Cataloguing in Publication Data

Rowland, Desmond, 1936–1998
    The law enforcement handbook

3rd ed.
Includes index.
ISBN-13: 978-0-17-616647-2
ISBN-10: 0-17-616647-5

1. Law enforcement – Handbooks, manuals, etc.   2. Criminal investigation –
Handbooks, manuals, etc.   I. Bailey, James, 1947– . II. Title.

HV7921.R68 1999   363.2'3   C98-932668-3

Director, Higher Education	Michael Young
Acquisitions Editor	Jessica Mosher
Senior Editor	Rosalyn Steiner
Project Editor	Evan Turner
Senior Production Coordinator	Brad Horning
Marketing Manager	Kevin Smulan
Art Direction/Cover Design	Sylvia Vander Schee
Composition Analyst	Elaine Andrews

Printed and bound in Canada
4   WC   06

CONTENTS

List of Illustrations

Foreword

The Law Enforcement Handbook, Third Edition, is a practical, highly readable guide that covers every aspect of normal police duties, from street patrol to major criminal investigations. As such, it is a valuable resource for everyone involved in law enforcement: college students and recruits, veteran police officers and criminal investigators.

Des Rowland, its author, was a close friend, a respected colleague, and an excellent police officer. As one who served under his command, I can attest that he was the ideal teacher, generously sharing with others the theoretical and practical knowledge that he had gleaned during his many years of police service.

He began his policing career in 1955, at the age of 18, with the Royal Ulster Constabulary in Northern Ireland. Four years later, he joined the Bermuda Police Force. In 1961, Des came to Canada and joined the Toronto Township Police, the forerunner of the Peel Regional Police, as a constable.

In the years that followed, he rose swiftly through the ranks, serving in many capacities, including patrol officer, detective, and divisional commander. He led homicide investigations, negotiated with barricaded suspects, directed security for VIP tours, carried out executive duties at headquarters, and performed many other roles. He was the first Peel officer to graduate from the FBI National Academy. In short, his police career covered virtually every element of policing, from routine traffic duties to managing highly complex criminal investigations. Every task he undertook was accomplished with enthusiasm, dedication, and professionalism.

Des retired from Peel Regional Police as a superintendent in 1994. He immediately entered a new career as a law-enforcement professor at Sheridan College in Oakville, Ontario. His students were fortunate to be guided by a teacher who so willingly shared his vast experience with them. Everyone who knew him was deeply saddened when he passed away on June 26, 1998, after a brief, courageous battle against cancer.

There is no more fitting tribute to Des's memory as a leader and a mentor than the successes that have been achieved by those who served under him. Many have gone on to become chiefs and deputy chiefs in police services across Canada, including Jim Wingate, Barry King, Peter Young, Denis O'Neill, Jack Delcourt, Rick Zanibbi, Mike Pearson, Lou Lawson, and myself. I know of no other commander who could claim such a tremendous record of achievement in developing the capabilities of those serving under him.

Those of us who knew him personally and professionally recognize that this book is an affirmation of Des's strong belief in the right of every citizen to live in peace and security. It is a fitting legacy to a fine man and a dedicated police officer whose impact on his community and profession will be felt for many years to come.

CHIEF NOEL P. CATNEY
Peel Regional Police

Preface

When the first edition of this handbook was published in 1983, such words as "crack," "ice," "free-basing," "narco-terrorism," and "AIDS" were unknown; today, all represent major threats to society. In a world of frequent and dramatic changes in technology, social attitudes, and legal thinking, the police officer plays an increasingly important role in protecting the human values that are essential in a civilized society. While still found walking a beat, today's police officer may just as easily be working in such specialties as computer fraud, tactical assault, hostage negotiation, or electronic surveillance.

This book is designed to provide the basic grounding a police officer requires to perform effectively while carrying out the duties of a patrol officer or criminal investigator. Because the division between patrol and investigative duties varies considerably among police forces, and may not exist in smaller departments, I have decided to take a comprehensive approach that follows the officer from the initial stop of a suspect on the street to testimony in court. *The Law Enforcement Handbook,* Third Edition, can be used as a core text for recruit training, as a handbook for more experienced officers, as a training manual for security personnel without prior police experience, or as a resource book in university police science courses. A thorough mastery of the material presented in this book will provide the information required to handle virtually all normal police duties, up to and including major criminal investigations.

As the courts make ever more complicated rulings to expand the rights of the criminally accused, the police officer must also be a skilled practitioner of such diverse skills as legal interpretation, psychology, and forensic science. The days when police officers were hired because of their sheer physical size are long gone. Extensive interviews, background investigations, and sophisticated psychological screening have become an integral part of the selection process of most police departments. Today's police officer is a professional. To perform effectively in this highly demanding environment, the police officer requires a solid understanding of investigative techniques. He needs both theoretical and practical knowledge to be successful in his chosen career.

This book has been written to serve that need, based on almost four decades of experience as a police officer. I believe that, aside from a few minor differences, the essentials of effective police work are the same in all democratic countries. The specific legal requirements for the admissibility of confessions may appear different in certain jurisdictions, but human nature is the same everywhere. The successful interrogator in Vancouver will be using the same psychological techniques as his counterpart in Toronto while questioning a suspect. And, of course, the same level of scientific knowledge is available everywhere, limited only by the budget, training, and expertise of local police officers.

I have attempted to take a practical approach to the police profession. There are many works of fiction and nonfiction published each year about police officers, written by authors who have never spent a night shift in a patrol car or subdued a violent, gun-wielding offender. This is a book written by a former police officer, designed to provide detailed information and quick reference access. I should add that, in the interests of readability, I have referred to both police officers and suspects in the masculine gender throughout this book. This does not imply a failure to recognize the equally vital contribution of female police officers in the field of law enforcement.

Much of what you will read here is personal opinion, based upon extensive research and my own experiences with three police forces. I suggest that you look upon this book as a guide to the policing profession; the application of the methods that I've outlined should, of course, be guided by the policies and procedures of your own police service or organization, as well as the legal requirements in effect within your jurisdiction.

As police officers, you are front-line troops in the war against the forces that would destroy the right of your fellow citizens to live in peace and security. Yours is an honourable task, one that requires your best. You can only offer your best by constantly working to improve your knowledge and skills. It is my hope that this handbook will help you to meet that challenge as you pursue one of the world's most interesting, important, and satisfying careers.

DESMOND ROWLAND

Acknowledgments

The authors would like to thank the following Peel Regional Police officers for their invaluable contributions to *The Law Enforcement Handbook,* Third Edition: Inspector David Price; Detective Sergeants Roy Morrison, Roy Hancock, and Fred Lemieux; and Constables Pat Moyston, James Murtland, Jay Quinlan, and Stephen Rowland. Special thanks to Paul Taylor, Crown Attorney of Peel Region, and Steven Sherriff, General Counsel, Ontario Ministry of the Attorney General, for reviewing the manuscript and providing their guidance and expert counsel. Christine Bailey's work in preparing and indexing the manuscript is also greatly appreciated.

In addition, we remain grateful to those officers, serving and retired, who assisted us with the previous editions of this handbook, including James Wingate, Denis O'Neill, Daniel Banting, Rod Piukkala, Michael Metcalf, D'Arcy Honer, Alfred Thomas, Boyd Brown, and William Sholdice. We also thank Mrs. Lorna Mays, librarian of Peel Regional Police, for her generous assistance.

PART ONE

PATROL

1. WORKING THE STREETS

I. Introduction

A. Purposes of Patrol

In carrying out routine patrol duties, a police officer is expected to fulfil several key responsibilities to the community, including:

1. Protection of life and property
2. Enforcement of laws and regulations
3. Detection and arrest of offenders and wanted persons
4. Crime prevention through the deterrent effect of high police visibility
5. Providing assistance to the public by offering advice, information, and direction

B. Theories of Patrol

As in many areas of policing, there are conflicting theories regarding how the patrol function can be employed most effectively. Some experts believe that high police visibility discourages criminals by causing them to fear detection and arrest. Others believe that low visibility increases the opportunity to apprehend criminals by lulling them into believing that their crimes will not be detected.

On the street, the effective officer will use both approaches. To deter criminals, the officer will on some occasions make his presence obvious, for example, by conducting a slow motor patrol through a high-crime area. In different circumstances, the officer may deliberately conceal himself to test the reaction of suspects before and after they become aware of his presence.

Although today's police services conduct patrols on land, over water, and in the air, the two traditional categories of patrol, foot and motor, still predominate; each offers distinct advantages and disadvantages in meeting the needs of the community.

C. Types of Patrol

1. Foot Patrol

    a. Advantages

        (1) Greater personal contact with the public, which can lead to increased community support for the police

            (2) In-depth knowledge of the character and problems of the patrol area

            (3) Greater opportunity to develop sources of information

            (4) High visibility and regular presence discourages criminal activity and provides a greater sense of security to merchants, females, elderly persons, and other high-victimization groups

    b. Disadvantages

            (1) Low mobility, resulting in limited coverage of the patrol area

            (2) Low response time to telephone complaints

2. Motor Patrol

    a. Advantages

            (1) High mobility, which allows coverage of greater area

            (2) Fast response to telephone complaints

            (3) More effective street pursuit of offenders

            (4) More effective traffic enforcement

    b. Disadvantages

            (1) Low personal contact

            (2) Little opportunity to develop sources of information

            (3) High visibility of marked police vehicles offers little opportunity for surveillance

II. Preparation for Patrol Duties

A. Equipment Check

1. Police uniform
2. Weapons
3. Watch
4. Money, including change for pay telephones
5. Flashlight, spare battery, and bulbs
6. Gloves
7. Notebook with ample supply of blank paper
8. Forms *re* reports, traffic violations, etc.
9. Current list of stolen and wanted vehicles
10. Portable radio
11. Pager or mobile telephone
12. Ammunition (for outdated rounds)
13. Handcuffs and key
14. Monadnock, nightstick, asp
15. Whistle
16. Warrant card or ID card

17. Penknife (for cutting seatbelts of accident victims trapped in motor vehicles)

B. *Information Check*

1. Secure and review descriptions of missing and wanted persons.
2. Arrange any follow-up work from previous shifts.
3. Check with the officer being relieved for any problems requiring your attention during the shift.
4. Check patrol area log for problem areas requiring extra surveillance.

C. *Vehicle Check*

1. Walk around cruiser to check for any damage.
2. Briefly turn on and off all lights and emergency equipment to ensure they are in working order.
3. Test the MDT (mobile digital terminal) and radio.
4. Check the inside of your patrol car, paying particular attention to the rear seat.
5. A prisoner may have hidden a weapon or evidence in the vehicle during the previous shift.
6. During your own tour of duty, a prisoner might try the same manoeuvre. If you haven't checked the vehicle, any evidence you recover might be ruled inadmissible in court; you would be unable to swear that the vehicle was empty before the suspect entered it.
7. Record the condition of your vehicle's interior in your notebook for possible later use as evidence.

TIP: You may be able to use this knowledge to obtain evidence when you don't have the legal authority to search a suspect. Here's how:

Place your suspect in the rear seat of your patrol car. Walk a few steps away from the vehicle and pretend to write something in your notebook. If he believes you aren't watching him, the suspect will probably try to hide any contraband or illegal weapons on his person in, or under, the seat. After giving him a few minutes to complete this transaction, remove the suspect from the vehicle. Search the seat and retrieve any incriminating evidence that he may have "voluntarily" turned over to you.

On one occasion, I placed a subject claiming to be the victim of a drug rip-off in the rear seat of my cruiser to await further questioning. A few minutes later, upon checking the vehicle, I discovered that he had left several thousand tablets of LSD concealed under the rear seat.

In employing this strategy, keep alert—the suspect may try to swallow narcotics or papers in an attempt to conceal evidence.

8. Check your vehicle's siren, roof light, and other equipment to ensure that they are in proper working order. Note any damage or mechanical problems.

III. Covering the Patrol Area

A. *Attitude*

1. Always present an alert, businesslike, and disciplined appearance while on patrol.
2. Do not loiter on the street, in business places, or in parked cars.
3. Do not engage in lengthy, idle conversation.
4. Be flexible in patrolling your area.

   a. Do not follow a fixed route or schedule.

   b. Backtrack and change directions frequently.

   c. Report to your dispatcher or supervisor as soon as possible whenever you are required to leave your patrol area on unassigned duties.

B. *Communications*

1. Radio:

   a. The primary method of maintaining communications between headquarters and the officer on patrol, and between patrol units.

   b. Because of the high volume of radio traffic and limited channels available to most police departments, messages must be clear, brief, and to the point.

   c. Most police departments use the 10-code or similar code systems to ensure brevity and confidentiality of transmissions.

TIP: Know exactly what you want to say before opening the microphone for transmission. This precaution will avoid hesitations and long pauses, which block other officers' messages.

   d. Speak into the microphone using a normal voice and rhythm. There is no need to slow down your normal rate of speech or to raise your voice.

   e. Every time you exit your vehicle, call in with your location and purpose in leaving.

   f. When requesting a records check, provide only relevant information to the dispatchers: names, dates of birth, vehicle licence numbers, etc. General descriptions of suspects or vehicles are of no value in retrieving records information.

    g. If you suspect that licence markers have been switched or that a subject is using false identification, have the dispatcher read back the description or other information on file.

    h. If you receive no calls for a lengthy period of time, ask your dispatcher to do a test. If the button on your microphone is jammed, you may be treating your superiors and fellow officers to a revealing personal commentary that may not be appreciated.

    i. Interrupt another officer's transmission only in the case of an emergency.

    j. Do not use the police radio for casual conversations.

2. Telephone:

    a. A vital supplement to radio communications.

    b. Use the telephone for lengthy, detailed, or highly confidential exchanges of information.

    c. Learn the locations of all the operative pay telephones in your patrol area.

    d. Refrain from using wireless telephones for sensitive conversations.

C. *Sources of Information*

1. Develop contacts in your patrol area by adopting a friendly, approachable attitude.

    a. Be helpful and grant reasonable requests whenever possible.

    b. Don't accept favours or take actions not appropriate to your role as a police officer.

2. Useful sources of information:

    a. Commercial or industrial security officers

    b. Delivery people (milk deliverers, mail carriers, bakers, dry cleaners, etc.)

    c. Newspaper distributors

    d. Drivers who make night deliveries to newspaper boxes

    e. Clean-up and maintenance people

    f. Taxi drivers

    g. Persons who frequent certain locations in the area regularly, such as bus stops, all-night restaurants, etc.

    h. Neighbourhood gossips

    i. Juveniles

3. Conduct yourself in a dignified manner, but never appear uninterested when people come to you with their problems. You will discourage them from approaching you when they may have important information.

4. Vary your approach to potential sources of information, according to the circumstances.

   a. Businesspeople such as merchants, news vendors, and restaurant owners may usually be approached openly.

   b. Persons with criminal backgrounds or connections may fear being seen with a police officer. They may sometimes engage you in apparently meaningless or unnecessary conversation. This could be a sign that they have important information for you.

      (1) Continue talking to allow them to indicate their message verbally, or through gestures.

      (2) Warn the informant off and walk away if you perceive a potential problem for him. Your discretion and good sense will encourage future cooperation.

5. Use names, preferably first names, unless you feel the person would like to be addressed more formally. People like being addressed by name, and are more cooperative if they feel known and respected as individuals.

6. Maintain a reference file on all the persons you contact.

   a. Use your notebook or file cards.

   b. List the subject's name, nicknames, address, and the time and date of each contact, with a brief description of the incident.

   c. Classify your sources according to the types of information they may have, indicating the best approach to use to obtain it.

   d. If you use cards, file them alphabetically by last name. A geographic cross-index can also be helpful.

EXAMPLE: During a major investigation, detectives in our drug squad discovered that a young rookie officer had maintained an extensive file of contacts he had developed during his routine patrol duties. The drug squad traced several persons through leads he provided and made several important arrests. His information was directly responsible for cracking a major drug ring.

I awarded the officer a letter of commendation for his initiative.

7. Your sources will judge you on your honesty and sensitivity in handling the information that they reveal. Avoid violating that trust whenever possible.

8. Paid informants can be a valuable resource, but use caution.

   a. Some persons may become offended at your offer of payment for information.

   b. Funds for information are usually available only to officers in criminal investigation units such as robbery, homicide, and drugs.

    c. The informant's motivation may be suspect.

        (1) He may be seeking revenge.

        (2) He may wish to get into your good graces because he anticipates having problems with the police in the future.

        (3) He may be trying to cover his own crimes by blaming somebody else.

        (4) He may be low in funds and hope to sell you useless information.

    d. Your informant may also be selling the same information to another officer without your knowledge.

9. Your contacts can save your life.

    a. If they know you, they will tend to watch out for you.

    b. They may warn you if a dangerous individual is in the neighbourhood.

    c. They may come to your aid in a physical conflict in which you are outmatched.

10. Members of the "criminal element" who are not currently wanted can sometimes be useful informants.

    a. They may wish to ensure the arrest of a criminal whose actions have frightened or outraged them.

    b. They may consider police officers as "fellow players"—i.e., as individuals on the opposite side of the same game.

    c. They may hope to establish their good citizenship in your eyes by offering information.

NOTE: Their cooperation will usually evaporate if they feel you are harassing them unnecessarily. Show them respect, but avoid becoming overly reliant upon their information. You may have to take action against them someday.

11. Daily newspapers and other publications that carry sales advertisements for used cars, heavy machinery, etc., can help you keep on top of what is happening in your patrol area.

    a. Reports on current events can indicate potential problem areas.

    b. Advertisements about sales can identify businesses that will have large amounts of cash on hand.

    c. Want ads can assist in locating stolen property, particularly motor vehicles, stereo equipment, cameras, and furniture.

D. Foot Patrol Procedures

1. Don't fall into a routine for covering your beat.

      a. If you patrol your beat along certain streets and make regular stops at specific times and locations, criminals will soon learn your habits and take steps to avoid you.

      b. Turn corners as often as possible to avoid being followed.

      c. Refrain from taking meal or coffee breaks at the same time and place during your shift.

      d. Reverse the direction of your patrol often and at random.

      e. Take shortcuts through lanes and alleys.

2. Pause often during your patrol and look around you. If you aren't paying attention to your surroundings, you aren't patrolling, you're strolling.

3. Walk near the curb during daylight patrol. This technique offers:

      a. A better view for observing street activity

      b. Less chance of obstruction by pedestrians on the sidewalk if you are required to take quick action

      c. Higher police visibility as a crime deterrent

4. Walk near buildings during night patrol.

      a. Check the glass on store fronts for cracks or broken glass.

         (1) Keep your eyes to the front to avoid tipping off burglars that you are aware of their presence.

         (2) Use the reflections in store windows to "see around corners."

      b. Pause frequently in shadows to observe without being seen yourself.

      c. Check the interiors of buildings and rattle doorknobs to ensure that the premises are secure.

      d. Watch for persons loitering or hiding in doorways and entrances.

      e. Listen carefully for the sound of breaking glass.

E. *Motor Patrol Procedures*

1. Get out of your vehicle regularly to develop personal contacts in the neighbourhood.

2. Obey all traffic laws, for both safety and public relations reasons, unless you are en route to an emergency.

3. Maintain a cruising speed of 30 km/h during your patrol. This is slow enough to allow you to make detailed observations without impeding the traffic flow.

4. Recommended patrol patterns:

      a. Zigzag (start at one corner of the patrol area and work your way diagonally across it to the opposite corner)

    b.   Cross

    c.   Cloverleaf

5. If you are patrolling with a partner, divide the observation area around your vehicle so that:

    a.   The officer driving covers his field of vision in a clockwise direction from 6 o'clock to 4 o'clock.

    b.   The passenger officer covers the area in a counterclockwise direction from 6 o'clock to 8 o'clock.

    c.   The officer who is driving has responsibility for, and control of, the police vehicle. He must not allow his observations to interfere with its safe operation.

6. Don't fall into the habit of using only the main arteries in your area. Most criminal activity occurs out of sight of busy streets.

7. Check the potential trouble spots in your patrol area frequently.

8. Don't hide behind hills, curves, or signboards to trap traffic violators. This is bad public relations and serves to erode community confidence in the police sense of fair play.

9. Stop periodically among parked cars or at the entrance to side streets to observe activity on the street.

10. Check the occupants of vehicles that stop beside or behind you at intersections and keep an escape route open.

11. Check parking lots in your patrol area regularly for abandoned or stolen vehicles.

IV. Street Knowledge

A. *Definition*

1. A thorough geographic knowledge of the patrol area

2. An understanding of the character, fears, concerns, problems, and attitudes of the local residents

B. *Familiarization with the Patrol Area*

1. Know where you are at all times.

    a.   In remote areas or at night, you may have difficulty in determining an address or exact location.

    b.   If your location has no street address, know in what direction you are going from a fixed point of reference such as a local landmark.

    c.   Know all the significant buildings in your patrol area.

    d.   Be familiar with the address numbering system in your patrol area—i.e., in some cities, even-numbered addresses are on the west and south sides of streets, while odd-numbered buildings are located on the north and east.

e. Keep your knowledge up to date by noting road construction and temporary closures of streets that could become emergency response or escape routes.

f. In a residential or commercial area, you should always know the approximate street number of your location.

g. Learn to identify the vehicles that are regularly parked overnight in your area; this will help you to spot suspicious vehicles.

2. Study a local map to develop a broad understanding of the layout of your patrol area.

3. Regularly examine crime reports to determine:

    a. Neighbourhood crime patterns

    b. Areas reporting a high number of robberies or burglaries

    c. Addresses where violent domestic conflicts occur

    d. Likely sites for gang fights

    e. Locations of gang clubhouses and meeting places

4. Develop personal contacts (see "Sources of Information," page 5).

5. Seek information from fellow officers on:

    a. Organizations or groups that meet regularly in your area

    b. Industrial or commercial premises, including:

        (1) Who should be on the premises after business hours

        (2) Names of authorized private security agencies and their personnel

    c. Background information on potential informants, troublemakers, and suspected criminals living or working in the patrol area, including:

        (1) Names and aliases

        (2) Characteristics

        (3) Habits

        (4) Occupation

        (5) Type of criminal activity, e.g., bookmaker, car thief, shoplifter, etc.

    d. Closing times of banks, stores, and entertainment facilities such as theatres and restaurants

C. *Important Locations*

1. Hospitals, particularly emergency department entrances

2. All-night retail businesses, particularly pharmacies, supermarkets, and gas stations

3. Bus depots

4. Major arterial roads and highways
5. Hotels
6. Major industrial plants, factories, and business premises
7. Pay telephones
8. Bus routes
9. Government buildings
10. Apartment buildings
11. Buildings with distinctive names
12. Restaurants
13. Theatres
14. Cab stands
15. Start and end points of major streets
16. Parks and playgrounds
17. Schools
18. Churches
19. Banks
20. Animal shelters
21. Sanitary landfills (dumps)
22. Liquor and beer stores
23. Construction areas

D. *Potential Trouble Spots*

1. Public parks and playgrounds

    a.   These locations are frequented by child molesters, exhibitionists, and other sexual deviants.

    b.   They may also be the scenes of illicit drinking or drug use.

2. Bars and taverns

    a.   Some of these establishments may be hangouts for prostitutes, narcotics addicts, bookmakers, deviants, and other unsavoury types.

    b.   Because these locations are frequently the scenes of armed robberies, fights, and other confrontations, use extreme caution. Always look inside before entering and go in with a partner, if possible.

    c.   Avoid lengthy conversations with bartenders or customers.

3. Bowling alleys
4. Drive-in theatres
5. Drive-in restaurants
6. Strip bars
7. Rear of schools
8. Pool halls

9. Roller rinks
10. Boxcars parked on railway sidings

TIP: Obtain maps of shopping malls in your area to identify the quickest and safest routes to stores and licensed premises that are likely to be the scene of fights, shoplifting, and credit card frauds.

E. *Public Transportation*

1. Learn bus and streetcar routes and schedules in your patrol area.
2. Maps and schedules are often available from the local transit company.

F. *Assistance to Persons in Need*

1. Learn the location and operating hours of:

    a. Hostels
    b. Family and children's bureaus
    c. Detoxification centres
    d. Welfare agencies
    e. Salvation Army
    f. Rape crisis centres
    g. Automobile clubs
    h. All-night garages
    i. Legal aid
    j. Employment offices
    k. Alcoholics Anonymous
    l. Travellers' Aid
    m. Any other services in your area offering assistance to the public

G. *Emergency Routes*

1. Identify useful routes of travel throughout your area.
2. These routes should avoid congested areas and permit rapid response time to emergency calls, especially during rush hours.

H. *Hotels and Motels*

1. Get to know the night managers, desk clerks, and other staff of hotels and motels in your area. Secure their cooperation to examine guest registration files for wanted or missing persons.
2. Check the licence numbers of vehicles in garages and parking lots for stolen and wanted vehicles.

V. Developing Your Powers of Observation

A. *Use of the Five Senses*

1. Sight

    a. The visibility of an object depends upon:

(1) Distance from the observer
(2) Size of the object
(3) Illumination the object receives

b. Recognition parameters:

(1) A person with highly distinctive features will be recognized in daylight by friends and relatives at a distance of up to 100 m.

(2) A person who is not known well by the observer can be identified at a distance of up to 27 m (30 yd.) in daylight.

(3) An individual can rarely be recognized beyond 10–12 m when illuminated by a full moon.

c. Night vision, unlike daylight vision, uses the periphery of the retina to receive light.

(1) If you look directly at an object at night, it tends to fade away because the image strikes a "dead spot."

(2) To examine an object in these circumstances, look slightly above, below, or to one side of the object.

d. The position of the observer in relation to the person or object viewed can affect his perception considerably.

(1) A seated person looking up will usually overestimate the height of a person standing beside him.

(2) Keep this factor in mind in recording descriptions from witnesses and identifying suspects.

e. Most observers see what they expect to see.

(1) If you view a familiar scene, you will often mentally insert missing items to fill in the gaps in your perception.

(2) Be aware that you may have adopted a mind set about certain locations or situations, and be alert to anything that is unusual or out of place.

2. Hearing

a. Hearing can be an important aid in identifying persons, places, and things.

b. Learn to recognize and differentiate between such sounds as:

(1) Activity noises (hammer pounding, glass breaking, footsteps, animals calling, etc.)

(2) Voices (volume, pitch, accents, intonation, etc.)

(3) Motors (drills, electric saws, foreign and domestic automobile engines, trucks, etc.)

(4) Firearms (pistols, rifles, shotguns, automobile backfires)

3. Smell

   a. Learn to distinguish between such potentially dangerous odours as:

     (1) Gasoline

     (2) Natural gas

     (3) Gunpowder (dynamite)

     (4) Coal oil and petroleum products

     (5) Other inflammable or explosive fumes or mixtures

     (6) Gas and fumes that might endanger life or health, e.g., chlorine, natural gas, etc.

   b. Remember that certain substances such as gas and ether may temporarily deaden your sense of smell and cause you to be unaware of additional dangers at the scene of fires, chemical spills, and other hazardous incidents.

   c. If you smell burning materials, particularly on the night shift, locate the source as quickly as possible. You may be able to prevent a major fire.

4. Touch

   a. The sense of touch can be helpful in:

     (1) Examining doors and windows in the dark

     (2) Checking tires, engines, or mufflers for warmth to determine if a car has been running recently

     (3) Identifying some types of cloth and paper, e.g., counterfeit money

   b. Touch can sometimes provide vital information that would be difficult to obtain any other way in the field, e.g.:

     (1) Feeling walls or glass surfaces for the heat from an unseen fire, or for vibrations created by sound, movement, or tools during a burglary in progress

     (2) Checking the pulse or heartbeat of an unconscious crime or accident victim

5. Taste

   a. Although the use of your sense of taste may occasionally prove convenient in identifying a substance, use EXTREME caution.

   b. NEVER taste any substance that may be a narcotic or poison

EXAMPLE: While searching a drug addict's residence, you might find a jar containing a white, powderlike substance that he claims is sugar. You suspect he is lying and the substance is heroin or cocaine.

By tasting the substance, you may quickly discover that he was only half-lying. The substance is sugar—laced with LSD.

You won't enjoy the trip.

B. Observation Skills

1. Description of persons:

    a. During your patrol, frequently examine pedestrians who walk past you and mentally record their appearance, including estimated height and weight, hair colour, clothing, facial features, etc.

    b. Double back and determine how close your mental record is to the subject's true appearance.

    c. Gradually cut back on the time you take to study the subject, and lengthen the time between your initial observation and your re-examination of the subject.

2. Descriptions of objects: Use the same technique to recall the items on display in store windows or other locations containing a variety of objects.

3. Discuss with other officers what events or characteristics arouse their suspicions about specific situations or persons.

4. Review your own arrest reports for the same purpose.

5. Study photographs, set them aside, then write out lists of the persons or objects they contained. Compare your lists with the photographs.

6. Interview persons in custody.

    a. Ask about their methods of operation.

    b. Encourage them to brag about the methods they used to elude police in the past. Avoid falling for the same tricks yourself.

7. Study a book on memory improvement to learn techniques that will assist you in recalling detailed observations.

VI. Checking Business Premises

A. Preparations

1. If your department doesn't have a store file or merchant index, create one for your personal use. The idea might catch on. Use it to record:

    a. Name and address of business

    b. Name, address, and telephone number of keyholder (person to be notified in case of emergency)

    c. Alternate keyholder's name and phone number

    d. Usual business days and hours of operation

   e.   Name and phone number of security company, if any
   f.   Date last checked

2. Learn the interior layouts of all stores in your area that are likely
   burglary targets so that you will know if something is out of place.
   A burglar may place a partition or a display counter in front of a
   safe to shield him from the view of passersby.

3. Pay close attention to:

   a.   The location and type of safes, cash registers, and alarm systems
   b.   The routine habits of the staff
   c.   Opening and closing times
   d.   The methods of locking windows and doors

4. Get to know the janitors and maintenance staff working on business premises in your area.

   a.   They know the buildings they work in intimately and can
   provide you with useful information.
   b.   Their legitimate presence in a building after normal working
   hours offers them a cover to commit thefts and burglaries on the
   premises or in neighbouring offices and factories.
   c.   Criminals often use coveralls and maintenance uniforms as
   disguises to gain entry to buildings, and to deceive police officers
   when they are confronted.

B. Precautions

  1. Approach the building quietly in your vehicle, ensuring that you
     do not squeal tires when turning corners or coming to a stop.
  2. When you leave the police vehicle to check premises, never
     travel more than two blocks on foot.
  3. While out of your vehicle, you should maintain a 360-degree
     awareness as you proceed with your security check.
  4. Take advantage of the darkness by walking close to the building
     and remaining in shadow.
  5. Don't allow your keys, flashlight, whistles, or other equipment to
     dangle loosely.
  6. Watch for unfamiliar vehicles.
  7. Take short, light steps.
  8. Check the rear doors and windows first.
  9. Minimize the use of your flashlight. Hold it out at arm's length to
     present a false target to armed burglars.
 10. Check vacant buildings for missing children, vagrants, fugitives,
     etc.

C. *Checking a Building*

1. Don't check all the doors in any business district at one time. Cover a portion, move to another area, and return to the original district to surprise any offenders who may have moved in behind you.
2. Always look for the unusual and out of place.
3. When checking doors, examine the hinges carefully before grasping the handle. If the door is partially latched and pulled in the wrong direction, it will lock; you will be unable to determine if there has been an illegal entry.
4. When checking windows, attempt to push them open and look around the edges for toolmarks.
5. Check skylights if they are easily accessible.
6. Check sidewalk elevators and gratings for signs of tampering, removal, or damage.
7. If the night or alley lights are not illuminated and appear to have been broken or tampered with, call for assistance immediately before checking further.
8. Don't walk down the middle of an alley or corridor; you may be silhouetted against any light source behind you.
9. If safe lights are not lit or appear to have been moved, use extreme caution. If you are alone, call for assistance. Safecrackers are a dying breed, but those who still practise this craft are often armed, experienced criminals.
10. Inspect *all* possible points of entry, including roofs and any locations where tunnels might have been dug. Use your flashlight to check for fresh pry marks around locks.
11. Be alert to the absence of animals such as alley cats or dogs that normally frequent the area. They may have been scared off by a prowler.

D. *Insecure Premises*

1. Be aware of any movement inside the premises, e.g., flashlight beams, footsteps, the sound of doors opening, etc.
2. Once you find anything out of the ordinary, call for assistance, both as a backup and as your witness in the event property is missing.
3. Conduct a thorough examination of the premises.
4. Lock the door upon leaving.
5. If your department has an official "notice of insecure premises" card, leave it inside in a visible place.

6. Do *not* hang it on the outside door handle or place it in a location where it can be seen from outside.
7. If you cannot lock the door, contact the owner.
8. Note the date and time of your inspection in your notebook and fill out any departmental form that may be required.
9. If the store has been burglarized, notify your dispatcher and the owner immediately.
   a. Remain at the scene until the owner or his representative arrives.
   b. Do not allow the owner to check the premises himself.
10. Avoid entering a room with a light source to your rear. You will present a silhouette in the darkness that will make you an excellent target.

VII. Suspicious Persons

A. Identification

1. Suspicious persons can be identified by their:
   a. Appearance
   b. Conduct
   c. Attitude
   d. Presence in unusual or inappropriate locations
2. They are often seen loitering about stores, warehouses, banks, service stations, bus stations, schools, theatres, railway stations, and hotels for no readily apparent reason.

B. Examples

1. Persons who engage children in lengthy conversations
2. Persons who appear to be following women whom they do not know
3. Persons carrying boxes, bags, and suitcases late at night in prosperous residential neighbourhoods
4. Persons carrying expensive stereos or television sets that they claim are being taken for repair when there are no repair shops in the vicinity
5. Persons who continually look into parked cars
6. Persons who are seen moving plates from one vehicle to another
7. Persons who make a special effort to avoid encountering a police officer
8. Persons who appear too nonchalant in the vicinity of a police officer, e.g., by staring straight ahead or making other obvious attempts to ignore his presence

9. Persons who appear to be tampering with vehicles
10. Persons driving vehicles that they don't seem familiar with
11. Persons operating commercial vehicles such as trucks or vans in residential or industrial areas after normal business hours
12. Persons who are walking in areas that do not have public transit service, and who do not appear to have a motor vehicle available
13. Persons selling products or services that do not seem in keeping with their appearance or with the neighbourhood they are working in
14. Persons loitering or prowling on dark streets, in alleys, or around residences
15. Persons who go to extraordinary lengths to prove to you that they have "nothing to hide"
16. Persons carrying goods in shopping bags in the late evening hours when stores are normally closed

NOTE: Be extremely cautious of strangers who attempt to engage you in lengthy or unnecessary conversation. They may be attempting to divert your attention from a crime in progress.

VIII. Suspicious Situations

A. Warning Signs

1. Vehicles parked improperly or with the motor running outside banks, stores, or other business premises. They could be getaway cars for crimes in progress.
2. Stacked boxes or ladders placed against the side or rear of buildings.
3. Store or business interiors in which large pieces of furniture or displays have been moved. This may indicate an attempt to conceal a tunnel or safecracking operation.
4. Banks or stores where people are seen entering but not leaving. This could indicate a holdup or hostage situation.
5. Parked vehicles in which persons are apparently sleeping. These subjects may be lookouts or missing or wanted persons seeking shelter, or they may be attempting suicide.

TIP: A stolen car that is found abandoned may be the "switch" car to be used in a getaway attempt from a robbery or other major crime. If you find a stolen car parked in an unusual place, notify your dispatcher and maintain surveillance on the vehicle from a concealed location before calling for a tow truck to take the vehicle into custody. Make the arrest if suspects appear on the scene to switch vehicles.

6. Any other activity or situation that does not reflect normal behaviour or routine activity.

B. *Criminal Subterfuges*

1. Criminals may try to lull you into thinking nothing is happening while a crime is in progress.
2. To counteract such tactics:
   a. Watch for reflections in store windows.
   b. Check your rear-view mirror as you drive past the scene where criminal activity may be taking place.
   c. Pretend to write reports or notes while keeping suspects in view.
3. Possible intentional distractions:
   a. Faked fights or arguments that erupt "spontaneously" as you approach
   b. Couples amorously intertwined in parked cars (they may be lookouts)
   c. Persons who encourage a crowd to gather by giving speeches expressing outrageous political or religious views
   d. Any person who attempts to attract police attention for no apparent reason
   e. Persons breaking away from a group
4. In these situations, approach slowly and deliberately, keeping all parties involved in view as long as possible.
5. Never rush blindly into the situation. Stay out of reach of the subjects and make your presence known by calling out.
6. Scan the surrounding area for signs of suspicious activity.

C. *"Gut Feelings"*

1. Do not ignore your so-called gut feelings.
2. Hunches are often important messages or warnings that are based upon information or experience recorded in your subconscious mind.
3. Although they may not seem logical, your hunches will often prove to be correct. They should be acted upon—with discretion—in appropriate circumstances.

IX. Public Hazards

A. *Examples*

1. Vacant buildings that juveniles may use as a playground
2. Ditches or open holes, particularly at construction sites, where deep water has accumulated

3. New construction
4. Unfenced swimming pools
5. Abandoned wells or shafts
6. Old refrigerators with locks
7. Utility poles that are mounted with cleats close to the ground
8. Unattended construction machinery
9. High scaffolding that can be reached by ladder
10. Storage magazines for explosives (often stored in steel boxes in open fields near construction sites; check to ensure that the boxes are locked and that all safety regulations are being complied with)
11. Defective roadways, street lights, or sidewalks
12. Obstructed fire escapes
13. Broken water mains (can cause a roadway to sink)
14. Leaking gas mains (danger of explosion)
15. Any object or situation that may present a hazard to children

B. Courses of Action

1. Contact the owner of the property and the appropriate government agencies.
2. If the owner is reluctant to make improvements because they are not required by law or municipal regulations, point out the severe consequences he would face in a successful civil action for damages.
3. Warn youngsters who live or play in the vicinity, and their parents, of the danger that the hazard presents.
4. If necessary, request approval from your superior to secure the area from public access until action has been taken to eliminate the hazard.

2. ON THE RECORD

I. Notebooks

A. The Limitations of Memory

1. Psychological studies have shown that the subconscious mind absorbs nearly 100 percent of the information it receives from the five senses of sight, hearing, touch, taste, and smell.
2. Immediately after an event, the conscious mind can recall only 10–30 percent of the impressions that the subconscious has received.
3. When the human memory is refreshed by notes or tape recordings, the conscious mind can recall about 75 percent of the information received.

B. The Mechanics of Note-Taking

1. All notes should be in your own handwriting.
2. Notes should be made at the time of your observations or as soon after as possible.
3. Your notes for each tour of duty should include:
   a. Date (preferably underlined)
   b. Time you began duty
   c. Nature of duties, e.g., routine patrol, prisoner escort, etc.
   d. Car number or patrol area
   e. Important radio messages or bulletins
   f. Names of all persons you came into contact with during the shift
   g. Rough sketches and detailed notes of all scenes you attended
   h. Weather conditions
   i. Lighting conditions
   j. Time you reported off duty
4. Record the names of *everyone* you speak to, not just the witnesses who agreed to give you information.
   a. Some persons have been known to tell police they didn't see anything, then appear in court with a detailed account of the incident that exonerates the accused.

b. Your notation that the witness claimed he had seen nothing when questioned at the scene can make an invaluable contribution to destroying his credibility.

c. If a witness's statement is doubtful, indicate that in your notebook. This will save the investigators wasted time checking out an unreliable story.

5. As a general rule, use only one type of pen to make notes. If your pen runs out of ink during note-taking and you are forced to change pens, the appearance of a different ink in your notebook could lead to a defence allegation that you had filled in your comments long after the event to support the prosecution's theory of the crime.

6. Do not erase any entries in your notebook.

a. Draw a fine line through the notation to be corrected, ensuring that you do not block out your original writing.

b. Initial the start point and end point of your correction.

7. Do not make personal notes, doodles, or other writings unrelated to your police duties in your notebook.

8. To avoid problems during cross-examination, clearly label your opinions as opinions.

EXAMPLE: If you are called to a death scene, unless the victim's death is obvious from the circumstances, e.g., decapitation or severe decomposition, you should make a notation that he *"appeared dead."* Similarly, if you believe that a suspect was intoxicated at the time of his arrest, your notebook should indicate the various symptoms of drunkenness that he displayed, rather than a flat declaration that he was intoxicated.

9. Abbreviations can be useful in reducing the length of your notes, but they should be consistent to avoid confusion and possible challenge in court.

a. If you use "S" to refer to the suspect, be sure to identify him clearly in the first reference in your notebook. Additional suspects can be identified as "S1," "S2," etc.

b. Other abbreviations:
    (1) W   = witness
    (2) C   = complainant
    (3) V   = victim
    (4) V.L. = vehicle licence number
    (5) ARR = arrest
    (6) A.I. = accident investigation

      (7) P.I. = person investigated

      (8) C.V. = condition of vehicle

  c. Use the radio 10-code system, Criminal Code section numbers, and other short forms where appropriate.

10. In preparing your notes, concentrate on developing an accurate, unbiased, and detailed record of the information you received or gained through personal observation.

  a. Always attribute information to its source, e.g., name of witness, weather bureau, departmental files, etc.

  b. Be careful not to record opinions or conclusions as fact.

EXAMPLE: You are dispatched to the scene of a sudden death. Upon arrival you note the time in your notebook as being 2130 hours and are advised by a bystander that the victim died about 10 minutes earlier. If you record the time of death in your notebook as 2120 hours, with no further comment, you might have great difficulty at a trial six months or a year later if you are asked to explain your notation. The forensic evidence might contradict your testimony.

Instead, your notebook should indicate your time of arrival and a notation of the name of the bystander and his statement that he had seen the victim die 10 minutes earlier. This is an accurate record of the information you received, not a conclusion based upon an unsubstantiated statement.

  c. Record key oral statements from witnesses as they were given, using quotation marks to indicate exact quotes.

11. Always note whether dates, times, or figures are exact or approximate.

12. Make your notes as detailed as possible.

  a. You can never fully reclaim a critical moment when all the facts were at your disposal but you failed to record them.

  b. Extra detail that is not apparently relevant to the specifics of your case can sometimes prove helpful in establishing your credibility.

EXAMPLE: During the trial of a drunk driver, I recited the familiar phrases that the accused had "bloodshot eyes" and "slurred speech," and was "unsteady on his feet" when I arrested him. The bored judge commented that my testimony was "the same old evidence." The defence lawyer, however, insisted upon reading my notes. When the judge looked them over, he read how the accused had left his car in gear when he got out to speak with me. I had been forced to chase it on foot, jump in, and apply the brakes to bring it

to a halt. The judge laughed, then registered a conviction against the driver. In this case, the extra detail in my notebook that had not been offered in evidence gave credibility to my testimony and established that I had not attempted to "get" the accused.

13. Begin every notation by recording the weather conditions at the time the notes were made. Defence lawyers routinely ask a question about the weather during cross-examination to test your powers of recall.

TIP: Before using a tape recorder to make notes, you may wish to consider these factors. You can't *see* what you have recorded so you may omit important details or duplicate information that you have already noted. You will often have to transcribe your notes, resulting in an unnecessary, time-wasting second step. In addition, a defence lawyer may require you to produce the tape recording of your notes in court, complicating your case considerably.

C. The Value of Notes

1. Notes can identify suspects who might otherwise go undetected.

EXAMPLE: You stop a delivery van driving through a residential neighbourhood late at night for a minor traffic violation. The driver identifies himself as a local resident who uses this vehicle to transport heavy objects to his cottage. You have no reason to search the vehicle or detain the subject, so you give him a verbal warning and return to your patrol. You do, however, record the incident and the identity of the driver in your notebook.

Later you discover that a serious sexual assault occurred a few kilometres away 20 minutes before you stopped the vehicle. The descriptions of the rapist and the driver of the suspect vehicle are similar. Although your reason for stopping the vehicle had nothing to do with the crime, you have now identified a suspect and established that he had the means and the opportunity to commit the crime.

If the suspect claims that he was home in bed when the offence occurred, your notes of an apparently innocuous traffic stop will destroy his alibi.

2. Your notes about seemingly unrelated events may eventually establish a pattern of criminal activity in your patrol area that will lead to the identification and arrest of a suspect.

EXAMPLE: In reviewing your notes over the course of several weeks, you notice that you have stopped several vehicles whose occupants were juveniles attending the same high school. These stops often occurred in neighbourhoods experiencing a high rate of break-ins.

In this case, through further investigation, your notes could lead to the arrest of a house-breaking gang.

3. Your notes could link together suspects who might not be connected in any other way.

EXAMPLE: You encounter two men late at night acting in a suspicious manner near a shopping centre. They respond cooperatively to your questions, and you have received no reports of a break-in in the area, so you allow them to go on their way.

Several weeks later, you learn that one of the subjects has been arrested at the scene of a burglary attempt, but a second unknown accomplice escaped. Your notes now reveal the identity and address of a possible second suspect.

D. *Creating a Complete Suspect Description*

1. As a patrol officer, you must have the ability to use your imagination to create an accurate word-picture of a suspect.

    a. You must also be able to transmit this image to others so that they can visualize the suspect through your description of his unique mannerisms, actions, or physical characteristics.

    b. The routine description "male, white, 25–30 years, blond hair, wearing a brown leather jacket" is virtually useless unless an officer happens to spot the suspect in the vicinity immediately after a crime has occurred.

    c. Unless the description identifies a specific person, it is normally of little value.

TIP: Many officers include in their notebooks a checklist that includes many of the descriptive elements needed for a good I.D.

2. Basic suspect/subject description checklist:
    a. Name
    b. Aliases
    c. Sex
    d. Race
    e. Nationality, if known
    f. Height
    g. Weight
    h. Colour of eyes
    i. Colour of hair
    j. Complexion
    k. Obvious distinguishing characteristics, e.g.:
        (1) Stammer
        (2) Limp

      (3) Facial scars
      (4) Unusual haircut
      (5) Blemishes
      (6) Unusual style of dress

NOTE: In taking a description, there is little point in noting the characteristics or features that the subject shares with most other human beings, e.g., "average height, average build, clear complexion," etc. To pinpoint your man and make him stand out from the crowd, you must know those things that are different and distinctive about him. It is the stammer that will identify your suspect, not the lack of a stammer.

Illustration 1

KEY WORD CHART FOR SUSPECT DESCRIPTIONS

a. **Build**

1. large
2. obese
3. stocky
4. medium/average
5. slender
6. thin
7. muscular/athletic

b. **Posture**

1. normal
2. very straight
3. military bearing
4. stooped
5. head protrudes
6. hunches over

c. **Complexion**

1. florid
2. ruddy
3. sallow
4. pale
5. fair
6. dark
7. clear
8. pimpled
9. blotched

d. Hair

1. colour—blond, red, strawberry, sandy, brown, black, grey, greying, bleached, dyed, etc.
2. thick or thin
3. curly
4. wavy
5. long
6. short
7. haircut or style
8. parted on left or right
9. thinning or balding
10. bald—completely, frontal, occipital
11. sideburns—long, bushy, grey

e. Face

1. Forehead—high or low, protruding or receding, wide or narrow, widow's peak
2. Eyes—colour (blue, grey, black, hazel/green, maroon, etc.), large, average or small, wide-eyed, watery, glassy, sunken, squinty, glasses (round, square, granny, type of frames, gold, silver, plastic, colour, horn-rimmed, etc.), artificial, crossed, wears contact lenses
3. Eyebrows—colour, thin, thick, bushy, sparse, plucked, up or down slant, arched, wavy, connected, pencilled, short or long hairs
4. Nose—large, small, pug, hooked, straight, Roman, flat, broken, angled to right or left, upturned, downturned, large or small nostrils, flared, bumps, scratches, freckles, pimples
5. Mustache—colour, shape, short, stubby, long, handlebar, Zapata, ends turned up or down, pointed, drooping, covers upper and lower lip
6. Beard—colour, size, shape, full, sparse, Vandyke, goatee, sideburns
7. Mouth—large, small, full or thin lips, drooping or upturned corners, open or crooked, any distortions during speech or laughter, harelip, puffy, cold sores, dry or moist
8. Teeth—large, small, colour, straight or projecting, even or uneven, apparent fillings, gold teeth, missing teeth, false teeth, broken, other dental work

9. Ears—small, large, covered by hair, close to head or projecting out, pierced, any earrings, long, short or no earlobes, cauliflower ears, clean or waxy
10. Chin—small, large, square, pointed, double chin, dimple, jutting, receding, flat, cleft
11. Shape—long, round, fat, thin, square, triangular, pear-shaped
12. Cheeks—high cheekbones, prominent cheekbones, pockmarked, freckles, blemishes
13. Distinguishing marks—moles, warts, pimples, acne scars, freckles, harelip, drooping eyelid

f. **Neck**

1. long
2. short
3. thick
4. thin
5. puffed
6. folds in back of neck
7. prominent or no Adam's apple
8. bull neck

g. **Shoulders**

1. broad
2. narrow
3. square
4. round
5. sloping
6. one lower than other

h. **Stomach**

1. flat
2. prominent
3. firm
4. soft-looking
5. spare tire

i. **Chest**

1. muscular
2. flat
3. indented
4. thin
5. buxom

j. Hands

   1. small

   2. large
   3. rings—type, colour, finger(s) worn on
   4. fingers—long or short, missing, nicotine stains, nails bitten
   5. liver spots
   6. protruding veins
   7. hairy or clear

k. Arms

   1. muscular
   2. thin
   3. hairy
   4. tattoos

l. Visible scars

   1. length
   2. location
   3. horizontal, vertical, or diagonal

m. Walk

   1. slow or fast
   2. long or short strides
   3. lumbering, shuffling, or bouncy gait

n. Dress

   1. neat, unkempt, or slovenly
   2. conservative or loud
   3. work clothes or business suit
   4. cheap or expensive
   5. wears hat—type
   6. shoes or boots—type and style
   7. any peculiarities of dress
   8. preference for certain colours

o. Jewellery

   1. kind
   2. where worn
   3. type of metal

    4. type of stones
    5. cheap or expensive

p. Tattoos

    1. initials

    2. name(s)
    3. words or phrases
    4. pictures or designs
    5. gang symbol
    6. numbers

q. Speech

    1. slow or rapid
    2. clear or mumbling
    3. any impediments—lisp, stutter, etc.
    4. type of accent
    5. effeminate or heavily masculine
    6. falsetto
    7. rasping
    8. loud or soft
    9. particular expressions or style of speech used

r. Habits

    1. clean or dirty
    2. chews gum, tobacco, etc. (brand)
    3. smokes—cigar, cigarette, pipe, brand, uses cigarette holder
    4. drinks—beer, type of liquor, wine, brand
    5. addicted to drugs—heroin, speed, etc.
    6. gambling—horses, cards, dice, etc.
    7. frequents pool halls, dance halls, taverns, discos, massage parlours, nightclubs
    8. goes to movies—type, favourite actor or actress, etc.

s. Diseases—any chronic disease: tuberculosis, ulcers, AIDS, diabetes, herpes, etc.

t. Disabilities—mental (specify), limbs or digits missing, stiffness, lame, broken arms or legs improperly healed, deafness, visually impaired, perceptual handicaps (mirror-reading, colour-blindness, etc.), crutch or cane, casts or bandages

u. Relatives—names and addresses

v. Known associates

    1. male and female—names and addresses, nicknames, aliases

    2. people who might know his whereabouts or other associates

w. Organization memberships—fraternal, political, social, trade, professional, etc.

x. Pastimes—hobbies, sports, academic or vocational studies

y. Other distinguishing features or peculiarities

    1. nose or eye twitch

    2. sexual perversions

    3. bad table manners

    4. gourmet

    5. never wears a hat

    6. always wears a certain type of hat

    7. clicks teeth while talking

    8. smacks or licks lips

    9. gestures with hands when talking

    10. poker-face

    11. shifty-eyed

    12. fast or slow driver

    13. preferred type of car

    14. introvert or extrovert

    15. bowlegged, pigeon-toed, knock-kneed

    16. any superstitions—refuses to walk under ladders, member of bizarre cult, etc.

TIP: Train yourself to perceive the more subtle nuances of appearance and behaviour. Use the Key Word Chart to work up detailed descriptions of several people you know well. When you meet them again, make a mental note of the distinguishing characteristics that you missed and the details in your description that were erroneous or misleading.

E. *Property Descriptions*

1. A property description should permit anyone who has read the description to pick the subject article out of a collection of similar articles.

EXAMPLE: A description such as "man's gold wristwatch, Rolex, with gold band" is virtually useless in identifying the object.

The description should read "man's gold wristwatch, Rolex, Oysterdate model, heavy scratches on crystal, gold expandable band, with date indicator in 3 o'clock position on face, engraved 'John, 1999' on back."

2. Although no list of characteristics will apply to all types of property, consider the following in preparing a description:

    a. Type of article
    b. Brand name
    c. Model name
    d. Serial number
    e. Identifying stains, marks, or scratches
    f. Colour
    g. Size
    h. Approximate weight
    i. Country where manufactured
    j. Optional equipment attached
    k. Any other special features

II. Reports

A. Clarity and Accuracy

1. As a police officer, your responsibility in preparing reports is to inform by stating clearly and accurately what happened and what you did.
2. You are not expected to be a creative writer in your reports. Use short, simple words and phrases that can be easily read and understood.
3. As a general rule, use the following grammatical pattern in writing sentences:
4. Subject (noun or pronoun)—Predicate (verb)—Object (noun or pronoun).
5. Use subordinate clauses where necessary, but keep them brief and to the point, e.g., "After questioning the suspect, I placed him under arrest on a charge of robbery."
6. Choose clear, familiar words in writing your sentences, e.g., *use* instead of *utilize; enough* instead of *sufficient; found out* instead of *ascertained.*
7. Sentence length should average between 15 and 20 words.

    a. To give a complex explanation, write two or three sentences rather than one long sentence.

Illustration 2
SAMPLE NOTEBOOK PAGE

	FRIDAY JANUARY 1ST 1999
	1400 - 0000 HRS
	AFTERNOON SHIFT
	CAR 22
	PORTABLE 7167
	AREA 12311
	LUNCH 1900
	WEATHER LIGHT SNOW
	ROADS WET/SLIPPERY
	VISIBILITY CLEAR
1400	REPORT FOR DUTY
	12 DIVISION
ZONE ALERT	PARADE
	STOLEN AUTO
	1997 FORD MUSTANG
	2 DOOR BLACK
	OWNERSHIP/INSURANCE IN
	VEHICLE ONTARIO MARKER
	PLATE DEZ 932
	NO CULPRIT INFORMATION

b. Not all sentences have to obey the 15–20 word rule, which is only an average. Vary sentence length to create more interest.

8. Personalize your writing.

a. Use a phrase like "I believe this action is necessary" rather than "It is believed that this action is necessary."

b. Use first person rather than third person. For example, "This officer is of the opinion that ..." sounds pretentious and overly formal. Instead, write "We recommend that ..."

9. Use a conversational style that is concise but grammatically correct. For example, "Upon exiting my police vehicle, I observed the alleged perpetrator proceeding in a northerly direction on foot" can be shortened to "As I got out of the patrol car, I saw the suspect walking north."

10. Use the active voice in preference to the passive. For example, "It has been observed by our officers on many occasions that ..." can be cut down to read "Our officers have often reported that ..." Not only is the second example shorter and less pompous, but it expresses the additional thought that the officers have not only made but reported their observations.

B. *Essential Information*

1. In most cases your report should outline the sequence of events in chronological order.

2. Your report will normally have covered all the essential information if it includes the following:

a. Who—victim, suspect (if known), witnesses

b. What—type of offence or situation requiring police action

c. When—date and time of occurrence, your time of arrival

d. Where—street address or specific description of the location (try to be concise)

e. Why—motive (if known or obvious from the nature of the offence, e.g., robbery)

f. How—details of the method used to commit the offence

g. What next—whether further investigation is required, follow-up work still to be completed (e.g., owner of stolen car to be notified, property to be returned to owner upon his return from vacation, etc.)

III. Obtaining Information

A. *Field Inquiries*

1. Purpose: To obtain information from persons not in custody.

2. Possible subjects:
   a. Suspects
   b. Suspicious persons
   c. Eyewitnesses
   d. Other persons who may have knowledge of value in a police investigation

3. Recommended procedure:

   a. Maintain a firm and professional attitude when you approach the subject, but offer a polite explanation of your reason for stopping the subject.

   b. Obtain the subject's identification and verify it quickly, through test questions or a radio check.

   c. Request the subject's cooperation in your investigation, but remain businesslike. Don't joke or act overly familiar toward the subject.

   d. Verify the subject's story or explanation for his presence by further test questions, radio checks, or other immediately available sources of information.

   e. Record the subject's name, address, and a brief account of his comments in your notebook, or on a suspect or field interrogation card, according to departmental policy.

   f. If the subject checks out, thank him for his cooperation and assistance.

   g. Obtain a full description of the subject, including such identifying characteristics as scars, tattoos, facial hair, earrings, glasses, and clothing. Also, make a written note of the description of his vehicle. Do not rely on your memory for this information.

   h. Do not turn your back on the suspect at the conclusion of the interview; remain alert until he is on his way.

B. *Questioning Eyewitnesses*

1. Psychologists have identified three stages involved in the recording of events in the human memory:

   a. Acquisition: Information is entered into the individual's memory system.

   b. Retention: Retention is the period of time that passes between the acquisition and recall of a specific piece of information.

   c. Retrieval: This stage occurs when the individual recalls stored information.

2. The retrieval stage is often of primary importance to police officers because it is during this stage that your subject will answer your questions, identify suspects from lineups, and testify in court.

3. Research has indicated that the quality of your subject's responses during retrieval can be dramatically affected by the types of questions you pose.

    a. Narrative questions—questions in which you ask the subject to tell you what happened in his own words—have been shown to elicit answers that are more accurate but offer less information than interrogatory questions.

    b. Interrogatory questions—specific questions that require specific answers—have been shown to provide more detail but are generally less accurate. More errors occur when subjects are forced to answer questions than when they are free to choose their own details.

    c. The wording of the question can suggest to the subject the answer you are seeking. Consider the following questions:

    (1) Did you see a gun?
    (2) Was there a gun?
    (3) Did you see *the* gun?

    Each question offers a different suggestion to the subject, though they are all based on the same facts. They could easily result in different answers.

4. When interviewing eyewitnesses, take the following approach:

    a. Ask the narrative question first, e.g., "What did you see?"

    b. Follow up the suspect's narrative account by asking specific questions, e.g., "How tall was he?" "What colour was his hair?"

    c. Choose your words carefully so that you don't plant a suggested response in the witness's mind. For example, ask "Did you see any weapon?" rather than "Was he carrying a gun?"

5. Studies have shown that the same principles apply to other police investigations, such as traffic accidents. If you ask a witness how fast two cars were going when they "smashed into each other," his estimate is likely to be higher than if you had asked how fast they were going when they "collided."

6. Make every effort to verify any important details in eyewitness accounts through other independent witnesses or, ideally, through physical evidence.

C. Questioning Victims

1. Children

    a.   If their child has been the victim of a violent crime, particularly a sex offence, parents are likely to be upset and extremely protective.

       (1) Assure the parents of your understanding and concern before questioning the child.

       (2) If the parents interrupt or become emotionally upset as the details of the offence are revealed, gently try to remove the child from their presence during your interview.

       (3) If the child is upset or unwilling, don't press for details during your initial interview.

       (4) If your uniform or questions are disturbing the child, ask the attending physician or nurse to obtain the necessary details for you.

    b.   Don't use expressions describing unnatural sex acts.

       (1) Use euphemistic words such as "the bad man" who "hurt you" or "beat you up."

       (2) Ask the child to describe the assault in his own words.

       (3) Don't use specific or biological terms in posing your questions. Children usually do not know the medical terms for genital organs and sexual activity.

       (4) If the child refuses to speak, interview the parents.

       (5) Ask them to tell you *exactly* what the child told them.

       (6) Be careful that you are getting an accurate account of what the child said, without the parents' embellishments or opinions added to the story.

2. Teenagers

    a.   The parents of a teenage victim may object to your questions, particularly in cases of sexual assault.

    b.   The victim may be reluctant to speak in front of her parents because of the circumstances of the assault, e.g., if she was picked up in a bar or on the street and taken to the suspect's apartment.

    c.   The victim may be reluctant to hurt her parents further with the details of what she went through.

    d.   If you cannot separate the victim from her parents:

       (1) Postpone the interview and ask her to come to the police station to look at photographs, or

       (2) Conduct a more detailed interview when she has been removed from her parents' presence.

e.   By the time you arrive at the parents' home, they may have discussed the case with the victim at great length, and embellished their version of the incident considerably. Be extremely cautious of accepting uncorroborated details that they provide.

f.   Many teenagers are adult in appearance but young in attitude and experience. Use tact and diplomacy in questioning them.

3.   Adults

a.   Adult victims are generally less reluctant to speak with police officers, but be sensitive to their concerns:

(1)   Allow no other officers or other persons to be present during your interview.

(2)   Ask the female rape victim if she would prefer to speak with a female officer.

(3)   Remove the victim from the presence of her husband if he appears to be upsetting her or making her reluctant to tell the whole story.

b.   When taking a report or conducting a preliminary investigation, NEVER indicate that you doubt the victim's story.

(1)   By expressing suspicion, you will likely cause her to refuse to speak at all or to demand that another officer take over the case.

(2)   Even if you suspect the story is false, by hearing the victim out you will learn details that can either verify or disprove the allegation.

TIP: Whenever you interview a witness or a victim, don't hesitate to ask the obvious question.

After a bank robbery in a small town near our jurisdiction, investigators arrived upon the scene and began the usual routine of photographing, taking fingerprints, and interviewing witnesses. One lady gave a particularly detailed description of the robber, which was duly noted by an investigating detective.

The same lady was interviewed later by another investigator. "I would have thought you'd have got him by now," she remarked.

"Why?" the detective answered, confused. Then he suddenly caught on. "Do you know who he is?"

"Sure," she said. "He's from around here."

After taking down the suspect's name and address, the exasperated investigator asked, "Why didn't you tell this to the other officers?"

"Nobody asked me," was the reply.

3. RESPONDING TO EMERGENCIES

I. Approaching Emergency Situations

A. Precautions

1. Your first responsibility is to get to the scene safely.
2. Use your vehicle's lights and siren in approaching emergency situations.

    a. Be aware that the public will probably not respond to these warnings as you might expect.

    b. Other drivers may not notice you because their car windows are closed, their radios or stereos are blaring, or they are distracted by children in their vehicle.

3. Keep the pitch of the siren fluctuating. A steady sound is less likely to be noticed.
4. Don't "overdrive" the siren.

    a. The sound of your siren will arrive at any given street location only seconds before you do and may not give other drivers enough time to react.

    b. Tall buildings and other obstructions tend to muffle the sound of the siren and cut down the distance at which it can be heard.

    c. Slow down and be prepared to stop when approaching blind intersections, intersections equipped with traffic signals or stop signs, and arterial roads.

5. Emergency vehicles such as police cars and ambulances sometimes collide at intersections because they cannot hear each other's sirens as they approach from different directions.
6. When approaching any serious domestic or emergency situation, do not allow the suspect to hear your siren. This will help you to avoid escalating the situation.
7. When responding to bank alarms and holdups, cut your siren and lights before coming into hearing distance of the crime scene. Failure to do so could create an avoidable hostage incident.
8. Take note of anyone sitting in a vehicle with the engine running in the immediate area .

B. *Use of Radio*

1. When responding to an emergency call, refrain from lengthy transmissions that may tie up the radio channel.
2. To assist the dispatcher in assigning other police cars and blocking possible escape routes, advise him of:

    a. The number of your patrol unit
    b. Your location
    c. Your intended route to the scene
    d. Any special equipment you have on board that may assist at the emergency
    e. The number of additional units needed

C. *Choosing Your Route*

1. Whenever possible, use major arterial roads to get to emergency scenes, even if you have to go a few blocks out of your way.

    a. Arterial roads usually provide the quickest route to locations at which emergencies are likely to take place.

    b. Motorists travelling these routes are generally more alert because of the greater traffic flow and pedestrian activity.

    c. Arterial roads should, however, be avoided during rush hours.

2. Drive defensively and maintain full control of your vehicle at all times. Saving a few seconds in arriving at an emergency scene is rarely worth the risk of causing a fatal accident.

D. *Vehicle Safety Precautions*

1. Don't keep pens, notebooks, papers, or other articles in the sun visor of your vehicle. If you have to stop suddenly, they may fall into your face and temporarily distract you.
2. Don't stuff pop cans and garbage under the front seat of your cruiser. They may fly forward and interfere with the operation of the gas and brake pedals.
3. Don't store objects on the rear seat shelf of your police vehicle. They could also fly forward during a sudden stop and cause injury, or be used as weapons by violent prisoners.
4. Keep articles in the trunk of your vehicle for easy access.
5. Secure objects or material to which you need immediate access in a specific place that will not create a hazard, such as the front seat beside the driver.

II. Approaching Accident Scenes

A. Hit-and-Run Drivers

1. Watch for hit-and-run drivers who may be fleeing from the scene. Their vehicles can often be identified by:

   a. Erratic driving at a high rate of speed

   b. Fluids leaking onto the roadway

   c. Signs of fresh damage

   d. Suspicious actions, such as the driver turning off onto a sideroad when he sees you approaching

2. If you spot a suspicious vehicle, radio the dispatcher immediately with:

   a. A description of the suspect vehicle

   b. Its direction of travel

   c. The licence number, if known

3. Request that another patrol car:

   a. Make the interception, or

   b. Proceed to the registered address of the vehicle owner to wait for him

B. The Accident Scene

1. Immediately upon arrival, check for gas leaks, fallen wires, and possible injuries.

   a. Do not attempt to move injured victims prior to the arrival of the ambulance unless there is an imminent danger of fire, electrocution, etc.

   b. Ensure that they have sufficient air and are kept warm to avoid the onset of shock.

2. Park well back to protect skid marks and other evidence left on the road that may be trampled or erased by tow truck drivers or other vehicles.

3. Notify the dispatcher if the assistance of the fire department, public utilities crews, ambulances, tow trucks, or other services is required.

III. Approaching Crime Scenes

A. Crimes in Progress

1. Be aware of the locations of other officers responding.

2. If you believe that criminals may still be present at the scene when you arrive, call for backup assistance before approaching the premises.

a. Turn down the volume of your radio.

b. Roll down your windows to listen for any suspicious sounds.

c. Shut off your motor and headlights as you coast to within three or four doors of the location.

d. Use the parking brake to stop your vehicle. This prevents the brakes from squealing and avoids illuminating the rear lights.

(1) Watch for manhole covers that may signal your arrival with a loud clang.

(2) Avoid scraping your tires against the curbside.

e. Remove your ignition keys and lock the doors of your patrol car after you get out. Close the doors softly.

f. Check for crowds, deliberate distractions, parked cars, or other suspicious signs.

3. You may encounter the criminal fleeing the scene as you arrive. Watch carefully any persons who come into view as you approach.

4. Always arrive from an unexpected direction.

EXAMPLE: Several years ago, two detectives and a patrol officer responded to a call concerning a man who was reportedly brandishing a "pellet gun" and threatening his neighbours. The man's residence was located in a high-rise apartment building. The three officers stepped off the elevator and were immediately confronted by a deranged man pointing a .22 calibre rifle. He squeezed off two quick shots that killed both detectives almost instantly. The uniformed officer gave chase and shot the suspect dead a few moments later.

If the two officers had gotten off the elevator one floor below the suspect's apartment and walked up one flight, they might have caught him off guard by approaching from the stairwell at the end of the corridor. A tragedy that claimed three lives might have been averted.

5. Keep away from light sources to avoid becoming a target.

a. Stay close to the sides of buildings, ensuring that you do not silhouette yourself against a lighted door or window.

b. If you use a flashlight, hold it away from your body, and turn it on only when necessary.

c. Don't outline a fellow officer in your beam of light.

6. Be alert for any lookouts that may be present.

NOTE: Use extreme caution, particularly if you are not in uniform. The complainant could also be out looking for the suspect, and he may be armed.

7. Watch for wire fences, bicycles, or other objects that could impede your movements.
8. Check for dogs or other animals that may be vicious or alarm the culprit.
9. Note the description of any vehicles in the immediate vicinity.
10. Using your knowledge of the neighbourhood, identify the most likely escape route from the premises and ensure that it is covered. In most cases, this is the rear entry.
11. If you encounter the complainant on prowler calls, tell him to remain inside until you have completed your search.

   a. Obtain a description from the complainant after you are satisfied the suspect is no longer in the area.
   b. Call for assistance and broadcast a description before continuing your search for evidence.
   c. Check in and under parked vehicles. If the engine of a suspicious vehicle is still warm, take down the licence number.
   d. If your search proves negative, advise the complainant before leaving the scene.

12. If you respond to a building alarm late at night, take up a corner position that offers you a view of two sides of the building you wish to investigate.

   a. When your backup arrives, alert him to your position with a short flash from your flashlight and use hand signals to communicate your instructions.
   b. The second officer should take a position at the corner diagonally opposite to your own so that all four sides are covered.
   c. When the building is surrounded, the officer in charge should knock on the front door, while standing clear to prevent being shot through the door.

      (1) This tactic will usually frighten the offenders into fleeing out the rear entry into the waiting arms of the officers who have taken covering positions.
      (2) If repeated knocking has no result, begin a search of the premises.

B. Searching the Premises

1. Prior to entry, notify communications that you are entering the premises.
2. Check on availability of a canine unit.
3. If the door to the premises is closed as you begin your search:

a. Shove it open forcefully with your foot so that the door strikes the wall. This should flush out anyone who may be hiding behind it.

b. Step back and listen before entering.

c. If you hear a noise, crouch down and douse your flashlight.

d. Call out to identify yourself and order anyone inside to come forward.

4. While conducting the search, be sure to close the door of each room that has been examined to prevent the suspect from hiding in a room that you have already covered.

5. Have your backup officer follow behind you a few paces to cover your back.

6. Never stand beside another officer while searching a crime scene. By separating, you present a smaller target and can view the scene from two different perspectives.

7. At a burglary in progress, you may find a suspicious vehicle parked nearby.

a. Check inside and call for another unit.

b. Have the second unit stake out the vehicle in case the subjects return while you are conducting your search.

8. Make a thorough, quiet, and methodical search of the entire building before clearing with the dispatcher.

C. Handling Suspects

1. If you encounter a possible suspect, check his:

a. Clothing—broken glass fragments, mud, grass stains, dust, oil, tears, etc.

b. Hands—cuts or scrapes, bleeding

c. Shoes—grass clippings, mud, wetness, etc.

d. General appearance—sweating, heavy breathing, alcohol on his breath, etc.

2. Conduct a field inquiry (see page 35), being particularly alert for vague or misleading answers.

TIP: A common excuse that prowlers use to justify their presence in places where they aren't supposed to be is that they were only seeking to relieve themselves. Ask the suspect to show you where he obeyed nature's call; unless there was a long delay in your arrival, the evidence to support his alibi should be easy to find.

3. When you apprehend a suspect, your first concern is your personal safety. Conduct a search immediately to ensure that he is not carrying any weapons.

4. Searches of female suspects:

   a. Although women should be searched by a female officer or matron whenever possible, a male officer is entitled to seize any weapons or evidence that he can see.

   b. If he only suspects that the female has weapons or evidence on her person, he should handcuff her behind her back and watch her carefully until she can be searched thoroughly by a female officer.

5. Handcuffing suspects:

   a. As you inform the suspect that he is under arrest, take hold of his elbow from the side.

   b. Tell the suspect to turn away from you and to place his hands behind his back.

NOTE: For safety reasons, all prisoners must be handcuffed behind their backs immediately upon arrest. The only exceptions are elderly and seriously disabled persons who obviously do not represent a physical threat. A detailed study of arrest procedures has shown that more than two-thirds of subjects demonstrate some degree of resistance when first touched by a police officer. Don't assume that a subject who impulsively flinches or pulls away from you on initial contact is about to initiate an assault.

   c. Speak calmly and quietly to the suspect, using this interval to gain his cooperation and assess the likelihood of resistance.

   d. Tell the suspect to turn around so that his back is facing you and his head is turned to the left.

   e. Order the suspect to position his arms away from his body at a 45-degree angle, with his palms facing up.

   f. Approach the suspect, also from a 45-degree angle, and take his outstretched left hand.

   g. Grip the thumb as you simultaneously apply the first (top) handcuff to his wrist. (This puts you in an excellent position to effect a takedown if you encounter resistance.)

   h. After the first cuff is secured, reach for the outstretched right hand and grip the thumb while quickly applying the second cuff.

6. Prone searches:

   a. Order high-risk suspects to lie face down on the ground, with both arms outstretched in the "crucifix" position.

   b. Approach and cuff the left arm as described above.

   c. Once the first cuff is secure, step toward the suspect's head, pulling his arm, and then kneel across his shoulders at a 45-degree angle.

d.   Ground-pin and lock the wrist joint, let go of the cuff, and then grip the suspect's other arm to apply the second cuff using the same technique.

7.   Standing searches:

a.   Wall searches are unsafe and to be avoided.

b.   To conduct a freestanding search, order the suspect to stand with his feet apart and his back to you.

c.   To put him off balance, order the suspect to bend over at the waist, with his hands outstretched and his head turned away from you.

d.   Take physical control by gripping his elbow and jamming your leg against the rear of his leg so you will be able to detect any resistance instantly.

NOTE: Do not place your leg between the prisoner's legs because this will provide him with an opportunity to take counter measures against you.

e.   Search the suspect's body by quarters, going from top to bottom.

f.   When you're finished checking one side, push the suspect gently away while holding on to him, further destabilizing him as you step around behind him to position yourself to search the other side of his body.

8.   Areas to search for weapons or drugs:

Hands
Forearms
Armpits
Small of the back
Inside and outside of his waistband

a.   Starting at the shoulders, run your hands lightly but firmly over the suspect's body in a continuous movement.

b.   Don't pat him or lift your hands to move them from place to place.

c.   Feel for any lumps or objects that may be

   (1)   In his pockets
   (2)   Taped or fitted to his side

d.   Turn the suspect around to check his

   (1)   Chest
   (2)   Sides
   (3)   Crotch (a common site of concealment for weapons and drugs)

    e. If necessary, remove his shoes and socks. Razor blades, shards of glass, and other potentially lethal objects are often hidden in the heels and soles of shoes.

NOTE: In recent years, the threat of contracting AIDS through contact with prisoners has become a matter of great concern to police officers. Other serious communicable diseases such as hepatitis can also be transmitted through contact with a prisoner's blood or saliva. If this happens to you, wash the affected area with an antiseptic solution immediately. If you are inflicted with a bite, scratch, or puncture wound that may have involved exposure to a suspect's body fluids, seek medical assistance as quickly as possible.

When investigating possible intravenous drug users, wear rubber gloves to check their pockets for syringes. Once you are sure you won't be pricked by a needle, you can check the pockets again for pills, folding money, and other items that the gloves might have prevented you from detecting.

Suspected AIDS carriers who bite or spit when handcuffed can be thwarted by placing an ordinary medium-sized paper shopping bag over their heads. With the bag secured by a small piece of tape under the chin, the prisoner will be able to breathe freely and faces no threat of strangulation or asphyxiation, but is effectively prevented from passing his bacteria orally to others.

9. Tools of crime you may find during a search:

    a. Burglary

        (1) "Cheaters"—strips of thin metal or celluloid

        (2) Skeleton or pass keys

        (3) Lock picks, jimmies, or screwdrivers

        (4) Punches, sledges, or drift pins for opening safes

        (5) Knotted ropes that can be used as ladders

        (6) Credit cards with worn edges (used for slipping locks)

        (7) Wire with magnet attached (used for taking money from newspaper boxes and vending machines)

    b. Narcotics

        (1) Bent spoon for heating and dissolving narcotics

        (2) "Hype Kit"—hypodermic syringe and piece of rubber tubing for making injections

        (3) Objects for concealing narcotics—aspirin bottles, matchbooks, cigarette packages, etc.

    c. Auto theft

        (1) Screwdrivers or ignition punches

(2) Jumper wires to short automobile ignition systems

(3) Pipe wrapped in newspaper for forcing door handles

(4) Bent coathangers for pulling up the latches inside locked doors

(5) Phony automobile registration documents

(6) Altered licence plates

(7) Dies for altering stamped automobile registration numbers

(8) "Slim Jim" car door-opener

(9) Spark plugs attached to a string for smashing windows

d. Gambling

(1) Betting "markers" and "owe sheets"

(2) Shaped, weighted, or capped dice

(3) Flash paper

(4) Sleeve "holdouts"

(5) Mirrored rings or eyeglasses

(6) Marked cards

e. Shoplifting

(1) Purses, boxes, or briefcases with open or spring-clip bottoms

(2) Wrapped packages with trapdoor bottoms

(3) Shoes with hollow heels

(4) Topcoats or jackets with linings that have inside pockets sewn in

(5) Sleeves with hooks suspended inside

D. *Taking Charge of the Scene*

1. When you have established that no criminals are present, you must take charge of the scene by:

   a. Excluding all unauthorized persons from entering

   b. Detaining all possible witnesses for interrogation by investigators

   c. Guarding the scene to prevent removal of any possible evidence

   d. Notifying the dispatcher of any services required such as ambulances, identification officers, and other resources

2. Retain control of the scene until relieved by a senior officer or an investigator assigned to the case.

3. Record the names and times of arrival and departure of all persons who enter the crime scene.

IV. Homicide and Other Violent Crimes

A. *Responsibilities of First Officer at Scene*

1. As first officer at the scene of a violent crime, remember that your first responsibility is to the victim.

    a. Never presume death unless there is no possibility that the victim is alive, e.g., decapitation, signs of decomposition, etc.

    b. Eliminate the source of danger, e.g., remove the garrote from the victim's neck, turn off leaking gas, etc.

    c. Summon medical assistance or have the victim transported to the hospital by ambulance.

    d. Apply first aid and artificial respiration, if necessary.

2. If the body is to be removed:

    a. Outline the position of the body with chalk.

    b. Disturb the area as little as possible.

    c. Clear all relatives and friends from the immediate area.

3. Enter and leave the scene by the same route. (Record this route in your notebook.)

4. Note the names and times of arrival and departure of all persons who attend the scene.

5. Preserve all exhibits in the condition in which they were found. For example, knots in ropes should remain tied, knives should not be removed from a dead body, and firearms found at the scene should not be unloaded or moved.

B. *Preservation of the Scene*

1. If the crime scene is indoors, all entrances and exits should be secured. Make a notation if there are signs of forced entry.

2. No person, including other police officers, should be permitted to enter unless he has a specific duty to perform.

3. If the crime scene is outdoors, roping off the area will usually provide a psychological deterrent to keep civilians away.

C. *Requesting Assistance*

1. Contact the dispatcher immediately, requesting:

    a. Additional officers to protect the scene and interview possible witnesses.

    b. Criminal investigation personnel, including homicide and identification officers.

    c. A police photographer. Photographs should be taken before the body is disturbed by the coroner and before any search of the scene is made. If the coroner arrives before the photographer, he should be allowed to examine the victim briefly but asked not to disturb the body further until photographs have been taken.

2. Advise the dispatcher of the address and telephone number at the scene to maintain communications.
3. While awaiting the arrival of assistance, make sure that the scene remains undisturbed. Do not smoke, walk around unnecessarily, or touch anything.

NOTE: Exclude from the crime scene all police officers who are not essential participants in the investigation.

D. *Identifying the Suspect*

1. Once you are certain the scene has been adequately protected, interview witnesses or other persons at the scene about the suspect to determine:

   a. His name and address, if known
   b. Description
   c. Whether he is armed
   d. His condition—intoxicated, on drugs, etc.
   e. How he escaped—vehicle (description, licence number), on foot
   f. Accomplices, if any
   g. Direction of travel

2. Transmit this information to the dispatcher as quickly as possible to initiate an immediate search for the suspect.

E. *Removal of the Body*

1. Normally the coroner will issue a warrant for the removal of the body for an autopsy.
2. As first officer at the scene, you should remain with the body to maintain continuity of the evidence.

   a. Escort the body to the mortuary in the ambulance.
   b. Stand guard over the body until the arrival of the identification officers and the pathologist.
   c. Remain present when the next of kin make the formal identification of the body to the pathologist.

   By remaining with the body from the time of its discovery to the beginning of the postmortem examination, you will eliminate the need for the testimony of many other police officers at trial who would otherwise be called to establish continuity.

F. *Use of the Notebook*

1. While awaiting the arrival of the coroner and investigating officers, use your time to make complete notes.

   a. Have your notebook out at all times.

   b. Write your observations down in the order that they occur.

2. Your notes should include the following:

   a. Time of the initial call

   b. Time of arrival on the scene

   c. Name of the person(s) who answer(s) the door when you arrive

   d. Position of the body

   e. Position of other articles, such as furniture, doors, windows, etc., in relation to the body

   f. Person who identifies the body, and the time of identification. (Try to ensure that you don't have a possible suspect identify the body.)

   g. Apparent blood stains

   h. A rough drawing of the scene that includes as much detail as possible

   i. Names and addresses of all persons present at the scene

   j. Names of all officers present with you at the scene, including their times of arrival and departure

   k. Physical conditions—weather, lighting, etc.

G. *Handling the Murder Suspect*

1. As first officer at the scene, you will often encounter the person responsible for the murder upon your arrival.

   a. Frequently this person will be under tremendous stress because of his actions and may make a spontaneous statement about the crime.

   b. You *must* record this statement carefully and accurately in your notebook as soon as possible.

   c. Make additional notes of any other statements he may make.

2. Conduct a preliminary search of the suspect to locate concealed weapons, but leave any detailed searches for evidence to the investigating officers.

3. As soon as the suspect makes an incriminating statement of any kind, e.g., "I didn't mean to do it," "I knew he'd push me too far one day," etc., *caution the suspect immediately.*

4. Also make notes of:

    a. His apparent mental state—upset, tense, calm, crying, sweating, shaking, etc.

    b. His sobriety—smell of liquor on his breath, rational, drunk, slurring words, etc.

    c. His physical condition—any apparent injuries, scratches, or bruises

    d. The condition of his clothing—normal, dishevelled, blood-stained, torn, etc.

    You will undoubtedly be asked to testify about all of these matters in court. Comprehensive notes will enable you to give complete, accurate evidence confidently.

5. Place the accused person under arrest and under guard.

    a. Inform the accused of his rights to legal counsel as soon as reasonably possible.

    b. Do not allow him to wander about the scene or to converse with relatives or friends.

    c. Do not permit other police officers to come into contact with the suspect.

6. Have the suspect removed from the scene as quickly as possible by a second officer.

    a. If a second officer has arrived at the scene with you and can corroborate your testimony regarding the suspect's statements, have that officer remove the accused.

    b. Give strict instructions that he is to be kept away from any other officers at the station until the case is taken over by the investigating officers.

        (1) All conversation with the accused should be kept as brief as possible.

        (2) Continue to record in your notebook any statements he may volunteer.

    By limiting the number of officers who come into contact with the accused, you increase the likelihood that his statements will be admitted in court as evidence.

4. STOPPING AND SEARCHING VEHICLES

I. Introduction

A. Hazards

1. The task of stopping vehicles is among the most common and hazardous in police work. One U.S. study has shown that 43 percent of police officers shot during routine vehicle checks were attacked *after* their initial contact with the driver, a startling statistic that underscores the need for alertness throughout the so-called routine check.

2. No vehicle check is routine; each places the officer in a potentially life-threatening situation. And, as the statistics show, an initial impression that you are in no danger is no guarantee of security. There is always an element of danger, and thus no vehicle check should ever be undertaken in a relaxed or complacent manner.

B. Courtesy

1. For most citizens, traffic stops are their only contact with police officers performing their duties.

   a. If you handle yourself in a courteous manner, even while giving out a ticket, your attitude will reflect favourably upon your department and police officers in general.

   b. By the same token, if you take a surly or authoritarian approach during the vehicle stop, the incident will become a favourite anecdote in the citizen's repertoire of stories and be repeated frequently——possibly for years. The public-relations effects are obvious.

II. Procedures

A. Location

1. When you decide to stop a vehicle, pick a location that will not place you, the motorist, or other drivers in danger. At night, choose a location in a well-lit area to:

   a. Provide a high level of visibility to other motorists
   b. Discourage the driver from attempting violent action

    c. Give yourself a better opportunity to watch the movements of the driver and any passengers in his vehicle

2. Avoid detaining vehicles in private or commercial parking areas during business hours.
3. Do not under any circumstances pull in front of a suspect vehicle or move between the suspect vehicle and another car.
4. Call for backup if necessary.

B. *Stopping the Suspect Vehicle*

1. On pulling abreast of the suspect vehicle, activate your emergency lights to signal him to stop.
2. Never pull completely abreast of the suspect vehicle. You will leave yourself open to being shot at, cut off, or forced into oncoming traffic.
3. If the use of your emergency lights is not appropriate, instruct the driver to stop by sounding your horn briefly and gesturing with your hand when he looks in your direction.

    a. At night, sound your horn and blink your headlights to attract his attention.

    b. If you activate your roof lights or siren during the stop, use caution:

        (1) They may unnecessarily embarrass or annoy the driver.

        (2) They could panic the driver, causing him to stop suddenly, lose control of the vehicle, or even attempt a high-speed escape.

    c. On major highways or expressways, after the suspect vehicle has been stopped, use your roof lights to alert other drivers to your presence.

4. If the driver does not stop immediately, remember that he may be preoccupied in a conversation, listening to a radio turned up to high volume, or simply daydreaming.

    a. If necessary, use your lights and siren to get his attention.

    b. If you are in plain clothes, signal the driver with your light, then shine it on your badge to identify yourself.

5. Drunken drivers react slowly and may continue to weave across the road after you signal them to stop.

    a. Keep a safe distance behind the suspect vehicle.

    b. Be prepared to move quickly to force the vehicle out of the direction of oncoming traffic if the driver wanders into the wrong lane.

III. The General Vehicle Stop

A. Precautions

1. After the vehicle has stopped, pull your patrol car up about half a metre (approx. 2 ft.) to the left and one car-length behind. This position protects you from traffic as you approach the vehicle.

2. Another method is to stop your patrol car behind the vehicle angled to the left, with your wheels turned to the extreme right.

   a. This position offers both protection from the traffic flow and defensive cover if the driver opens fire.

   b. The angle and distance of your vehicle also protects against injury if your patrol car is struck by another vehicle.

3. Activate your overhead lights in appropriate weather, lighting, or traffic conditions.

4. Before getting out of your vehicle:

   a. Request a check from your dispatcher by advising him of:

      (1) Your unit number

      (2) Your location

      (3) The licence number of the stopped vehicle

   b. Mentally review the elements of the violation or reason for the stop so that you do not appear hesitant or unsure of yourself while speaking to the driver.

   c. Leave your ticket book in your vehicle, since it can be a mental distraction during your initial encounter with the suspect.

5. Upon receiving the results of your radio check, approach the vehicle cautiously from the passenger side. This will mean that both his vehicle and your own are blocking his potential line of fire during most of your approach.

   a. During darkness, take the additional precaution of walking around behind your police vehicle to avoid being silhouetted in its headlights. You will also obtain a clear view of the suspect before he knows where you are located.

   b. Watch for any sudden movements from the driver or passengers, such as weapons being drawn, drugs being thrown out the window, etc.

   c. Check the rear seat for hidden or reclining passengers.

   d. Check the trunk to ensure it is secure.

   e. Angle your body so that your chest and shoulders are parallel with the car.

6. Stop to the rear of the driver's car door. This strategy will place the driver in an awkward position, forcing him to talk to you over his left shoulder. It also ensures that:

    a. You will be able to watch his hands for any sign of weapons or aggressive action.

    b. You can keep an eye on the other passengers in the rear.

    c. The driver will not be able to shove the door violently into you or knock you into traffic.

7. Never lean into the car window or place your hands where the driver can grab them. If he decides to flee, you could be dragged and seriously injured.

8. Once you have safely reached the vehicle and determined the driver's attitude, you can initiate tactical communications, i.e.,

    a. Greeting ("Good evening, sir. How are you tonight?")

    b. Self-identification ("I'm Officer Jones.")

    c. Reason for stop ("I noticed that your vehicle ran a red light at the last intersection.")

    d. Legal justification ("Running a red light is contrary to the provisions of the Highway Traffic Act.")

    e. Request for driver's licence, registration, and insurance

    f. Decision—summons or caution

    g. Closure ("Thank you for your cooperation. Have a good evening.")

B. *Questioning the Driver*

1. Through your body language and positioning, project an attitude of alertness and objectivity during your conversation.

2. Address the driver politely, using expressions such as, "Good morning," "May I see your driver's licence and registration, please?" etc. A friendly smile and courteous manner can take much of the heat out of a potentially antagonistic situation.

    a. Use the subject's name and the appropriate polite form of address—Mr., Mrs., Miss, or Ms—frequently. Everyone loves the sound of his own name.

    b. Never chastise the driver in front of his family or other passengers.

    c. Explain immediately why you stopped the driver and what action you intend to take.

3. Ask for the driver's operator licence, registration, and insurance immediately.

a. Do not accept these items in a wallet or any type of folder; request that he remove them and hand them to you.

b. Do not be drawn into a discussion or argument over the merits of your case.

c. Watch closely if the driver reaches over to the glove compartment, under the seat, or anywhere else where a weapon could be hidden.

d. If you suspect that the identification is false, quickly ask the driver his date of birth and the name of his insurance company while you are holding his documentation.

4. Hold the papers in your weak hand to keep your strong hand ready for quick action.

   a. Keep your hand above your belt.

   b. If you are still suspicious:

      (1) Ask the driver to step out of the vehicle and tell you the mileage on his car.

      (2) Check the sticker on the left door panel for the last date of servicing. Most bona fide owners know it.

5. Most honest drivers will appreciate your professionalism in conducting a thorough check. If the driver objects to your actions, remind him that you've acted exactly as he would have wanted you to if *his* vehicle had been stolen.

6. Do not ask the driver to join you in your police vehicle. Contact should be kept to a minimum.

7. Return to your cruiser, walking slowly backward on the shoulder of the road or highway. Always keep a vehicle between yourself and the subject.

8. If you are not comfortable with the driver's attitude or behaviour:

   a. Call for backup.

   b. Increase the distance between your vehicle and the driver's to improve survival reaction time.

9. If two officers are present and no threat is suspected:

   a. The passenger officer should stand near the rear of the violator vehicle in a position where he or she can see the driver clearly.

   b. The passenger officer then signals the driver officer to approach the driver and initiate contact.

   c. Once the driver officer has concluded the conversation, the passenger officer remains in the cover position as the driver officer returns to the police vehicle to write the ticket.

C. Issuing a Summons or Warning

1. Check with the dispatcher for outstanding warrants or suspensions.
2. Write out the summons or warning clearly and legibly.
3. Hand the summons to the driver as soon as possible to avoid provoking him through unnecessary delay.

TIP: Keep your head up and eyes on the car. Write the ticket while resting the pad on your steering wheel so that you can keep the violator vehicle in full view.

4. If the driver insists upon arguing, listen attentively and sympathetically, but make no comment.
5. When he is finished, advise him courteously of the steps he may take to contest the matter in court.
6. After returning the driver's documents, assist him in pulling back into the flow of traffic.
7. Do not turn your back on the violator vehicle.
8. To avoid creating the impression you are harassing the subject, wait until he is out of sight before resuming your patrol.

IV. The High-Risk Stop

A. Procedure in Dangerous Situations

1. Upon making the decision to stop a high-risk vehicle, pick a location that is most tactically advantageous to you.
2. Activate your emergency equipment.
3. Open the window on the driver's side to:

   a. Allow yourself a better opportunity to hear while approaching.

   b. Be in a position to return fire more easily from a position of cover.

   c. Protect against eye or other injuries that might be inflicted by broken glass fragments.

4. Contact the dispatcher, advising him of:

   a. The description of the vehicle and occupants

   b. The licence number of the suspect vehicle

   c. Your location

   d. The fact that you are making a possible high-risk stop

   e. The reason you believe the risk exists

5. Place the microphone on the left side of the steering column for easy access in an emergency.
6. Stop your vehicle about 6 m to the rear of the suspect vehicle.

a.   Turn your steering wheel to the left so that your left front end is offset about 1 m outside of the left side of the suspect vehicle.

b.   Step out of the cruiser behind the door on the driver's side, keeping the engine block of your vehicle between you and the suspect.

c.   If possible, wait for backup.

NOTE: Automobile doors do not stop high-velocity bullets. Never use them to provide cover in dangerous situations.

7.   When backup arrives, one officer should begin issuing commands to the suspect while the other provides cover. Both should have their guns drawn and sighted on the suspect.

8.   Commands:

a.   "Driver, with your left hand throw the ignition keys out of the driver's window."

b.   "Driver, place both hands outside the window and open the door from the outside."

c.   "Driver, get out of the vehicle and stand facing away from us with your hands in the air."

d.   "Driver, any moves that you make without instructions may be taken as hostile. Do you understand?"

e.   "Driver, walk slowly backward toward my voice."

9.   When the suspect has reached a point midway between the vehicles:

a.   Order him to do a slow 360-degree turn. This will enable you to conduct a preliminary visual search for weapons.

b.   If a weapon is seen, shout a warning to your partner and order the suspect clearly and loudly to keep his hands away from it.

c.   With the suspect facing away from you, instruct him to continue moving slowly toward the sound of your voice.

d.   As he does so, move quietly to a different point of cover, such as behind the police cruiser, so that if he attempts an assault, it will be made toward the wrong location.

e.   Once the suspect is between the vehicles, advise him as to the reasons that he has been stopped.

f.   As one officer provides cover, the other should holster his weapon and handcuff the suspect.

g.   Once cuffed, the suspect should be quickly searched for weapons, illegal drugs, and possible evidence.

10. Repeat this procedure for each passenger in the vehicle.

Illustration 3
A HIGH-RISK STOP

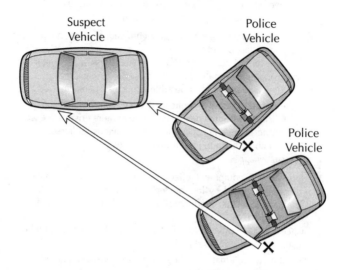

Suspect Vehicle

Police Vehicle

Police Vehicle

11. Once the passengers have been secured, await the arrival of the tactical unit, if available, to obtain vehicle clearance.

TIP: Use caution with drunken drivers—they could stagger out into oncoming traffic. Remove the ignition keys from the vehicle immediately and do not allow the drunken driver to pull his vehicle over to the side of the road. Not only might he try to escape, but in court his defence lawyer could demand to know why you allowed the suspect to continue driving if you truly believed he was intoxicated.

V. Checking the Driver

A. Identifying Suspicious Drivers

1. If possible, obtain the driver's home telephone number so that you can contact someone there to confirm his identity if necessary.
2. Be alert to unusual smells and sights, e.g., liquor, drugs, fresh paint, combustible fumes, etc.
3. Examine the attitudes of the vehicle occupants closely.
4. Ask the driver for his date of birth *after* he has given you his licence in case it doesn't belong to him.

a. Check the expiry date.

b. If the licence is in unreadable condition, call in a radio check or have the driver produce a new licence at a later date.

5. If the driver doesn't have his licence with him:

a. Check some other piece of identification to get his proper name and date of birth.

b. Ask him to stand aside for a moment; ask a passenger his name and approximate age.

c. Check his name for a possible licence suspension.

6. If the driver produces a duplicate licence, you should also check for a suspension. Some people have two or more driver's licences.

7. Check the driver's licence history for previous addresses. Then ask him about them to confirm his identity.

B. *Vehicle Check*

1. Do a quick equipment check of the vehicle. Take whatever action is required by law or departmental policy if defects are found, e.g., ticket, warning slip, removal of licence markers, checkup slip, etc.

2. Check the type of vehicle and the vehicle identification number against the registration slip.

a. If they don't match or they appear to have been altered, call in for a stolen vehicle check.

b. Do not rely completely upon a radio check with the police computer to determine vehicle status. The vehicle may have just been stolen and not yet reported, or the owner may be on holidays and unaware that his vehicle is missing.

3. Check for proper licence plates on the vehicle. One set of markers is sometimes used on two vehicles.

TIP: When checking drivers of heavy truck transports, be sure you know your law. An experienced, road-savvy trucker can easily make you look foolish if your questions reveal that you really don't know what you're talking about.

4. Check the expiry dates on all rental and leasing contracts. The vehicle may be stolen or overdue.

5. Do a radio check of the vehicle occupants with the police computer.

6. If everything is in order but you are still suspicious, make a note in your notebook or on a suspect card. This information may be useful in later investigations or in solving a crime that has not yet been reported.

VI. Searching the Suspect Vehicle

A. Primary Considerations

1. Your personal safety
2. Control of the suspect(s)
3. Locating and protecting evidence

B. Conducting the Search

1. You will have to establish a chain of custody for any evidence found during your search.

    a. Do not lock up the vehicle and leave it with the intention of conducting a search later. A court may rule that your evidence could have been planted by another person who entered the vehicle, either with a duplicate set of keys or by force.

    b. If you are accompanied by another officer, before beginning the search decide immediately who will take custody of the prisoners and who will take custody of the vehicle.

    c. If you take the vehicle into custody, place seals on the doors, hood, and trunk to establish your chain of custody from the time the vehicle was towed away until its arrival at the police vehicle pound.

    d. If your department does not use seals, follow the tow truck that picks up the vehicle to the police pound.

    (1) Keep the vehicle in sight at all times during the trip.

    (2) Upon arrival, obtain written certification that the attendant or officer in charge has taken over custody of the vehicle.

2. If you decide to conduct the search at the scene of the stop, be systematic but avoid adopting any preconceived ideas of what you will find.

EXAMPLE: If you have captured an armed-robbery suspect, you may search for concealed weapons in the vehicle but fail to notice an innocuous matchbox or discarded gum wrapper containing narcotics.

3. Any evidence found should be tagged or marked and delivered immediately to the property room.

C. Possible Search Areas

1. Consider searching the following areas, according to the circumstances and the legal justification for your search:

    a. Behind the headlights and taillights
    b. Hubcaps
    c. Inside the horn

d. Air filter
e. Spare tire
f. Windshield washer container
g. Shift knobs
h. Under the dashboard
i. Sun visors
j. Carburetor
k. Under the floor mats
l. In or behind the upholstery
m. Under the steering post
n. Under the tire air valve caps
o. In motorcycle handlebar covers
p. Inside tubing on roof racks
q. Behind bumpers (placed or taped)
r. Tailpipe
s. In insulation of hood
t. Voltage regulator
u. Heater
v. Glove compartment
w. Inside trunk, bottom or fuse box
x. Under the seats
y. Under the arm rest
z. Axle
aa. Magnetic key box
bb. Inside gear box
cc. Under horn rims
dd. Inside door panel
ee. Behind licence plates
ff. Inside cassette or CD player
gg. Under the fender wells
hh. Engine pans and motor (weapons or drugs may be taped on)
ii. Trunk, including the spare tire and jack
jj. Any other compartments large enough to conceal any object
kk. Convertibles—the well where the roof folds down behind the rear seat
ll. Station wagons—the rear deck

TIP: Whenever possible, have photographs taken of false-bottomed trunks and other locations where weapons, drugs, and evidence have been concealed. They can be valuable evidence in court.

VII. Abandoned Vehicles

A. *Indicators*

1. Exterior:
    a. Dirty or dusty windshields
    b. Litter or debris under the vehicle
    c. Weather-beaten parking tags attached to the vehicle
    d. Heavy accumulation of snow during winter
    e. Windows left partially open in bad weather
    f. Broken or cracked windows

2. Interior:
    a. Sleeping or reclining persons
    b. A "lived-in" look
    c. Gas cans, siphon hoses, coat hangers, or other jimmying devices in the rear seat
    d. Punched ignitions or wires hanging beneath the dashboard
    e. Aluminum foil in the front seat on the driver's side (used for hot-wiring vehicles)

NOTE: Conduct your search in a manner that avoids the destruction of fingerprints, footprints, and other evidence that may be present on or near the vehicle. There is always the possibility that the vehicle was stolen or involved in an unreported crime.

B. *Signs of Theft*

1. Keys left on the tops of tires
2. Clean licence plates that do not match the dirty appearance of the vehicle
3. Bugs or stone chips on a rear licence plate, indicating that the plate may have been switched from the front of another vehicle
4. Dealer logos, particularly on trucks, that indicate that the vehicle is a long way from where it was purchased
5. Licence plates that have been deliberately bent or repainted to conceal their identification numbers
6. Phony licence plates made of fibreglass, cardboard, or other non-metallic materials

5. TRAFFIC ACCIDENT INVESTIGATION

I. Introduction

Traffic accident investigation is a duty that will fall upon virtually every police officer at some point during his career, and is among the most important tasks he will be assigned. For most civilians, a traffic accident is a highly traumatic experience; it may be the first occasion in their lives in which they have come into contact with a police officer on duty. Your performance can have an important effect on their perception of the skill and professionalism of all police officers.

Your responsibility is to *investigate,* not merely report, traffic accidents. The principles of good investigation are as applicable to a so-called routine traffic accident as they are to a homicide. You must determine:

1. What happened
2. How it happened
3. Why it happened
4. Who was legally responsible

As an investigator, you must develop information based on hard evidence, and never assume anything. Too many officers use the phrases "rear-end collision" or "driver inattention" to cover a multitude of situations whose real cause might have been determined by more extensive investigation effort.

II. The Accident Scene

A. *Upon Arrival at the Scene*

The scene of a major accident will be filled with vehicles, tire marks, debris, and people. Your first concern, of course, is for the welfare of anyone involved in the accident. Your immediate priority is to request the necessary assistance, including ambulances, fire service, environmental control, and other appropriate agencies.

1. Note the conditions that the driver involved in the accident may have encountered, such as:

   a. Road obstructions (potholes, cave-ins, roadworks)
   b. Slippery road surface (wet, icy, snow-covered)
   c. Low visibility (fog, heavy rain, blizzard)

d. Inoperative or defective traffic signals

e. Warning signs that have been altered or removed

2. Park your vehicle in a safe location that does not block traffic.

   a. At night, if possible, position your vehicle to allow your headlights to illuminate the accident scene.

   b. Do not drive over tire marks at the scene or on the shoulders of the road. They may become important evidence.

3. Reduce potential traffic hazards by:

   a. Activating your roof lights

   b. Assigning another officer to direct traffic around the scene

   c. Clearing pedestrians from the roadway

   d. Placing flares a suitable distance from the front and rear of the accident scene

4. Immediately check for any potential fire or electrical hazards such as spilled gasoline or fallen wires.

5. Determine the severity of the accident by identifying persons who have been killed or injured.

6. Make injured victims as comfortable as possible.

   a. Loosen their clothing.

   b. Cover them with blankets or coats to provide warmth and delay the onset of shock.

   c. Give the victims plenty of air by clearing away curious bystanders.

   d. Stop arterial bleeding as soon as possible through the use of tourniquets or hand pressure.

7. Call for ambulances, tow trucks, fire equipment, hydro repair crews, additional police assistance, and other services as required.

8. Do *not* move injured victims until the ambulance has arrived, unless there is no ambulance available or there is an imminent life-threatening danger such as explosion, fire, or electrocution.

9. Remove obstacles from the roadway that may present a danger to traffic.

10. Be alert to any attempts to steal the personal property of victims, or equipment and merchandise from damaged vehicles.

11. Locate the drivers involved and any potential witnesses.

    a. Ask these persons to wait in your cruiser or another safe, easily accessible location.

    b. If the accident is a hit-and-run, quickly obtain a description of the suspect driver, vehicle, and direction of travel for broadcast to the dispatcher.

c.   Note the licence numbers of all vehicles at or near the scene in case you need to locate further witnesses later.

12. Mark the position of the vehicles involved in the accident before allowing them to be removed from the roadway.

13. If the accident involves a serious injury or fatality:

a.   Take action to protect the scene on the same basis that you would for a major criminal investigation.

b.   Request the accident investigation specialists, photographers, and identification officers to attend the scene.

c.   Request the attendance of the coroner if required.

d.   Conduct a quick search of the surrounding area for:

(1) Other bodies that may have been thrown clear
(2) Seriously injured persons who may have crawled away and fallen unconscious

B. *Conducting the Accident Investigation*

1.   Question the drivers involved *separately* to determine:

a.   Who was driving each vehicle
b.   Their direction of travel
c.   Their activities prior to the accident

2.   Record any statements the drivers may volunteer, but refrain from making any comment yourself. Note the time and the location at which you took the statement.

3.   Be alert to signs of alcohol or drug impairment, confusion, nervousness, or extreme feeling of guilt.

a.   Check the interior of the vehicles involved for alcohol or drugs.

b.   Question the drivers about any drinking that may have occurred prior to the accident.

c.   If appropriate, request that the driver(s) take a breathalyzer or chemical test to determine blood-alcohol levels.

d.   Ask the subjects when they slept last, to determine if fatigue may have been a factor in the accident.

4.   Check the drivers' licences, registration, and insurance documents.

a.   Verify the identity and address of the drivers by asking particulars such as their ages, middle names, names of insurers, etc., *after* you have possession of the documents.

b.   Check the expiry dates of the documents closely and make sure that the ages indicated correspond with the appearance of the drivers.

5. Take down a step-by-step account of what each driver saw and did prior to, during, and after the accident.
6. Check the condition of the vehicles involved, noting:
   a. Headlights—on, off, or inoperable
   b. Light switches—on or off
   c. Gear shift—in what position
   d. Tires—condition and turn position
   e. Brakes—any loss of brake fluid or other possible cause of failure
   f. Steering gear, wheels, and springs—broken parts, wear, or misalignment
   g. Directional lights—check switch position
   h. Rear-view mirrors—check for correct adjustment
   i. Damage—location, extent, old or new
7. Take measurements of any skid or other relevant marks on the roadway.

NOTE: Be sure the marks relate to the accident you are investigating.

8. Note also:
   a. Final position of vehicles
   b. Location of debris and vehicle parts (debris may consist of cargo and vehicle liquids, broken glass, plastic and metal parts, and "soil cake"—the undercarriage and underbody rust that accumulates naturally under vehicles)
   c. Significant distance relationships such as:
      (1) Width of the roadway
      (2) Width and height of the curbs
      (3) Location of traffic lights and signs
      (4) Sizes and locations of potholes
      (5) Distance to the nearest intersection
      (6) Point of impact
      (7) Position of injured or deceased persons
      (8) Sight distances
9. Secure their personal belongings (i.e., handbag, wireless phone, etc.)

TIP: Tire marks might be tire prints from a rolling tire; scuff marks from a tire that is side-slipping or yawing, rolling, and sliding; or skid marks from a tire that experienced breaking or metal collapse around the wheel during the collision.

10. Note the times when injured persons and damaged vehicles were transported from the scene and the locations to which they were taken.

11. Have the roadway cleared of any traffic obstructions caused by the accident.

12. Decide if charges are warranted. If so, take appropriate action by making an arrest or issuing a court summons.

13. Advise the drivers to:

    a. Exchange names and insurance information
    b. Prepare any reports that may be required of them

14. Take statements from witnesses to the accident.

    a. Allow the witnesses to give full accounts of what they saw in their own words, then ask specific questions to fill in any gaps in the accounts (see page 36).
    b. Keep the witnesses apart when taking statements. They may alter their stories consciously or unconsciously to fit the facts given in an earlier version.

15. Conduct a complete, detailed examination of the vehicles and make additional notes as required.

TIP: Avoid having police officers or other persons appear in photographs taken at the scene. A defence lawyer may insist on calling them as witnesses or test your credibility in court by asking if you know who they are.

16. Make a sketch of the location and position of the vehicles, indicating the measurements recorded earlier. Your sketch should indicate the positions of:

    a. Utility poles
    b. Mailboxes
    c. Traffic signs
    d. Guardrails
    e. Potholes
    f. Dirt piles
    g. Snow drifts
    h. All other physical objects that may have played a role in the accident

NOTE: Accurate and complete sketches are invaluable records of accidents, and can be useful as photographs in presenting your case in court.

17. Arrange for a complete clean-up of the scene.

18. Report to the dispatcher upon completion of the on-the-scene investigation.

III. Completing the Accident Investigation

A. Follow-up to On-the-Scene Investigation

1. Notify the relatives of the dead or injured and the owners of the vehicles involved as soon as possible.
2. Inform other agencies such as public utilities, the roads department, and others if conditions require their attention.
3. Complete the departmental accident report form and transmit it through normal channels.
4. Note any further court appearance dates or other follow-up work that may be required.

B. Common Faults in Traffic Accident Investigations

1. Vehicle damage or marks on the roadway incorrectly identified as resulting from the accident under investigation, e.g., unrelated tire marks being indicated as skid marks that occurred during the collision.
2. No attempt made to match the gouges and scratches on the road or vicinity of the accident scene with corresponding abrasion marks or other damage to the vehicles.
3. Measurements taken through guesswork, pacing, or other unreliable and unprofessional methods.
4. Measurements recorded in such a way as to be useless in determining what happened. For example, "skidmarks 12 long" does not indicate which vehicle is referred to or whether the measurements refer to the front or rear wheels of the vehicle.

IV. Hit-and-Run Accidents

A. Investigation Procedure

1. Investigation of the hit-and-run accident follows many of the same procedures that are employed in other accident investigations.
2. Because one of the drivers responsible for the accident is not present, however, and because he has committed a serious criminal offence by fleeing, you must take extra measures to identify and successfully prosecute him.
3. Interview the victim and witnesses immediately to obtain:
   a. Description of the suspect vehicle
   b. Description of the driver and other occupants
   c. Vehicle's direction of travel

4. Transmit this information to your dispatcher to permit other officers to make an interception.

5. Isolate the area surrounding the accident to preserve any evidence at the scene that would assist in identifying the suspect vehicle.

6. Conduct a thorough search, collecting everything that might be related to the accident. Objects can sometimes fly several hundred metres after an automobile collision, so be generous in determining your search area. Pay particular attention to:

   a. Glass fragments (can sometimes be "matched" to the suspect vehicle)

   b. Blood and tissue

   c. Hair

   d. Fibres

   e. Paint chips

   f. Small pieces of debris (can usually be positively identified with suspect vehicle)

   g. Foreign mud or dirt that may have shaken loose from the underside of the suspect vehicle

   h. Liquids on the roadway that may have come from the suspect vehicle, e.g., radiator water, engine oil, transmission oil, brake fluid

   i. Type of tire mark known as the "print," which is left when a tire has run through tar, oil, dirt, or water while rolling free (indicates vehicle direction and confirms positively that the wheel on which it was mounted was not locked)

7. Record licence numbers and descriptions of all vehicles in the immediate area.

8. A police officer should accompany the victim to the hospital or the morgue.

   a. If the hit-and-run involves a fatality, ask the attending physician or coroner to preserve any foreign material found in the skin or in lacerated areas of the victim's body.

   b. The victim's clothing or body may contain paint, glass particles, tire marks, or impressions made by ornamental objects affixed to the suspect vehicle.

      (1) Make sure that attending medical personnel do not cut through holes or tears.

      (2) Wrap the clothing securely to avoid contamination by other evidence during shipment to the crime laboratory.

(3) Ensure that photographs of the victim are taken as soon as possible to record the extent, type, and location of all injuries received in the accident.

B. *Locating the Suspect Driver*

1. Imagine yourself in the hit-and-run driver's predicament and try to determine what action he might have taken, e.g.:

    a. What route he might have chosen for his escape

    b. Whether he might have parked in a nearby parking lot until the "heat was off"

    c. If he might have taken the vehicle immediately to a nearby body shop for repair

    d. If the damage to his vehicle was so severe that he would have been forced to abandon it a few blocks away

2. If you locate a parked suspect vehicle soon after the accident, check for warmth from the radiator and muffler, and record your findings in your notebook. (The owner may claim the car hasn't been driven for hours.) Protect the vehicle for fingerprint examination and photographs.

3. Do a computer check of all vehicles that were reported stolen or burned around the time of the accident.

4. Canvass all garages, repair shops, service stations, and parking lots in the area.

5. Check hospitals and doctors' offices if you believe the driver or occupants may be injured.

6. Return to the accident scene periodically. The hit-and-run driver or an eyewitness may pass the scene regularly as part of his routine, e.g., to go to work, visit friends, go shopping, etc.

TIP: The majority of drivers involved in hit-and-run accidents have been found to live or work within a 3 km radius of the accident scene.

7. When you encounter the hit-and-run suspect, record carefully and completely any statements he may make to you. Note also his apparent physical and mental condition, e.g., inebriated, nervous, frightened, etc.

V. Accidents Causing Death or Serious Injury

A. *Notifying Next of Kin*

1. Do *not* use the telephone to make a death notification.

2. Demonstrate a tactful and sympathetic attitude in speaking to the next of kin, showing a sincere interest and concern for their loss.

3. Before revealing the bad news, ensure that you have the relatives' full attention and that they are aware of the seriousness of what you have to say.

4. Be sensitive to the emotional response you are receiving and pace your delivery of the notification accordingly.

   a. If the relatives begin to cry or become hysterical, give them time to express their emotions and to calm down before continuing.

   b. If the death was extremely violent or painful, e.g., the victim was decapitated or burned alive, avoid giving specific details until the initial shock has worn off. By being too graphic too soon, you could cause an emotional overload and complicate an already difficult and tragic situation.

5. Before leaving, ensure that a close relative, friend, physician, or member of the clergy remains behind to offer comfort.

B. Other Agencies

1. If you must contact other police officers or agencies to make the death notification, request that the next of kin be informed *in person* as soon as possible.

2. If there will be a lengthy delay, ask that the quickest means of communication available be used.

3. Request that you receive immediate verification that the next of kin have been notified.

6. HAZARDS AND DISASTERS
I. General Procedures
A. *Precautions*
1. Use extreme caution when approaching the scene of any hazard or disaster.
2. Park your vehicle safely. Do not obstruct the route or park in a manner that prevents other emergency vehicles from gaining access to the scene.

B. *Courses of Action*
1. Advise your dispatcher of:
   a. Nature of the hazard or disaster
   b. Exact location
   c. Estimated loss of life
   d. Estimated number of injured persons
   e. Estimated extent of the damage
   f. Assistance required
   g. Most direct route for emergency response
2. Take immediate action to safeguard lives.
3. Detain witnesses for interviewing later.
4. Maintain radio communications at all times.
5. Brief the first supervisory officer upon his arrival at the scene.

II. Fallen Wires
A. *Precautions*
1. Consider all wires at an accident or disaster scene to be live.

   a. Warn any approaching police officers, firefighters, or citizens of the danger.
   b. Ask your dispatcher to contact the power company for emergency assistance.
   c. Keep all bystanders well away from the scene.
2. Remember that there is no "safe" voltage—any voltage can kill, or cause serious injury, in certain circumstances.
3. *Never* allow anyone to get into the circuit between one wire and another, or between a wire and the ground.

4. *Never* rely on rubber boots, raincoats, or rubber gloves.
5. *Never* touch—or permit your clothing to touch—the wire or the victim of an electrical accident.

B. *Procedures*

1. If a victim is trapped in a vehicle that is in contact with a live wire, instruct him to remain inside until you are assured the power has been cut off.
2. If the person must get out of the vehicle because of a fire or other immediate hazard, tell him to jump clear so that no part of his body is touching the vehicle when he lands.
3. *Never* allow the victim to step down out of the vehicle by placing one foot on the ground while the other is still in contact with the vehicle. He will create an electrical ground and be electrocuted instantly.

III. Fires

A. *Patrol Officer's Responsibilities*

1. Traffic direction
2. Pedestrian control so that bystanders do not impede firefighters in their rescue and fire control efforts
3. Assistance in rescue operations to save lives and prevent injuries
4. Preservation of crime scene in arson cases

NOTE: Upon arrival at a fire scene, park your vehicle in a location that does not obstruct fire engines and other emergency vehicles.

B. *Procedures*

1. If you are required to enter a burning building:

    a. Keep low—on your hands and knees if necessary—to avoid smoke and heat.

    b. *Never* open a door if the doorknob is too hot to touch with your bare hands.

    c. Always feel a door with the palms of your hands before opening it. There may be fire on the other side.

    (1) If the door opens inward, stand to the side as you open it to protect yourself from a sudden blast of heat or flame.

    (2) If the door opens outward, keep your foot in place as a doorstop. Pressure may have built up behind the door and could blow it into you violently as it opens.

2. Assist fire department personnel as requested.
3. Your record of your observations at the scene can be of value in the subsequent police investigation.

a.   Record the licence numbers of vehicles in the area.

b.   Note the condition of external openings such as doors and windows, paying close attention to any signs of forced entry.

c.   Watch the crowd that gathers at the scene carefully. If the fire was caused by arson, you may be able to spot a pyromaniac in the crowd through his:

    (1)   Extreme excitement

    (2)   Repeated presence at fire scenes

    (3)   Gregarious attitude toward firefighters and news reporters, and avoidance of police officers

    (4)   Overeagerness to assist in firefighting operations

EXAMPLE: A major fire broke out at an oil refinery in our jurisdiction. The blaze grew rapidly into an inferno, which caused $7 million in damage, although, fortunately, no one was killed or seriously injured.

One refinery employee distinguished himself by his repeated efforts to assist firefighters in several difficult and dangerous situations. He was briefly considered to be almost a hero for the courage and dedication he displayed in combatting the conflagration.

Subsequent investigation revealed that the fire was caused by arson and, yes, the heroic employee was the party responsible. He was convicted of arson and sentenced to a seven-year penitentiary term.

4.   If you discover a fire while on patrol, advise your dispatcher before taking any other action.

5.   When the fire has been extinguished, begin your preliminary investigation by searching for the apparent point of origin of the fire.

a.   If the fire has more than one point of origin, arson has been committed. Call in fire investigation specialists.

b.   Take action to collect and preserve all relevant evidence (see page 178).

IV. Explosives

A. Precautions

1.   Do *not under any circumstances* touch or remove any package that is suspected to contain an explosive device.

a.   Leave the package exactly as it was when you found it.

b.   Do *not* cut any strings or wires.

c.   Do *not* remove or insert any component of the package.

2. Evacuate the area immediately, removing people from the vicinity of the package, *not* the package from the people.

    a. Isolate the package to a distance of at least 100 m.

    b. Take into account the floors above and below the package in establishing an evacuation area in a multi-storey building.

    c. If a container of inflammable liquids or gas is attached to the package, the evacuation distance should be *greatly* increased.

B. *Procedures*

1. If the suspected package is in a building or enclosed area, ventilate the scene immediately by opening doors and windows, if practicable.

    a. Do not cover the package with a bomb blanket or any other covering material.

    b. Do not attempt to remove explosives or inflammable liquids and gases from the area of the suspected package.

2. Do *not* transmit on your police radio. Radio-frequency energy can set off an explosive device.

3. Request the assistance of an explosives disposal unit immediately *by telephone.* If you cannot safely leave the scene, ask a civilian or other officer to make the call.

4. Try to locate the owner of the suspected package.

    a. This preliminary investigation can save valuable time for the explosives disposal unit in determining the degree of danger that the package may present.

    b. Keep the owner with you until the explosives disposal unit arrives.

5. Do not allow any other police officer to handle the package, with the exception of members of the explosives disposal unit.

6. Don't feel compelled to perform a display of false heroics. Your first wrong move could be your last.

V. Ice Storms

A. *Introduction*

On January 5, 1998, large sections of Ontario, Quebec, and the Atlantic provinces were struck with the worst ice storm in Canada's recent history. Many hospitals lost hydro power and were forced to rely on generators, thousands of traffic lights failed, Montreal's subway system was closed, and numerous radio and television stations stopped broadcasting.

Millions of Canadians suddenly found themselves stranded in their homes without heat, light, electrical service, or the means to cook food. Across stricken areas, schools, libraries, shopping malls, curling clubs, hockey arenas, fitness centres—every kind of large building—were turned into shelters.

Power lines remained down for weeks as residents relied on candles, kerosene, and propane to provide the necessities of life while they waited for service to return. In disaster situations such as this, police officers have a vital role to play in saving lives, controlling crime, and maintaining public order.

B. Patrol Officer's Responsibilities

1. Directing traffic
2. Keeping pedestrians away from areas with fallen wires
3. Checking for citizens sleeping in idling cars who may be at risk of carbon monoxide poisoning
4. Assisting rescue operations to save lives and prevent injuries
5. Checking homes for elderly persons without heat, food, or proper clothing
6. Assisting hydro, fire, and other services as requested
7. Conducting security checks on closed businesses, vacant homes, and temporarily abandoned farms, all of which are vulnerable to looters and vandals

VI. Dangerous Gases and Chemicals

A. Introduction

A few minutes before midnight on Saturday, November 10, 1979, a Canadian Pacific train from London, Ontario, bound for its Toronto yards, derailed in Mississauga, a city on the western boundary of Toronto. The first tank car to leave the rails was the thirty-third car in the 106-car train. It pulled 23 other cars off the tracks; 21 were tank cars, 18 of which contained dangerous goods. The first tank car was itself loaded with toluene, another dangerous commodity.

Fire spread through almost all of the derailed cars, including three that contained propane. They promptly exploded, causing $1.5 million damage to the surrounding area and shattering window panes up to a kilometre away.

The seventh car in the wreck was loaded with chlorine, a deadly gas that was used to devastating effect as a poison gas during the First World War. This car had suffered a hole of about 1 m in diameter in its shell.

Because of the very real possibility of massive death if the chlorine escaped in large amounts, virtually the entire population of Mississauga—almost 250,000 people—was evacuated for a period of up to five days. This was the largest peacetime evacuation of a civilian population in North American history.

Almost 10 years earlier, on June 21, 1970, a similar disaster had occurred at a derailment in Crescent City, Illinois. Fifteen cars of a 109-car train derailed, including nine loaded with liquefied petroleum gases. One of these cars was punctured, and leaking propane ignited. This resulted in a series of explosions that caused injuries to 66 persons and more than $2.1 million in damage.

Investigation revealed that the derailment had been caused by a "hot box," a burned-out bearing that erupted into flame. The heat generated from the fire from the initial puncture caused the other cars to rupture and explode. Safety valves on the tank cars were useless in preventing the explosions; many firefighters at the scene, however, believed that had the valves been working, the tanks would not have ruptured.

In Waverley, Tennessee, a freight train bearing dangerous commodities jumped its tracks on February 22, 1978. Two days later, as workers continued their efforts to clear the scene, a massive explosion left 14 persons dead and 43 injured.

Clearly, the safe transportation of dangerous goods is an issue worthy of serious study by all police officers—their own safety and that of the public depend on it.

B. Precautions

1. Upon arrival at the scene of a rail or truck disaster involving gases or chemicals, check immediately for warning placards on the containers.

   a. These placards indicate the type of substance you are dealing with and the danger it represents.

   b. Do not assume there is no danger because you don't see these placards. They may have been burned off, blown off, or, through human error, never been attached to the shipment.

2. Never approach a container containing a gas or chemical until you have seen the shipping papers or emergency response bill that identifies the contents.

   a. If you must approach a container to rescue an injured victim, walk toward it from the side.

   b. Stay away from the ends of the tanks. They may blow out.

3. Take action to ensure there are no flames, flares, or persons smoking in the hazard area. They could ignite vapours that would cause the container to explode.

4. Listen for "venting," a whistling noise that indicates the contents are escaping under pressure. Some gases, such as propane, will explode if they come into contact with a spark.

5. Do not touch spilled material.

6. If possible, stay above and upwind from the spill or leak.

7. Be cautious of manhole covers and sewer systems in the immediate area.

8. Remember that most vapours are heavier than air and will tend to concentrate near the ground or inside covered areas.

9. Inflammable vapours may spread away from the spill.

Illustration 4
DANGEROUS GOODS CHART

10. Potential hazards:

    a. BLEVE (Boiling Liquid Expanding Vapour Explosion)

    b. Asphyxiation

    c. Explosion or fire

    d. Rupture of the container

    e. "Rocketing" of the container (the rear end blows out, propelling the container forward like a rocket—known as a "flying cigar")

    f. Toxicity

    g. Frostbite

C. *Course of Action*

1. Eliminate all flames and other sources of ignition, e.g., sparks, cigarettes, live wires, etc.

2. Isolate the area to keep all unauthorized persons away.

3. If necessary, evacuate the area.

4. Shut off all public utilities such as natural gas and electricity.

5. Request an explosives disposal unit to attend the scene as soon as possible.

6. Consider the following factors as you take action or request assistance:

    a. Kind of gas or chemical involved, e.g., poisonous, inflammable, suffocating

    b. Volume and concentration of the gas or chemical released

    c. Size and nature of the area involved, e.g., residential, industrial, etc.

    d. Number of persons affected

    e. Wind direction and velocity

7. Do not move packages or articles after exposure to heat and fire, except under the supervision of an expert. The likelihood of explosion increases substantially when a dangerous commodity is subjected to heat.

D. *Handling Victims*

1. Move the victim into fresh air as quickly as possible.

2. Request emergency assistance from medical personnel.

3. If the subject is not breathing, give mouth-to-mouth resuscitation.

NOTE: Do not use the mouth-to-mouth techniques to resuscitate victims of cyanide gas poisoning. If you do not know what material is involved, use artificial respiration.

4. Remove, isolate, and package any clothing that may have been contaminated by the hazardous substance.

5. Attempt to identify the hazardous materials to assist in determining the medical treatment required.
6. If the victim's skin or eyes have come into contact with a toxic or dangerous substance, flush with running water for at least 15 minutes.
7. Keep the victim warm and quiet until the ambulance arrives.

E. *Possible Locations of Shipping Papers (To Identify Contents)*

1. Trucks
   a. In the possession of the driver
   b. In the pocket inside the door on the driver's side of the cab
   c. Anywhere else in the cab

2. Trains
   a. In the possession of the conductor
   b. In the caboose
   c. May be in the possession of the engineer or another crew member
   d. If none of the above, contact the railway's chief dispatcher

3. Aircraft
   a. In the possession of the captain
   b. In the possession of the shipping agent
   c. If neither the above, call the airline involved or the nearest airport

4. Ships
   a. Ask the captain for the Dangerous Cargo Manifest
   b. If the vessel is a barge at anchor, contact the local harbour master

F. *Gases Commonly Transported in North America*

1. Chlorine—used in the pulp and paper industry and for water purification
2. Oxygen—used in hospitals and for producing steel
3. Acetylene—used for welding
4. Propane—used as a household, industrial, and automotive fuel, and in the manufacturing of ethylene, refrigerant, and aerosol propellant
5. Anhydrous ammonia—used as a fertilizer and for nitric acid manufacturing and refrigeration
6. Ethylene oxide—used as a fumigant and petroleum demulsifier, and in the manufacture of ethylene glycol used in antifreeze and explosives

7. Butane—used in synthetic rubber, high-octane liquid fuels, and propellant in aerosols; as a food additive; and as a fuel for household and industrial purposes

8. Aerosols—used in perfumes, inhalants, antiperspirants, insecticides, and paints

9. Argon—used in light bulbs and arc welding

10. Helium—used in luminous signs, leak detection, geological dating, weather balloons, and welding

11. Carbon dioxide—used in carbonating beverages and extinguishing agents

12. Tear gas grenades—used in crowd control by police and military

13. Hydrogen—used in the production of edible oils and margarine; in metal processes, electronics, glass manufacturing, and drug manufacturing; and in the production of ammonia and methanol

VII. Radioactive Materials

A. Precautions

1. Spend as little time as possible near the radiation source.
2. Ensure that personnel at the scene are changed frequently.
3. Stay as far away from the radioactive material as possible.
4. Use shielding as a protective barrier between yourself and the radiation source.

B. General Procedures

1. Do *not* touch a damaged container or any spilled materials that may be radioactive.
2. Keep all unauthorized persons as far away as possible from the containers and wreckage.
3. Notify an explosives disposal unit as quickly as possible.
4. Keep upwind of the spill site.
5. Isolate and evacuate the area as quickly as possible.
6. If you must remain in the vicinity, wear self-contained breathing apparatus and full protective clothing.
7. If an aircraft is involved, set up a perimeter around the scene of at least 650 m (approximately 2000 ft.).
8. Avoid inhaling, ingesting, or touching the radioactive material.
9. Advise any ambulance personnel who arrive at the scene of possible radioactivity and alert the hospital that will be receiving the victims.
10. Direct any other persons who may have been contaminated to remove their outer clothing, wash the exposed skin, and remain at the scene until they have been examined by a radiation expert.

C. *Possible Hazards*

1. Exposure may lead to radiation sickness and death.
2. Contamination may be spread to other persons.
3. Fire may melt down shielding around the radioactive material. (See "Dangerous Gases and Chemicals," page 79.)

D. *Radioactive Materials Commonly Transported in North America*

1. Low Specific Activity (L.S.A.)
    a. Uranium chemical precipitants (yellowcake)
    b. Uranium hexafluoride
    c. Heavy water
    d. Thorium compounds
2. Medical radionuclides
    a. Molybdenum
    b. Iodine
3. Industrial
    a. Cobalt
    b. Iridium
    c. Cesium
4. Radioactive wastes
    a. From nuclear reactors
    b. From hospitals
    c. From nuclear plants

E. *Possible Locations of Radioactive Materials*

1. Medical and research facilities
2. Industrial facilities
3. Universities
4. Military bases
5. Waste-disposal sites
6. Transportation facilities, including major ports

VIII. Aircraft Accidents Involving Nuclear Weapons

A. *Authorities Responsible*

1. In the event of an accident involving an aircraft equipped with nuclear weapons, all levels of government will become involved.
2. Primary responsibility for dealing with the emergency will rest with radiation experts, who will require the highest level of co-operation from civilian authorities, including police, to deal with the crisis.

B. *Before Radiation Experts Arrive*

1. Secure the area and clear all nonessential personnel to a distance of at least 650 m (approximately 2000 ft.).
2. Do not allow anyone to remove, examine, or touch *anything* in the vicinity of the accident.
3. Advise your dispatcher to report the accident and location to the nearest military agency.
4. Notify fire departments and other police forces as required.
5. Keep away from the accident area, except to save lives.
6. Take firefighting precautions to prevent the spread of the accident effects to the surrounding area.
7. Identify all persons who may have been exposed to the radioactive material, dust, or cloud.
8. Record all available information to assist in their treatment.
9. Make sure that all persons who may have been contaminated are labelled with identifying tags and attended by medical personnel.
10. Rope off a 650 m (2000 ft.) area around the accident and prohibit entry by unauthorized persons.
11. Avoid any dust or smoke clouds at the accident site and limit your exposure as much as possible.
12. If you must expose yourself to save lives, use a cloth, goggles, or other objects to filter the air you breathe and protect your eyes.
13. Wash possible exposed areas, particularly cuts, with soap and water as soon as possible.
14. Cover injured skin surfaces to prevent contamination from smoke or dust.
15. Maintain a log of your activities, indicating names, times, and actions taken.

C. *Hazards*

1. The hazards presented by an accident involving nuclear weapons vary greatly, depending upon the factors involved.
2. Transmit a complete description of the situation as soon as possible, including:

   a. Number of people in the vicinity of the scene and the type of buildings in which they are located
   b. Type of terrain
   c. Weather conditions
   d. Type of vegetation (forested, bare, sand, bush, etc.)

7. STREET PSYCHOLOGY

I. Domestic Gun Calls

A. Approaching the Scene

1. In approaching a location at which a person with a gun has been reported:

    a. Confirm that a supervisor and the tactical unit are en route.

    b. Check your body armour.

    c. Ensure that all civilians are immediately removed from any possible lines of fire.

    d. Await arrival of the tactical unit.

2. If circumstances require that you take immediate action to protect lives:

    a. Never have more than two officers present on the porch or in the vicinity of the front door. If too many police officers are bunched together and a gun battle breaks out, they could wind up shooting each other.

    b. Other officers attending should be located at other exit points, particularly near the rear or side door to prevent a bid for escape.

B. Handling the Suspect

1. If you encounter a distraught but apparently unarmed subject, remove your hat at the first opportunity. This action suggests to the subject that you are not about to take immediate action and will help to calm down disturbed and frightened persons.

2. Do *not* allow the subject to leave your view under any circumstances. He may say he is going to get his coat or a package of cigarettes, but can just as easily return with a weapon.

3. If the subject has a dog, tell him to remove it. The dog may attack if you have to move against the owner.

4. Ask the subject to join you outside.

    a. This will eliminate his access to any hidden weapons.

    b. He will also be at a greater psychological disadvantage in a less familiar environment.

5. If the suspect refuses to come out, get him to invite you inside.

6. Once inside, ask if you can take a seat to reinforce once again your nonthreatening attitude.

NOTE: Do not make any gestures that he might interpret as provocative, e.g., placing your hand on your holster, fingering your baton, etc. He may interpret these actions as meaning that you are secretly planning to attack him when his guard is down.

7. As you talk, a second officer should try to remove any members of the subject's family or other persons who may be present:

   a. For their own safety
   b. To prevent them from goading him into violence
   c. To make it easier for the subject to back down

8. The second officer should question the family members as to the subject's psychiatric history to learn:

   a. If he has undergone psychiatric treatment and, if so, for what problem
   b. If he has ever been hospitalized for mental or emotional disorders
   c. If he has a problem with drugs or alcohol
   d. If there are any guns in the house and, if so, where they are located
   e. If the subject has a history of violent behaviour
   f. If he has any military, police, or other special training in the handling of weapons
   g. If there are any special people in his life such as a friend, parent, priest, or co-worker to whom he might listen

9. The second officer can also reassure the family members by advising them how the police can help by calling an ambulance, physician, or social service agency.

10. The second officer's presence nearby also reminds the subject that there is a world outside that can respond if he takes action against you.

C. Confrontation at Gunpoint

1. If the subject actually pulls a gun on you without warning, do not use threats to force him to put the weapon down. They will probably only inflame him even more.

2. An appeal to spare you because of your spouse and children is unlikely to be effective.

   a. The subject's mental state may have resulted from his own difficulties with his family. He may take grim satisfaction in destroying your family's happiness in retribution.

b. He may seek to punish you for his inadequate relationship with his own family.

3. If the suspect is a professional killer, suffers from a severe organic medical problem, or is heavily intoxicated with drugs or alcohol, there may be nothing you can do to influence his actions.

a. You may be forced to take surprise physical action when his guard is down.

b. Only *you* can make that judgment.

4. If the subject is emotionally disturbed, you can usually persuade him to put down his weapon.

a. Tell him that he is in control of the situation and assure him that you do not intend to harm him.

b. If he asks you to hand over your handgun to him, DON'T DO IT. His weapon may be unloaded or even a toy replica; yours isn't.

c. Tell him that his gun makes you feel nervous and makes it difficult for you to concentrate on his problems.

(1) If the subject is unwilling to hand over his weapon, ask him to put the gun down next to him, with the barrel pointed to the wall, to avoid an accidental discharge.

(2) Advise him that you understand that, although he has put the gun down, he is still in charge of the situation.

d. Always address the subject as "Mr. Jones" or "sir," or by his first name.

e. Speak in a low, calm, reassuring voice without making any threats or insults.

f. If he has any questions, answer them sympathetically but carefully.

g. Constantly stress that you are there to help him.

h. Suggest repeatedly that he allow you to take him to someone who can provide professional assistance.

i. If you can establish yourself as a personal friend in his mind, he will be much more receptive to your suggestion that he surrender his weapon.

NOTE: Most mentally and emotionally disturbed people who threaten death to others are really crying out for help for themselves. They often become involved in gun confrontations with police simply to prove to a coldly bureaucratic, uncaring world that they really do *need* help. In some cases, they hope to provoke the police into shooting them, thereby relieving themselves of personal responsibility for an act of suicide they can't commit themselves.

5. Your attitude to the subject after he has surrendered his weapon is extremely important.

   a. He will likely be released from custody in a short period of time, either by the courts or by the psychiatric hospital to which he is sent. Your behaviour could determine his attitude toward the next police officer he may confront.

   b. Continue speaking to him in the calm, reassuring voice that you employed during the confrontation.

   c. If you have to use pepper spray on a subject, use it once only. If the spray is ineffective the first time, it won't work any better on the second application.

   d. Avoid offering putdowns or using strong-arm tactics while taking the suspect into custody. The emotionally disturbed subject is ill, not evil. Leave him with his dignity intact.

   e. Apply handcuffs gently, explaining that this procedure is required by departmental policy and beyond your control.

   f. Conduct a careful search for any hidden weapons.

   g. Praise the subject for being cooperative.

   h. Advise him of the excellent professional help available to assist him with his problem.

   i. During transport to the station or psychiatric facility, ensure that the suspect is seated in the rear of the cruiser, that the "cage" is operative, and that the suspect is handcuffed and, if necessary, shackled.

II. Family Disputes

A. Potential for Violence

Family disputes are among the most dangerous and potentially violent calls you will respond to. They can result in death or serious injury. They are dangerous not only to the participants, but also to the police officer who intervenes.

B. Intervention Techniques

1. Take an extremely low-key approach to dealing with family disputes.

   a. You are intervening in a highly emotional, painful, and personal situation that may be the result of longstanding and deep-seated difficulties.

   b. You are an "outsider"; at least one of the parties involved probably resents your being there.

2. Speak in a calm, soft voice when addressing the disputants. This technique will sometimes cause them to lower their voices—and their emotional level—in order to hear you.

3. Give only a minimal amount of advice and avoid being drawn into the debate.

   a. Your role as a police officer is limited to restoring order, providing protection, or making an arrest, as the circumstances dictate.

   b. You do not have the experience, training, or time to conduct a marriage counselling session.

   c. Above all, don't take sides in the dispute.

4. Separate all the parties immediately and establish yourself as a "referee" who will mediate the conflict.

   a. As referee, lay down some ground rules for the discussion. You may suggest, for example, that you are prepared to listen to their concerns, but only if they stop shouting.

   b. If the husband's drinking is antagonizing his wife, instruct him to put away the bottle before allowing him to speak.

   c. You may attempt to conduct "shuttle diplomacy" between rooms until both parties have calmed down enough to talk to each other.

   d. By keeping the parties apart, you can help them to back down without losing face in front of their partner.

5. In most cases, however heated the discussion, threats of violence are unlikely to be carried out.

   a. Never touch either of the parties unless absolutely necessary. Love and hate are contradictory emotions that are deeply intertwined in many relationships. Your intervention against one partner could quickly transfer much of that hate to you, provoking the other partner into violence to protect his mate.

   b. If a weapon appears, your responsibility is, of course, to disarm, arrest, and restrain the would-be assailant.

6. If one party attacks the other in your presence, do *not* get into a wrestling match.

   a. Place the subject under arrest for assault, and remove him from the scene quickly.

   b. If the subject offers any resistance, indicate clearly and firmly that the dispute is no longer a family matter—he is under arrest and must comply.

    c.   Do not get into a lengthy argument or explanation about your actions. You will appear indecisive and may encourage a more aggressive, violent response.

7. If a fight appears likely, remove any children from the residence as soon as possible.

    a.   The sight of their parents physically attacking each other could have a long-term psychological effect on the children.

    b.   Watching their father or mother being arrested and taken away in handcuffs could also be extremely damaging.

8. Do not make unfounded threats of arrest to control behaviour. If there are grounds to make an arrest, do so; otherwise, try to resolve the problem as best you can and withdraw.

9. Occasionally one of the parties involved in a family dispute will use your presence to:

    a.   Goad the other person involved into an act of violence, thereby forcing you to make an arrest.

    b.   Threaten the other person with arrest unless he makes changes in behaviour, e.g., "I'll have them lock you up unless you promise to stop drinking."

    c.   Embellish his description of the conflict with fake accusations of assault to compel you to make an arrest.

10. Be on the alert for this kind of manipulation. If you detect that it is taking place:

    a.   Advise the subject that you have no authority to make an arrest under the circumstances.

    b.   Inform him of the steps required to make a private complaint.

    c.   Record the subject's threats or aggressive behaviour in your notebook or in an occurrence report. This will protect you if he later charges you with failure to perform your duty.

11. Before withdrawing, advise the couple where to go for help to resolve their personal problems. Suggest an appropriate social service agency that specializes in counselling families in difficulty.

NOTE: Remember that in *all* cases in which a spousal assault has actually occurred, you are required to make an arrest. You do not have the discretion *not* to arrest and charge in these circumstances.

III. **Hostage Situations**

A. Initial Response

1. If no rescue attempt is immediately launched by the responding officers, the most dangerous time in a hostage crisis is during the first 15 to 45 minutes.

2. Crisis management teams normally require 45 minutes to an hour to respond, so the first officer on the scene has a critical role to play in controlling the situation and preserving lives.

3. Isolate yourself and others from danger by taking cover and, if you can do so safely, evacuating the area along routes that are out of sight of the subject.

4. If possible, get the suspect to agree to allow as many civilians as possible to leave the scene.

5. Reassure the subject that the situation is under control and no one is going to be hurt, and inquire as to the safety of the person(s) under his control.

6. Request that any injured parties be released for immediate medical attention.

7. If possible, avoid getting into a continuing conversation; if this is unavoidable, act friendly and concerned, but do not bargain or make any concessions—tell the suspect that you do not have the authority to make such decisions.

B. The Next Stage

1. Keep a record in your notebook of all events, conversations, and personal impressions as you await the crisis management team and pass this information on to them immediately upon arrival.

2. Although you may want to relieve your nervousness by speaking with the subject, let him do the talking so that you learn more about him.

3. Do not give orders or make demands on him that could lead to a heightened level of confrontation. Act and sound thoughtful and conciliatory.

4. Minimize the importance of the events up to the current moment.

   a. Do not admit that any deaths or serious injuries have occurred.

   b. If the suspect has access to a radio or television, say that you have no information because you have been busy with him.

5. Do not offer the subject any physical comforts such as food, coffee, or blankets. (These will be important bargaining points for the negotiating team.)

6. Do not appear to be overly concerned about the victims.

   a.   At the outset, and in a matter-of-fact way, question the suspect as to the victims' names, ages, families, and physical condition.

   b.   Do not belabour these points because this may embolden the hostage-taker and make him feel he has greater power.

7. Do not mislead the suspect unless absolutely necessary. You need his trust. If he thinks he is being tricked, the result will be, at best, lengthier negotiations and, at worst, a dead hostage.

8. Do not respond to specific demands. For example, if he says, "I want my brother here with $1 million in an hour," your response should be, "I can see that you'd like to talk to somebody and get some money as soon as possible. I'll get someone working on it right away."

9. Do not set deadlines for your own performance and try not to let the suspect set them for you.

   a.   If you agree to providing the suspect with, say, coffee or cigarettes in 15 minutes, you may find it impossible to keep your promise, with the hostages paying the price for the delay.

   b.   Even when you are ready, wait until the suspect brings up the request again himself.

     (1) This will use up extra time, which is to your advantage.

     (2) A delay may divert his attention from a more critical deadline, e.g., when money or transportation should have been delivered.

10. Never say no or suggest alternatives, unless you have discussed it first with the on-scene commander.

11. Do not allow civilians such as family members or journalists to be introduced into the situation without the express approval of the head negotiator.

12. Do not under any circumstances allow an exchange of persons not at risk—including yourself—for hostages.

13. Do not negotiate face to face. Speaking by telephone or from cover has proven to be more successful and obviously involves far less risk.

14. Plan the suspect's surrender carefully to avoid taking the weapon from him directly.

15. The two possible approaches to exiting the crisis site are:

   a.   Hostages first—removes the hostages from danger within a brief period of time, but presents the risk that the suspect will change his mind and barricade himself in as they are leaving

b. Suspect first—removes the threat to the hostages immediately, but prevents ordering the suspect to leave his weapon behind (because this would give the hostages access to it)

IV. Nuisance Offences

A. *Obsessive-Compulsive Behaviour*

1. Many so-called nuisance behaviours, such as exhibitionism, kleptomania, and voyeurism, are manifestations of obsessive-compulsive behaviour.

2. Definitions:

a. Obsession—spontaneous, persistent, irrational, and often repetitive thoughts that force themselves into the subject's mind.

b. Examples:

(1) Fantasies of perverted sexual activity

(2) Unwarranted and excessive anxiety about disease

(3) Aggressive or hostile mental images of the subject's parents, spouse, or close relatives

(4) Blasphemous thoughts against Christ or important religious figures such as the Pope (especially if the suspect has a highly religious or moral background)

c. Compulsion—an act that a person commits to relieve his anxieties about an obsession, such as:

(1) Repeated washing of the hands

(2) Incoherent, irrational mumbling about imagined acts of persecution

(3) Complicated rituals for dressing, beginning work, cleaning, or other routine activities

d. Ritualistic patterns that appear in the commission of criminal acts differentiate obsessive-compulsive behaviour from the actions of the psychopathic personality.

3. Obsessive-compulsive behaviour does not always involve criminality.

EXAMPLE: Some individuals may insist that their undershorts or pyjamas be ironed and folded in a certain way, or that their food be arranged on the plate according to a specific layout. These mild obsessions can be found in many normal persons, who can dismiss them from their minds at will. The major distinguishing characteristic of obsessive-compulsive behaviour is an inability to rid the mind of the obsession.

4. As a police officer, your knowledge of the ritualistic nature of obsessive-compulsive behaviour can be an important investigation aid. If you detect a ritualistic pattern in a series of otherwise unrelated crimes, you may be able to:

   a. Link them to a single suspect
   b. Predict his future actions

5. Characteristics of an obsessive-compulsive suspect:

   a. A need to maintain control and appear perfect at all times
   b. A fear of change (which, in his mind, leads to a loss of control and sense of perfection)
   c. A sense of frustration, anxiety, or even guilt if he resists his compulsions

NOTE: This does not necessarily mean that the person *cannot* resist his compulsions. He may feel more comfortable in obeying his compulsions, just as a highly superstitious person may prefer not to step on cracks in the sidewalk. But there is no evidence to suggest that these compulsions are irresistible.

B. *Exhibitionists*

1. Persons who commit acts of indecent exposure are often exhibitionists, but not always.

   a. Some individuals who expose themselves do so:
      (1) As a joke, e.g., mooning
      (2) In response to a dare
      (3) As a gesture of contempt for authority

   b. The exhibitionist exposes himself to the opposite sex to obtain sexual gratification.

      (1) His purpose is to assert his manhood symbolically.
      (2) Although his victim may believe that she is about to be raped, this fear rarely proves to be well-founded.
      (3) The exhibitionist may be exposing himself to prove that he doesn't need women.
      (4) He normally has no intention of having sex with his victim, despite his obscene questions or suggestions.

2. Profile of the exhibitionist:

   a. Most offenders are white males in their mid-20s.
   b. Most are or have been married.
   c. They often stammer when speaking.
   d. Many are intelligent and well educated.
   e. Exhibitionists rarely, if ever, know their victims.

    f.   Most operate in the same type of neighbourhood, at the same time, and most follow the same behaviour pattern in each offence, e.g., using the same expressions in speaking to the victim, wearing the same type of clothing, confronting the same type of victim, etc.

3. By identifying the ritual that the exhibitionist employs, you can often predict where and how he will strike next, and be there to make the arrest.

C. *Kleptomaniacs*

1. Kleptomaniacs differ from common thieves in that they usually steal small, inexpensive, or valueless items.

2. Profile of the kleptomaniac:

    a.   Most are females.

    b.   Many are middle-aged women with no children left at home.

    c.   Most steal openly, making no attempt to conceal their thefts.

    d.   Kleptomaniacs often cry or cause a disturbance during their apprehension (in an effort, perhaps, to attract the attention that they are subconsciously seeking through theft).

    e.   Offenders are frequently, although not always, among those in the upper-income bracket.

    f.   These individuals tend to be evasive during questioning, adamantly refusing to admit their guilt.

    g.   Quite often, kleptomaniacs already possess the stolen object or have sufficient funds on their person when arrested to have purchased the item.

NOTE: Many authorities believe that there is no such clinical condition as kleptomania.

D. *Voyeurs (Peeping Toms)*

1. The voyeur obtains sexual gratification from viewing sexual intercourse, or nude and seminude females.

2. Although most normal men will experience some sexual excitement in this way, the voyeur can be identified by the extent of his efforts to obtain visual stimulation.

3. He will prowl residential neighbourhoods late at night, climb fire escapes, wait for hours in promising locations, and take other extraordinary measures to find what he is looking for.

4. For these persons, the voyeuristic act, usually accompanied by masturbation, *replaces* the sex act as the outlet for sexual satisfaction.

5. Characteristics of the voyeur:

    a.   Usually a young male

    b.   Normally operates close to his own neighbourhood

    c.   Frequently follows a predetermined route where he knows he will find targets of opportunity

    d.   Often operates at the same time each evening

    e.   Frequently masks his prowling activities with some legitimate action such as going to the store or walking the dog

    f.   Usually operates at night to avoid detection

5. Although the voyeur is ritualistic in his operating pattern, he may vary his timetable according to the showering or undressing routines of his victims.

E. *Fetishists*

1. Fetishists use nonsexual, inanimate objects such as shoes or women's underclothes as a replacement for a sex partner to achieve physical gratification.

2. The fetishist may taste, kiss, fondle, embrace, or masturbate over the object to obtain sexual release.

3. Fetishism normally becomes a police matter only when the subject attempts to increase his thrills by stealing the fetish object, e.g., shoes from a woman sitting on a park bench, underwear from a clothesline.

4. Profile of the fetishist:

    a.   Usually male, although incidents involving females have sometimes occurred

    b.   Can be from any age group

    c.   Men more likely to commit theft to obtain fetish objects

5. A fetishist is generally nothing more than a nuisance offender, but male fetishists have been known to commit acts of violence while stealing the fetish object.

F. *Investigating the Nuisance Offender*

1. Because of the ritualistic behaviour commonly associated with nuisance crimes, important evidence can often be found in the suspect's home.

    a.   The voyeur or stalker may have a diary; the fetishist or kleptomaniac will likely have stolen property in his home.

    b.   By executing a search warrant or conducting a search by consent, you may be able to obtain the necessary information to substantiate your case.

    c.   The diary or other evidence found may also assist psychiatric counsellors in treating the suspect's problem.

2. During questioning of the obsessive-compulsive suspect, do not be deterred by the suspect's strong denials or apparently kind, friendly personality.

   a. These subjects need to feel in control and must always attempt to appear perfect.

   b. The moral outrage that your questions elicit may simply reflect the suspect's belief that if he did it, it must have been the right thing to do.

3. Too many police officers view interrogation of nuisance offenders as mere routine, not really expecting to obtain an inculpatory statement.

   a. Often they feel that the minor nature of the offence does not demand the extra effort required to secure an admission of guilt. This kind of attitude guarantees failure.

   b. Although nuisance offences may not seem important in comparison to such serious crimes as rape and homicide, they can have a devastating psychological effect on their victims, sometimes to the point of changing their lives.

   c. Some nuisance offenders go on to commit major, violent crimes.

   d. You should always conduct a thorough investigation and interview of nuisance offenders; you may be able to get them help for their problems and spare future victims pain and embarrassment.

8. COMMUNITY POLICING

I. Introduction

Police agencies throughout North America are implementing community-oriented policing programs. Community policing is an operating philosophy, not a specific tactic. It requires a proactive, decentralized approach that emphasizes increasing citizen satisfaction with the policing service they receive, rather than simply increasing arrests and clearance rates.

The objective of community policing is to reduce crime—and, just as important, fear of crime—by involving the same officer in a particular community on a long-term basis. In this way, residents develop trust in the police and are more likely to provide information and assistance to help officers achieve their goals.

Despite the views of some hard-core traditionalists, community policing is not "soft on crime." Quite the opposite. Its purpose is to reduce the incidence of crime by forging an effective partnership between police officers and the community that they serve. In discussing the huge challenge of fighting crime, senior police officers often tell the media, "We can't do it alone." Community policing is intended to ensure that we don't have to.

II. The Principles and Practices of Community Policing

Implementing a successful community-oriented approach to policing has been shown to require the adoption of several well-tested principles and practices. They include:

1. Establishing a department-wide strategy that encompasses all officers and civilian employees
2. Integrating all divisions into the community-policing process, rather than building special units that remain isolated from the mainstream of departmental activity
3. Providing line officers with the authority to exercise their individual discretion in finding solutions to community problems
4. Assigning officers to work exclusively on community-policing initiatives
5. Initiating specific training programs to support community-policing skills such as problem solving, interpersonal communication, and consensus building

6. Establishing effective working partnerships with the community
7. Increasing citizen participation in dealing with issues of community security

III. Building Community Partnerships

1. The primary objective of community policing is to obtain citizen input and participation.
2. People who come to know and trust the community police officer assigned to their neighbourhood will be more inclined to provide information and assistance.
3. Community spirit can be enhanced by giving citizens a greater voice in setting police priorities.
4. Residents can help identify key neighbourhood problem areas and assist in the creation of locally tailored solutions.
5. Community police officers are allowed to determine the enforcement activities needed for their individual areas and to use their own judgment in providing them.
6. In responding to 911 calls for service, the community police officer is encouraged to follow up during downtimes, to gather intelligence, to help solve continuing problems, and to call in other police or community resources as needed.

IV. Officer Qualifications

1. The ability to identify and analyze recurring or potential crimes and acts of public disorder
2. Strong interpersonal and social interaction skills
3. The willingness and patience to work effectively with local residents, merchants, community leaders, schools, service organizations, associations, and others
4. An interest in uncovering the root causes of neighbourhood problems, and a desire to develop proactive, creative solutions to them
5. Several years of "on the street" police experience

V. Skills and Training Required

Officers involved in community policing must have, or develop, the following skills:

1. Public speaking
2. Problem solving
3. Conflict resolution
4. Team building
5. Interpersonal communication

VI. Community Policing Tactics

1. Operate storefront substations in high-traffic areas such as shopping malls, recreational areas, and downtown shopping districts
2. Interact with the community in resolving problems of crime and disorder (e.g., organizing seminars and meetings to educate citizens on crime prevention techniques, visiting schools and community centres, etc.)
3. Organize neighbourhood organizations to gather information on criminal activity
4. Target for close attention high-risk groups such as biker gangs, prostitutes, and drug traffickers
5. Maintain up-to-date records on local criminal activity, wanted suspects, and crime patterns
6. Meet frequently with residents and local business owners to identify problem areas and develop solutions (e.g., obtaining restraining orders against prostitutes who deter potential customers from entering local stores and other commercial premises, moving benches and other public facilities at which disorderlies tend to gather, etc.)
7. Seek out or initiate conversations with high-risk individuals, such as recently released parolees, suspected drug traffickers, and burglars, to make them aware that you know who they are and where they can be found
8. Support the establishment of citizen advisory committees consisting of:
   a. Homeowners
   b. Business operators
   c. Public housing residents
   d. Church representatives
   e. School representatives
   f. Politicians
   g. Neighbourhood Watch
   h. Service clubs
   i. Community representatives
   j. Social organizations

VII. Measuring Success

1. By its nature, community policing does not lend itself to traditional measures of officer performance, such as number of suspects arrested, tickets and warnings issued, calls handled, and cases cleared. In fact, an officer who is a top performer with respect to these standard measures may actually be a detriment

to the implementation of a successful community-policing program.

2. Police executives may have to employ more subjective measures to determine the success of their community-policing programs. These measures might include:
   a. Surveys of citizen attitudes
   b. Personal interviews
   c. Feedback from community groups
   d. Supervisors' performance appraisals

3. More quantifiable measures include:
   a. Crime statistics
   b. Numbers of justified internal complaints
   c. Numbers of complimentary letters and expressions of gratitude from community members

VIII. Benefits of Community Policing

1. Breaks down the "them vs. us" barrier between police officers and the community they serve
2. Improves morale among officers by empowering them to use their own creativity to solve multidimensional problems
3. Provides the entire police service with more accurate and precise criminal intelligence
4. Inspires greater community support for police officers
5. Focuses on achieving enduring solutions, rather than simply shoving suspects through the "revolving door" of the criminal justice system
6. Reduces the number of calls for service
7. Reduces the number of complaints about police conduct

EXAMPLE: Our police service received frequent complaints that youths using a basketball court in a public park were shouting obscenities at each other that were disturbing to persons strolling nearby, particularly those accompanied by young children. The traditional police response would have been to caution the youths repeatedly and, ultimately, to lay charges of disorderly conduct if they failed to comply.

Such action might have solved the problem; on the other hand, it might simply have inspired the youths to become more defiant of authority, leading to more serious antisocial behaviour and perhaps even more serious charges.

Instead, working with community organizations and the Parks and Recreation Department, our officers arranged to have the basketball net moved to a more remote section of the park where the youths could shout whatever they wanted at each other without disturbing anyone: a win-win situation for everyone concerned.

PART TWO

CRIMINAL INVESTIGATION

9. SUSPECT INTERVIEWS

I. Introduction

Everyone knows how police officers solve crimes. Citizens have seen it done thousands of times on television and in films. It takes only a single tire track in a muddy road, or a smudged fingerprint from a cocktail glass that the detective has surreptitiously slipped into his coat pocket. The case is wrapped up within the hour and the suspect makes a voluntary confession as soon as he is confronted with the facts.

Real police officers can only shake their heads in amazement. They know that in most cases the wonders of scientific investigations only confirm the guilt of a suspect who has already been identified by the age-old technique of asking questions.

Fingerprints and other forms of physical evidence are helpful in establishing guilt. But judges and juries are most likely to be swayed by the accused's voluntary confession, on videotape, that he committed the crime.

Of all the skills demanded by modern police work, skill at interviewing is still the most important. The police officer who is adept at developing informants, who is tenacious in tracking down suspects, and who is expert in collecting physical evidence can still be an ineffective investigator if he is incapable of obtaining video confessions. The officer who is relatively weak in these other areas can earn an excellent reputation for solving crimes if he has an aptitude for interpersonal skills in dealing with suspects.

A solid understanding of human nature is without a doubt the most important weapon in the police officer's arsenal of investigative techniques.

II. Prerequisites for a Successful Interview

A. Attitude of the Investigator

1. Although you may be disgusted or repelled by the nature of the crime you are investigating, during the interview you must display an attitude that shows respect for the subject as a human being.
2. A bullying attitude or physical threats will serve only to:

    a. Jeopardize the admissibility of the confession you do obtain

    b. Cause the suspect to become so defiant that he refuses to talk at all

    c. Result in a public loss of confidence and respect for police officers

    d. Raise the possibility of your facing criminal charges

3. Many suspects want to confess to somebody about their crimes but will not open up to an officer who is unsympathetic or intimidating.

B. Need for Privacy

1. Many experienced officers believe that privacy is the principal psychological factor in obtaining confidential or embarrassing disclosures.

2. Only two officers should be present during an interview—one to ask questions, the other to take notes. (Some officers feel more comfortable with a one-on-one approach, and choose to have their partner monitor the interview on video from outside the interview room.)

    a. The suspect may feel a strong sense of shame over what he has done; he will be understandably reluctant to discuss his crime in front of a crowd.

    b. Unnecessary persons in the interview room may:

        (1) Divert the suspect's attention from your questions

        (2) Transmit their feelings of disapproval to the suspect

        (3) Interrupt you unexpectedly and destroy your line of questioning

        (4) Complicate your court case when they are called to give testimony in voir dire proceedings to determine the admissibility of a statement

3. The second officer, by nodding and making appropriate gestures, can indicate his approval of your statements as they are made to the suspect.

4. The suspect's denials or evasions may well be shaken by this visible third-party endorsement as you recite the evidence against him.

5. Every suspect and crime is different; experience will guide your judgment of privacy issues.

C. Suitable Setting

1. Every police station should have at least one room that is reserved for questioning purposes only.

a.   If possible, this room should be located on an upper level. This precaution will prevent a judge from inferring that the suspect was intimidated into confessing because he was locked up in a dungeon in the basement.

b.   If the layout of the station permits, the room should be located near a regular office area—provided, of course, that security can be maintained.

2.   For security reasons, a squad room or other police work area should be situated between the interview room and areas in which civilian office staff are working.

3.   The interview room should have only one entrance, with a locking door and a sign indicating whether the room is vacant or in use.

4.   The interview room should be stripped of all pictures, posters, and small loose objects such as pens and paper clips, which could serve to distract the suspect's attention during questioning. (Some of these items could also be used as weapons in an escape attempt.)

5.   The interview room should not contain any windows or pictures that may distract the suspect.

a.   If the only room available has windows, they should not be barred. Bars only remind the suspect that he is in police custody.

b.   Visible indicators of confinement can destroy any rapport that you have established whenever they fall into the suspect's view.

6.   Retain normal overhead lighting.

a.   You must present a normal, human image to the suspect.

b.   If a jury hears that your interview room contains desk or spot lamps, it might conclude that the accused's confession resulted from so-called third-degree tactics.

7.   A video camera should be positioned unobtrusively in a corner of the room that provides a complete picture of the scene. The microphone should be located in a position that clearly picks up all conversations in the room, not just those between the subject and the interviewer. Test the audio function before beginning the interview to ensure that it is working properly.

8.   Although you should ensure that the suspect has had full opportunity to contact his legal counsel prior to questioning, no telephones should be located in the interview room.

NOTE: If the interview room has a drop ceiling, it should be removed. The suspect may hide in it when he is left alone in an effort to attempt an escape.

D. *Preparation for the Interview*

1. The success of your interview will usually depend upon the amount of work you have done to prepare for it.

   a. Interview in detail the victim, the complainant, and the person who discovered the crime, as well as any possible witnesses or informants, before beginning any interview.

   b. You must know *all* of the facts that have been established in the case up to that time.

   c. Be sure that your information is *accurate*.

NOTE: An experienced criminal will quickly lose respect for an investigator who is obviously not in command of the facts.

You must remain the psychological master of the situation. Small errors will chip away at the aura of competence that is so crucial to your winning the accused's respect and confidence.

2. As part of your preparation, carefully review and commit to memory all oral, written, or recorded statements of anyone with informed knowledge of the case, including:

   a. Notes of the officers who originally responded to the call

   b. Reports prepared by doctors, fingerprint experts, laboratory technicians, and other specialists

   c. Any available background information on the suspect, such as his criminal record, prior arrest reports, medical records, etc.

3. If the suspect has offered an alibi prior to the interview, check it out. Note any inconsistencies with other evidence.

   a. The skillful destruction of an alibi will often contribute to the "break" that results in a full confession.

   b. The effects of inaccuracy can rebound in many ways, depending upon the personality of the subject:

      (1) If he has a belligerent nature, an unfounded allegation may enrage him to the point that he refuses to talk.

      (2) If your questions reveal that you are not aware of the true seriousness of his involvement, the suspect may offer an incomplete or twisted version of the truth. This will lead to wasted time and effort spent in investigating false leads.

4. The time element is an important factor in determining the admissibility of a statement.

a. In some cases, although the suspect is in custody, you will not have had time to prepare yourself or your partner to conduct an interview properly.

b. In these cases, you are entitled to hold the suspect alone in a cell for a few hours until you are ready to proceed.

c. The courts have ruled that spending several hours in a cell awaiting questioning is not prejudicial to the accused.

III. Conduct of the Interview

A. Interviewing Techniques

1. On initial contact with the suspect, identify yourself with a statement such as "I'm Sergeant Jones. I have been assigned to your case."

   a. This statement implies that you are not out to "get" him, but simply wish to clear up a difficult situation.

   b. At all costs, avoid giving him the impression that you are seeking to exact punishment for his crime.

   c. If circumstances permit, don't wear your uniform, badge, identification card, gun, handcuffs, or any other sign of your official status.

   d. You must establish as quickly as possible that the interview is between two human beings, not simply police officer and suspect.

2. Immediately tell the suspect why he has been brought to you and give him the standard warnings required by statutory and case law.

3. During your preliminary conversation, state clearly that your only goal in speaking with the suspect is to find the truth.

4. Flattery, in the initial stage, can be a powerful weapon.

EXAMPLE: One of my colleagues often used the "show me your hands" technique to start the interview on the proper note: If the subject's hands were rough, he'd say, "You know, your hands tell me that you're a man who works for a living. You're not one of those low-lifes we get in here all the time, the kind who's out for a free ride and doesn't care how he gets it. You work for a living just like I do. Now, let's get this thing cleared up. What got you into this mess?"

Or, if the suspect had smooth hands, the approach would be, "Your hands tell me that you're an intelligent, educated man. You've got smooth hands. You use your head to make a living. You're not one of those dummies we get in here every day. I'm not even going to try to play games with a man like you. Let's get this thing resolved

quickly. There's no sense in wasting your time or mine. How did this happen?"

On another occasion, this detective asked a rape suspect to "prove" that he had a job by telephoning his employer on the police telephone. The officer offered to listen in on the extension, if the suspect agreed. The suspect willingly consented and made the call. After his somewhat confused employer agreed that yes, he did indeed have a job, the suspect hung up and was escorted back to the interview room. "Okay," the investigator continued, "I believe you. You're a working man with a steady job. Now, tell me, how did you get into this mess?"

The suspect willingly offered all the facts and signed a detailed confession. He was duly charged and taken to the station cells to await transport.

A few hours later, the officer received a call from an officer on the prison escort detail who had just made a delivery to the county lockup. "I called," he said, "because I want to make sure there hasn't been a mix-up. This may sound strange, but I was talking to a rape suspect that I just dropped off at the jail. He seemed so sure I thought I better check with you. Is he supposed to be going to work tomorrow?"

By asserting that the suspect is a unique individual, worthy of respect, you can often obtain a statement quickly, without resorting to threats or other tactics that would render the statement inadmissible in court.

5. Establish your dominant role in the situation immediately by issuing brief, sharp commands in an authoritative voice. Tell the suspect where to sit and where to hang up his coat, to put out his cigarette and to take his hands out of his pockets, and so forth.

6. Sit as close to the suspect as possible. Do not allow a desk or other piece of furniture in the room to become a psychological defence barrier that he can hide behind.

a. Don't wander around the room during questioning. The suspect may feel that you lack confidence or are becoming impatient and will soon give up questioning him.

b. Limit the amount of smoking that takes place during the interview.

(1) Smoking creates a relaxed atmosphere from which the suspect may draw comfort.

(2) He may also use his cigarette as a psychological crutch to prop him up during stressful questioning.

(3) The occasional offer of a cigarette will, however, assist in establishing in court that the accused was well treated while in custody.

7. Use language that reflects the level of the suspect's verbal comprehension.

a. A subject with little education or intellectual ability may hesitate to answer your questions because he simply doesn't understand them.

b. Your goal is to obtain a confession in clear, simple English, not to impress the suspect with your command of polysyllabic words.

8. Have the accused relate exactly what he did in his own words.

9. Make sure he continues speaking in the direction of the microphone.

10. Ask specific questions to get him to explain portions of his statement and to get him back on track if he wanders.

11. Ensure that relevant portions of the videotape record are clearly marked. If necessary, have transcripts of these portions of the tape prepared for distribution to other officers or the Crown Attorney's office, or as evidence for court.

12. At no time during the interview should the suspect be handcuffed or shackled.

a. If the suspect arrives for the interview in handcuffs, remove them immediately.

b. Tell him that you want him to be comfortable and are concerned about his sense of dignity.

13. Be cautious of the suspect who offers a full, voluntary confession too easily.

a. Many disturbed people are eager to confess to serious crimes that they did not commit.

b. Their motivations are many:

(1) To gain sympathy

(2) To obtain free room and board at government expense

(3) To get their names in the newspaper

(4) To receive punishment and psychological redemption for moral wrongs they may have committed that are not crimes

EXAMPLE: On one occasion, I arrested a drunk who immediately confessed to a major bank robbery. Under intensive questioning, he revealed that he had not robbed the bank; he had confessed only to

increase his status among his fellow prisoners. He was tired of being a nobody in the inmate hierarchy. He was so ambitious to move up in the jailhouse social set that, shortly after his release, he robbed the same bank that he had described during our interview.

14. False confessions need not always be psychologically motivated.

    a. Use caution in dismissing a confession as the work of a crank.

    b. Some clever suspects will confess to a relatively minor offence in order to appear truthful and divert your attention from their involvement in a more serious crime.

B. Nonverbal Communication

1. Actions, as well as words, can communicate a suspect's opinions, feelings, and attitudes during questioning.

    a. Although, in theory, gestures and body positions are consciously controlled, in fact they often reveal the subject's most deeply concealed thoughts.

    b. To be a skilled interviewer, you must:

        (1) Know the hidden meaning of gestures

        (2) Constantly be alert to nonverbal cues

2. Nonverbal signs indicating deception:

    a. A hesitant pause before answering your question

    b. A break in eye contact during an important question

    c. A reluctance to look you in the face

    d. An excessive amount of time spent stubbing out a cigarette

    e. Staring at the walls or floor

    f. Constant repetition of your questions before answering

    g. Placing a hand over his mouth while responding

    h. Inability to sit still in the chair

    i. Nervous manipulation of jewellery, small change, or bits of paper

    j. A dry mouth that creates a clicking sound while the subject is talking

    k. Removal of wallet from a pocket to look over family photographs

    l. Pallid skin colour

    m. Constant checking of watch

    n. Tapping of the fingers (could also indicate boredom)

    o. Picking imaginary lint from clothing

    p. Sitting with head bowed, slumped forward in the chair

    q. Arms crossed in front of his body

    r.   Frequent touching of the nose area (as if flicking away an imaginary fly)

3. Nonverbal signals indicating truthfulness:

    a. Willingness to answer questions freely

    b. No hesitation in replies

    c. Detailed answers

    d. Nondefensive stance, e.g.,

        (1) Feet remain uncrossed

        (2) Arms on armrests

        (3) Clasps hands behind his head while answering

    e. Looks directly at interviewer

    f. Willingly offers sources of confirmation for his statements

NOTE: A study of nonverbal cues has revealed that truthful persons exhibit friendly, light-hearted, and well-composed behaviour three times more often than liars. This study, however, also showed that composed and relaxed attitudes were the least reliable of all indicators of truthfulness.

The skillful liar apparently has little difficulty in presenting a relaxed, confident image. Do not rely upon the subject's state of composure to interpret nonverbal cues.

The same study reported that such indicators as evasiveness, nervous body movements, poor eye contact, and frightened or uncooperative attitude were displayed 10 times more often by untruthful subjects.

4. Nonverbal signals indicating anger:

    a. Clenched fists rested on the hips

    b. Legs placed apart

    c. Gritted teeth

    d. Squinting eyes

    e. Flushed face

    f. Change in voice pitch

    g. Use of profanities directed at victim or police in general

5. Interpretation of nonverbal cues:

    a. Do not draw any conclusions about the subject on the basis of one or two gestures.

    b. Nonverbal signals must be interpreted in *clusters,* taking into account:

        (1) The context in which the signal occurred

        (2) How long into the interview the cue occurred

        (3) What was being discussed

EXAMPLE: During the initial stages of the interview, most citizens, particularly those who have had no previous contact with police officers, will be extremely nervous. Their natural rhythm of speech may be slow and hesitant. They may even present a deceptive appearance over a minor personal transgression for which they feel deep guilt, but which has nothing to do with your investigation.

   Begin serious interpretation of nonverbal signals only after you feel certain you have established a sufficiently strong rapport with your subject that these external influences are not affecting his behaviour.

6. Remember that the suspect is also picking up nonverbal cues from you, e.g.:

   a. If your eyes widen with surprise, he will know he has said something significant.

   b. If your face is impassive and you begin looking at your watch, he may be hesitant to continue with his answer.

   c. Use nonverbal signals consciously to guide your subject in the directions you wish him to go during questioning.

IV. The Type A Suspect

A. Definition

1. For the purposes of the interview, many investigators distinguish between two types of suspects:

   a. Type A suspect: guilt is virtually certain

   b. Type B suspect: guilt is uncertain

B. Approach

1. In dealing with the Type A suspect, all your actions and questions must demonstrate complete confidence in his guilt.

   a. Make him believe that lies, evasions, or emotional protests are not going to dissuade you from a cool, measured search for the truth.

   b. Use nonverbal cues such as an understanding smile or a weary shake of the head to show the suspect that his guilt is obvious and his attempts to escape the truth are ineffective.

2. In questioning the Type A suspect, feed him small pieces of circumstantial evidence that suggest his guilt, such as:

   a. His proximity to the crime scene at the time of the offence

   b. His resemblance to the description given by witnesses

   c. His lack of an alibi

   d. His past history of committing similar types of crimes

NOTE: Never reveal all that you know. You will need more facts for further questioning if he attempts to alter his story to suit the facts that you disclose.

3. Indicate that you feel sympathy for his predicament.
4. If the suspect asks if he can make restitution, this offer usually indicates guilt.
5. Suggest that an accomplice or someone else involved is really responsible for the crime.
6. Make the suspect feel that nothing he says will surprise you, that you've been through this hundreds of times before.
7. Be careful not to suggest that this means he will not be prosecuted or that you will attempt to have his penalty reduced.
8. If he asks for something in return for his confession, reply that those decisions are up to the prosecutor.
9. Make no promises, but point out that he will have every opportunity to tell his side of the story to the judge and jury, just as he is telling it to you on videotape.
10. If the suspect continues to maintain his innocence, suggest that his nonverbal cues are evidence of his guilt.

    a.   If he licks his lips, tell him his mouth is dry because he is not telling the truth.
    b.   Take the same approach if he won't look you in the eye or stares at the floor.
    c.   Point out that his hand wringing, foot jiggling, gulping, reddened face, or excessive sweating are all signs of falsehood.
    d.   Ask him if he has a "peculiar feeling inside" and link that sensation to his deceitful words.

NOTE: Members of some ethnic groups who are completely innocent may demonstrate these behaviours simply because they are in the presence of an authority figure. Be sensitive to these cultural differences in assessing their credibility.

11. If the suspect continues making strenuous denials:

    a.   Divert your line of questioning from seeking an admission of guilt to obtaining an admission that he was at or near the scene of the crime when it occurred.
    b.   If he admits to having been at the scene, ask him to justify his presence.
    c.   If he denies being present when the crime was committed, try to place him there at some other time.

EXAMPLE: "You live a few blocks over from the store that was held up, don't you? Have you ever seen it open late at night? Did you ever stop in to pick up a pack of cigarettes?"

12. If that approach doesn't work, try to establish some prior contact with the victim. Use apparently innocent questions such as "Have you known Mary long?" or "This guy Jones is pretty hard to get along with, isn't he?"

13. If, during the course of these questions, you catch the suspect in a small lie, tell him why you know he has not told the truth, and then move on to further questions.

    a.   At a critical moment later, when he swears that he is now telling the truth, tell the suspect that he was caught lying before and is doing so again.

    b.   If he becomes angry or annoyed, remind him in a disappointed tone that you are only reacting to his own words.

    c.   Follow through by saying his lies and evasions prove that he committed the crime.

    d.   Constantly remind the subject of the futility of not telling the truth.

    e.   Remind him that you already have enough evidence to convict him, and that you are merely tying up "loose ends."

    f.   Tell him, "Everyone makes mistakes, but you're getting a chance—right now—to put things right."

    g.   Use phrases that imply finality, such as "Let's clear this up once and for all."

    h.   Tell the suspect how much you personally respect a person who is brave enough to admit his mistakes and make amends.

14. When the suspect begins to confess, don't interrupt until he has finished his story.

    a.   Only after he has purged his sense of guilt should you attempt to clear up ambiguities in his story or seek clarifying details.

    b.   Even if you know that elements of his confession are false, let him keep talking.

    c.   Make mental notes of any inconsistencies or lies and clear them up later.

15. Although questioning an unresponsive suspect can be a difficult, frustrating experience, don't give up until you have absolutely no other choice.

a. A subject's lack of response to your questions may signify that a major break is coming.

b. If you've exhausted one line of questioning, keep things moving.

    (1) Begin a new dialogue by asking the subject if he would be willing to appear in a lineup.

    (2) If he refuses, ask for an explanation.

    (3) His response could open up a whole new area of questioning.

c. Offer the suspect the opportunity to clear himself by taking a polygraph test (even if your department doesn't have a polygraph).

d. A refusal indicates probable guilt and opens up a new line of questioning.

TIP: After cautioning the accused and allowing him to make a telephone call to legal aid duty counsel, keep talking even if he refuses to speak. Start with his personal details for the record of arrest. Once he begins to talk, you can quickly get him back to the reason that he is speaking to you today. In some cases, he will forget the advice of the legal aid lawyer and make a legally admissible confession.

V. The Type B Suspect

A. *Preliminary Questions*

1. In dealing with the Type B suspect, the person whose guilt is uncertain or doubtful, direct your questions toward establishing that he has some knowledge of the crime under investigation.

a. Ask the suspect if he knows why he is being questioned. (This approach can be used only if the suspect is speaking voluntarily. If the suspect is under arrest, he will, of course, have been cautioned and know what crime is under investigation.)

b. If his response is negative, when he clearly has some knowledge of the crime under investigation, the suspect is either guilty or in some way involved.

c. If his reply is affirmative, you have put him on the defensive. Now he is compelled to justify his answer with an explanation. If he doesn't offer anything further, ask, "Well, what do you know about it?"

d. This line of questioning will often reveal solutions to other unsolved crimes.

(1) The suspect may begin talking about an offence you are not aware of.

(2) Be quick to recognize the opportunity and allow him to continue without interruption.

(3) The suspect may reveal his knowledge of a more serious crime.

(4) You can bring him back to the offence under investigation later.

(5) Ensure that you caution the suspect for the fresh crime once you are satisfied that it merits investigation.

NOTE: Not only does this tactic quickly implicate the guilty, but it also serves to avoid creating needless difficulties for the innocent. If, in your judgment, the subject is completely confused by your initial question and has no other evidence against him, you can safely move on to other suspects.

Even if later developments reveal that the suspect put on a successful deception, you've won something. When you question him again, you will have established your competence as an investigator by demonstrating that he can't lie to you and get away with it for long.

2. Once you have established that the subject has knowledge of the crime, ask him to tell you everything he knows about it, to the smallest detail.

a. This will help you either to confirm his story independently or to refute any lies or inconsistencies.

b. If there are multiple suspects involved, ask your subject who he thinks did it.

c. Often the guilty party will not want to involve innocent friends or acquaintances and will refuse to name anyone, no matter how hard you push.

d. The completely innocent subject, fearful of being jailed for a crime he didn't commit, will probably identify someone.

3. If the subject holds strong views about "stooling" on others, ask him to identify the persons he feels sure did *not* do it.

4. Either way, his willingness to give a name indicates probable innocence.

B. Testing the Suspect's Credibility

1. To test credibility:

a. Ask for details of events that occurred before and after the time the crime was committed, through a series of questions that require precise answers.

b. Ask for details of the time period during which the crime occurred.

c. If the suspect's recollection of events that took place at the time of the crime is in much sharper detail than the other events of the same day, use this inconsistency to attack his credibility.

2. When the suspect offers an alibi, the ideal method of verification is, of course, investigation, checking the places he supposedly visited and the people he claims to have talked to. You can avoid wasting time and effort, however, by asking the right questions during the interview.

a. Obtain detailed information about his activities before, at the time of, and after the occurrence in question.

b. Ask him to provide as many details as possible and be obvious about taking detailed notes.

(1) If he is guilty, there may be a time gap in his alibi, a period of one or two hours that he cannot account for or in which he claims he neither spoke to nor met anyone.

(2) If he is guilty, this time period will coincide exactly with the time of the offence.

c. Challenge him on this point immediately, arguing that it could hardly be coincidental that his memory falls apart at the precise moment the crime was committed.

EXAMPLE: Tell him that since there are 24 hours in a day and 365 days in a year, the likelihood of the two times corresponding is about 9000 to 1.

You can also throw in a "red herring" such as "You say you were driving along the downtown expressway at 8 p.m. Didn't you get caught in the traffic jam? Our accident reports show that a tractor trailer overturned at 7:30 p.m. and traffic was held up for over an hour."

If he believes your story, his guilt is almost certain. If, on the other hand, he is clearly confused and emphatically denies seeing the accident, he is probably telling the truth.

d. Ask the suspect to give you his alibi.

(1) Prepare a written statement and ask him to sign it.

(2) Later, you can ask for a second oral statement of his alibi.

(3) Because it is almost impossible for a liar to remember all the details of a false story, a quick comparison of the two statements will show whether or not he is telling the truth.

3.   Your initial goal in interviewing the Type B suspect is to catch him in a lie and to build upon this weakness, using any other evidence you have gathered.

   a.   If he is truly innocent, he knows he has nothing to fear from you and is unlikely to lie.

   b.   Sometimes, however, the suspect may lie or evade your questions for personal reasons unrelated to the crime.

EXAMPLE: The suspect may fear that an act of adultery will be discovered or that his employer will learn that he spent a sick day at the racetrack.

You can usually shatter this sort of posturing by reminding him that the legal consequences of a serious criminal offence are far worse than anything he might face for his personal indiscretions. You can also assure the suspect that you have no interest in, or judgment to make about, his personal life, and that his answers will remain confidential.

4.   Question the suspect about nonexistent incriminating evidence such as fingerprints or witness statements.

   a.   If he accepts the existence of this evidence but tries to offer an explanation, your suspect is probably guilty.

   b.   On the other hand, the innocent person will become confused and extremely anxious, and may suspect a conspiracy to frame him.

EXAMPLE: If the offence is a break-in, you might ask, "Is there any reason why your fingerprints were found on the inside doorknob?" If the offence is armed robbery, you might ask, "Is there any reason why three different witnesses would have taken down your licence number when they saw the getaway car leaving the bank?"

The guilty man will try to explain; the innocent will probably say, "No, there isn't, because I wasn't there." His immediate recognition of your deception suggests that he is telling the truth.

5.   Ask the suspect to take a lie detector test. A negative response, while not conclusive, is again an indication of possible guilt.

6.   If the suspect continues to deny any involvement in the offence, ask him if he ever *thought* about committing this type of crime. His reaction could be very revealing.

7.   If two suspects are involved, separate them immediately upon their arrest.

    a.   Question each suspect individually, suggesting that the other was the prime mover in the crime and that the person being questioned played only a minimal role.

8.   This technique can be embellished in a number of ways.

    a.   If both men are hard cases, they are probably as distrustful of each other as they are of you.

    b.   This distrust can be a highly effective aid in securing a confession; use it to play one against the other.

VI. Conclusion

If you feel any personal misgivings about using trickery to obtain confessions, remember that the courts over the years have ruled that confessions obtained in this manner are admissible so long as the tricks employed would not be likely to inspire a false confession or bring our system of justice into disrepute.

Although the use of trickery during an interview will often result in defence counsel and even judges making disparaging comments about police tactics, such comments should not deter you from using these techniques when required. Your responsibility is to produce a truthful confession that is legally admissible and will result in the conviction of a guilty person. Clearly, however, deception should be reserved for the investigation of serious crimes that justify its use.

The law recognizes the hard reality that the police need to use trickery to solve crimes. The techniques outlined in this chapter are effective only when applied against guilty suspects. The innocent need have no fear of a skilled interviewer.

10. THE CRIME SCENE

I. Introduction

The criminal investigator is a seeker of truth, but truth is elusive and easily concealed. Witnesses can be imprecise, inaccurate, or deceitful in giving their version of the truth. The suspect, faced with a possible jail term or fine, has little incentive to reveal the truth. Even when they are *trying* to be helpful, human beings can offer only their interpretation of the truth as they perceive it, based upon their physical and mental abilities, biases, personal opinion, and verbal skills. The objective truth will often be found through the skillful collection of physical evidence. Unlike witness or suspect statements, physical evidence provides hard facts that cannot be challenged (although the *interpretation* of these facts may be hotly disputed in court).

In most cases, some physical evidence will be found at the scene of the crime. Within the boundaries of that crime scene are the clues that will enable you to identify and charge the person responsible. As an investigator, your responsibility is to ensure that all relevant information at the crime scene is discovered and intelligently interpreted. Equally important, evidence must be preserved and recorded according to procedures that satisfy the rules of legal admissibility.

Cases can be won or lost depending upon your ability to investigate and manage evidence. Improperly handled, this evidence may solve the crime in *your* mind, but have no value in the forum that really counts—the criminal court. Gathering physical evidence can be difficult and painstaking work; however, you will often find that it plays a decisive role in a successful investigation.

II. The Crime Scene

A. *Preliminary Considerations*

1. The police investigator must determine the answers to six fundamental questions to solve his case:
    a. Who?
    b. What?
    c. When?
    d. Where?

    e.   Why?

    f.   How?

2.   Your first responsibilities upon arrival at a crime scene are to:

    a.   Obtain an initial overview of the situation

    b.   Choose a starting point of reference from which to make a detailed, well-planned examination

3.   You must keep an open mind about what you observe until all the facts are in.

EXAMPLE: An investigator who attends a sudden-death call where the victim was found hanging by his belt from a garage rafter could assume suicide and not take the precautions necessary to ensure that the scene remains free of contamination by cigarette butts, fingerprints, and footprints. His assumption that the death was a routine suicide might be disproved by an autopsy revealing that the victim died of poisoning, not strangulation. A great deal of vital evidence could be lost because of his erroneous assumption that the victim had "obviously" killed himself.

B.   Observing the Scene

1.   Rather than be satisfied with the obvious, adopt the "worst possible" scenario upon arriving at the scene of any crime, particularly a sudden death.

    a.   Once you have permitted evidence to be destroyed or removed, you can never go back and correct an error of omission. The past can never be replayed.

    b.   If you find that an apparently serious crime was in fact an accident, your efforts to note and preserve potential evidence have certainly done no harm.

    c.   There is always a possibility that the real truth about an incident will be found out only at a much later date. Your notes and observations could suddenly prove to be vital in proving a complex or difficult case.

2.   Make observations, not assumptions, during your examination of the crime scene.

    a.   Objects are often moved in order to lead the police into developing a false theory of the crime. Note any inconsistencies between the way things are and the way they should be, e.g.:

        (1)   If a suicide victim is right-handed, why is his wallet in his left back pocket?

        (2)   If the victim always writes his correspondence out longhand, why is the suicide note typewritten?

(3) If it's a hot day, why are the ashes in the fireplace warm?

(4) If the victim apparently died alone, why are there two brands of cigarette butts in the ashtray?

b. Noting such questions, and finding the answers, can build a total picture of what actually happened, rather than what apparently happened.

3. In addition to noting what *is* at the crime scene, pay careful attention to what isn't and should be, e.g.:

a. If the victim apparently walked into the room alone, why are there no fingerprints on the doorknob?

b. If he was a fastidious gun collector, why has a shotgun been mounted in a rifle rack?

c. If a house has been broken into, why did the burglar smash through the basement window when he could have entered noiselessly through the rear kitchen door?

NOTE: To keep an open mind while examining a crime scene, you must develop a systematic approach in conducting your search for evidence. Wandering about the scene hoping that your eye will pick up something interesting may work occasionally, but in the long run the officer who relies on inspiration or intuition will fail to find a piece of important evidence.

C. *Securing the Scene*

1. Do not touch or move anything until the entire scene has been recorded through notes, photographs, and sketches.

a. These notes and photographs should show clearly the location and condition of all objects at the scene, both movable and fixed.

b. Note your time of arrival at the scene and also the weather conditions.

c. Confirm that the first officer to arrive at the scene has made a similar notation.

2. Prevent any persons who may have witnessed or been aware of the crime from leaving the area until they have been questioned in detail.

3. Remove all persons from the room or vicinity of the crime to prevent destruction of evidence.

a. If possible, prevent unauthorized entry to the scene by locking entrances where necessary. (Be careful not to wipe any fingerprints off windows and doors.)

b. Post guards or rope off the area to unauthorized persons.

4. Make a permanent record of the area by describing the scene and evidence in your police notebook.

   a. If expert assistance is not available, immediately photograph the scene yourself and make sketches.

   b. Record in your notebook:

     (1) All observations made at the scene

     (2) Suggestions, leads, and any other useful information obtained from other officers or through interviews of witnesses

D. Examining the Crime Scene

1. Note the general appearance of the scene from the principal point of entry.

2. Step forward carefully, checking the floor for:

   a. Marks
   b. Traces
   c. Stains
   d. Scratches
   e. Small objects

3. Disregard large objects such as the body, furniture, or pools of blood at this stage of the examination.

4. After completing a minute examination of the floor or ground area, you may begin examining larger objects with the confidence that you will not be treading on important, hard-to-see evidence.

   a. Examine all large objects that might have any conceivable bearing on the case—which means *everything.*

   b. Starting from a fixed point such as a corner of the room:

     (1) Check each wall thoroughly from floor to ceiling, including doors and windows.

     (2) Try to determine the direction from which the offender gained entry to and exited the scene.

     (3) Examine the ceiling carefully, noting any marks, stains, holes, or other items that might be relevant.

5. Check the contents of furniture and containers such as wastebaskets, sinks, desk drawers, bottles, and jars.

   a. Read any letters, documents, or other papers found at the scene. List them in your notebook and hold them as evidence.

   b. Hold any papers or other objects at their edges or corners to avoid destroying latent fingerprints.

6. If you are going to leave the scene for any reason, exit along the same path along which you entered.
7. If the crime involves a death, examine the body carefully, noting:

   a. Position of the entire body, with particular attention to the placement of the hands, feet, head, trunk, and legs

   b. Distance of the head, side, crotch, and limbs of the body from other objects in the room

   c. Condition of individual parts of the body, e.g.:

   (1) Head wounds?
   (2) Hair combed?
   (3) Hair and skin—dirty or clean?
   (4) Bruises, scars?
   (5) Dirt?
   (6) Haircut?
   (7) Distinctive marks?
   (8) Eyes and mouth—open or closed?
   (9) Facial expression?
   (10) Teeth—clean or dirty? straight or broken? discoloured or white?
   (11) Lividity

   d. Condition of clothing

   (1) Shoes—colour, material, worn, scuffed, polished, any marks, cracks in leather, anything stuck to soles?
   (2) Jacket and pants—clean or dirty, pressed or rumpled, cuts or tears, stains, missing buttons, anything in cuffs, labels, lapel pins, holes, wear marks, colour and pattern, apparent fabric, vents or pleats, cuffs, wet or dry?

NOTE: If you remove clothing, wrap it carefully in paper for expert examination by the forensic science specialists. (See "The Search for Evidence," page 128.)

8. Check the terrain around the crime scene for any traces of the suspect's movement such as:

   a. Disturbed soil
   b. Footprints
   c. Damaged grass or plants
   d. Broken twigs

9. Record all details noted as quickly as possible, remembering that:

   a. Conditions change rapidly at a major crime scene (e.g., room temperature, condition of ground or floor, etc.), which may be visited by coroners, senior police officers, forensic science experts, and others who may or may not have a legitimate reason to be there.

b.   Unauthorized persons may blunder into the scene, contaminating it beyond salvation.

c.   The information you record at this stage of your crime scene examination could very well determine the outcome of the investigation.

NOTE: A significant mistake at this stage could ruin your investigation, no matter how expert the follow-up work might be. On the other hand, an effective job of handling the crime scene evidence can often narrow down the field of suspects considerably and lead to a quick arrest in what would otherwise be a lengthy and difficult investigation.

E.   Videos, Photographs, and Sketches

1.   Videos, photographs, and sketches offer a valuable and permanent record of the crime scene.

a.   Many cases have been lost because an accurate photograph of the scene was not taken immediately upon discovery of the crime.

b.   If you are required to take the photographs personally, record each exposure in your notebook, noting:

(1)   Exact location and angle of the camera in relation to the scene

(2)   Name, make, and model of the camera

(3)   Lighting conditions when the photographs were taken, e.g., bright sunlight, cloudy, photoflash, floodlights, etc.

(4)   Type of film

(5)   Lens opening

(6)   Aperture setting

(7)   Shutter speed

(8)   Whether flash was used

NOTE: If you have discovered a body, ensure that it has been photographed in detail from every conceivable angle before allowing it to be removed.

2.   Prepare a sketch of the scene after the photographs have been taken, indicating:

a.   Location

b.   Approaches and entrances to the building or area

c.   Size and number of rooms

d.   Location of fingerprints, footprints, or tracks

    e.   Position and relative size of objects on the floor, ceiling, or walls

    f.   If the windows were open or closed

    g.   All other objects or distance relationships of value to your investigation

3.   Indicate the angle and location of the camera used at the scene so that the photographs and sketch may be tied together.

4.   The sketch and the description of objects in your notebook should include:

    a.   Date and time when they were made

    b.   Your signature

5.   Your preliminary sketch should later be redrawn to scale for use as an exhibit in court. (Your original rough sketch should be preserved even after it has been redrawn. It may be needed in court.)

TIP: If you have access to a personal computer equipped with graphics software and a plotter, you can save a great deal of time when preparing these sketches.

6.   Designate objects in your sketch by numbers, letters, or symbols if necessary.

    a.   Include a full explanation of each designation in case you forget them at a later date.

    b.   Be consistent in the use of designations to avoid confusion.

7.   Consider videotaping the entire scene.

III. The Search for Evidence

A. *Definition of Evidence*

1.   As a professional investigator, your skills must include an ability to recognize evidence and to relate it to the offence under investigation.

2.   The definition of evidence is extremely broad:

    a.   Anything that may be presented to determine the truth about a fact in question

    b.   Any fact from which another fact may be inferred

3.   As a rule of thumb, everything at the scene of a crime that can be used to determine what really occurred is evidence.

    a.   Evidence can be seen, heard, felt, smelled, or tasted.

    b.   Evidence can not only assist in identifying the person or persons responsible for a crime, but may also reveal how the crime was committed.

B.   *Classification of Evidence*

1.   Class characteristics:

a.   Laboratory examination of some types of evidence can indicate only that the evidence falls within certain class characteristics, because it could have come from more than one source. Examples are hair and fibres, blood, single-layered paint, soil, etc.

b.   Evidence that originally would provide positive identification, such as bullets, shoe prints, and tool marks, may fall into this classification if its markings are not clear enough for positive identification.

c.   Although this type of evidence cannot positively prove a given theory of the crime, it can have great value in eliminating certain possibilities. For example, if fingernail scrapings show that a rape victim's attacker has type O blood, you can safely eliminate persons with other blood types from your list of suspects.

d.   This evidence can be highly suggestive of guilt in certain circumstances. For example, a burglary suspect may be found to have the seeds of a rare type of flower in his cuffs, and the victim's garden is the only location in the immediate area where such flowers are grown.

2.   Individual identifying characteristics:

a.   In most circumstances, evidence such as handwriting, tool marks, bullets, or shoe prints can be positively identified because of unique markings or other characteristics.

b.   Other items such as pieces of glass and wood can be positively identified as coming from specific sources if they can be physically matched with the broken or cut edges of other samples.

C.   *Importance of Physical Evidence*

1.   During your examination of the crime scene, keep a checklist of the elements of the offence in the back of your mind and review them constantly as you conduct your search.

a.   Too often the investigator is so intent on trying to find out who committed an offence that he fails to do the groundwork necessary to show that a crime did in fact occur.

b.   Although some of these elements may seem obvious, this constant mental review is extremely helpful in determining what is or is not worthy of attention and identification as evidence.

EXAMPLE: During an investigation of the crime of murder, you must establish:

    a. That a human being is dead

    b. That the death resulted from an act or an omission of the accused

    c. That the accused had an intention to kill or to inflict grievous bodily harm, knowing that his actions were likely to cause death; or was engaged in an illegal act or in an act that showed a wanton disregard for human life

Unless all these elements are established, you have not proven the crime of murder. Any efforts you make to track down a suspect will be pointless—unless, of course, you can prove that some other crime has been committed.

2.   Physical evidence can often eliminate the possibility that the incident under investigation involved an accident, suicide, or non-criminal act.

EXAMPLE: Several bullet holes in the wall of a murder victim's home suggest that he was cut down in a fusillade of bullets. They also provide a court with the strong suggestion that the homicide was deliberate, because the accused obviously fired several times. Extrapolating the trajectory of the bullets can show where they were fired from, at what distance, and occasionally by whom if the persons present at the time of the occurrence can be identified and positioned.

They certainly establish that the death was not a suicide or an accident, arguments that a defence attorney might make in the absence of facts to support a murder theory.

3.   Be careful not to make any assumptions about physical evidence that lead to important items being ignored.

EXAMPLE: In one murder case I can recall, the accused, a female who had lived with the victim, was charged with first-degree murder after her lover was found stabbed to death in their living room. Several witnesses stated that they saw her with a knife in her belt several hours before the stabbing. Because she had also made numerous death threats to the deceased in the presence of others, the case looked extremely solid. The knife was, of course, seized, bagged, and held as evidence, and the usual photography, finger-printing, and other identification procedures were performed.

Unfortunately, the investigator in charge assumed that a portable radio in the room would be dusted for fingerprints. It wasn't.

At trial, the defence argued self-defence, claiming that the accused stabbed the victim because he was attacking her, waving the portable radio over his head as a weapon.

The defence wasn't entirely successful. The accused was convicted of manslaughter and sentenced to four years in prison. She did, however, escape the mandatory life sentence that would have resulted from a conviction for first-degree murder. Clearly, the jury felt she did not deserve to be acquitted. On the other hand, her story aroused enough doubt in the jurors' minds to cause them to reduce the charge considerably. Had the radio been dusted for fingerprints, who knows what the verdict might have been?

Murder is a particularly difficult crime to prove because the victim, who is frequently the only witness, is not available to testify.

Physical evidence is often the principal avenue to conviction.

4. NOTHING AT THE CRIME SCENE IS TOO INSIGNIFICANT TO BE RECORDED.

   a. You will never lose a case by collecting and preserving too much evidence.

   b. You can lose—badly—by making a premature decision that a certain article or mark is unimportant or unworthy of your attention.

5. Evidence is *always* present at the scene of the crime, to varying degrees. You may or may not find it, but it is there. Keep at your search of the crime scene until you are absolutely certain that there is not a single detail or potential item of evidence that has gone unrecorded.

D. *Handling Physical Evidence*

1. Physical evidence must reach the forensic science laboratory in the condition in which it was found, if at all possible.

   a. Forensic evidence should receive a minimal amount of handling.

   b. Forensic evidence should be delivered to the forensic science laboratory immediately.

2. Physical evidence must be held in a complete chain of custody from its time of recovery until it is presented in court.

   a. Any officer who handles evidence may be called to testify in court to establish continuous possession.

   b. Evidence should pass through the custody of as few persons as possible.

3. Evidence should be securely packed for shipment to the laboratory.

    a.   If an object is damaged or otherwise altered during shipment, it could be rendered inadmissible in court.

    b.   Each article should be wrapped and labelled separately. (If a number of articles are placed in the same container, this procedure is particularly vital to ensure that the evidence items do not contaminate each other.)

    c.   Latent fingerprint evidence should be packed so that nothing can come into contact with any surfaces where fingerprints may be found.

4.   Liquids should be:

    a.   Placed in well-sealed vials or containers
    b.   Properly labelled and initialled
    c.   Packed to avoid breakage or leakage in transit

5.   Wet stains upon cloth, paper, or other objects should be air-dried before packing to avoid putrefaction.

    a.   Do *not* dry wet articles with fans or artificial heat sources.
    b.   Allow wet articles to dry through evaporation in a secure, well-ventilated room before packing.

6.   Powder, dust, hair, specks of paint, and other minute particles of evidence should be:

    a.   Collected on a clean sheet of white paper
    b.   Wrapped in a druggist's fold
    c.   Placed in an envelope

NOTE: Evidence should *never* be sent loose in an envelope.

7.   Every evidence item must be properly marked, labelled, and initialled to enable you to identify it easily, and with confidence, when you testify in court.

NOTE: An evidence item should be initialled or otherwise marked by *every* officer who handles it.

IV. Latent Fingerprint Evidence

A. Possible Sources

1.   Weapons
2.   Tools
3.   Documents
4.   Glass surfaces
5.   Metal surfaces
6.   Any objects at the scene that could have been touched by the suspect
7.   Human skin

NOTE: Identifiable fingerprints can be obtained from human skin. This information can, of course, be an invaluable aid to solving rape-murders and other violent crimes. Remember, however, to advise hospital and ambulance personnel *not* to handle exposed skin or refrigerate the body.

B.   Techniques for Obtaining Fingerprints from Human Skin

1.   Kromekote technique:

    a.   Place a piece of Kromekote paper over the suspected fingerprint.

    b.   Lift the paper and apply powder to its surface.

    c.   Photograph the surface.

Illustration 5
DRUGGIST'S FOLD

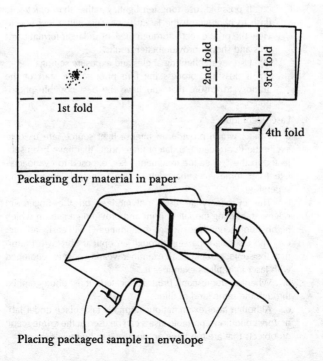

Packaging dry material in paper

Placing packaged sample in envelope

2. Iodine fuming technique:

    a. Blow iodine fumes over the skin surface using a small rubber pipe or hose.

    b. Place a silver plate over the fingerprint that appears.

    c. Expose the silver plate to sunlight and the print will appear on its surface.

    d. Photograph.

3. Magnabrush technique:

    a. If the victim is deceased, do not refrigerate the body.

    b. Dust the suspected area carefully with MacDonell Magna Jet Black Powder, using a Magnabrush.

    c. Examine the area with a large hand-held magnifying glass.

    d. If any ridges appear, photograph them through the magnifying glass.

        (1) Use both Kodak VPS and Kodacolor films.

        (2) If possible, use tungsten lighting rather than electronic flash to photograph the latent print. This will allow you to view the print directly through the lens of larger-format cameras and should provide better results.

        (3) Use several lighting angles and exposure settings.

        (4) If possible, process the film prior to the start of the autopsy to ensure that you have the best possible photograph.

4. Laser technique:

    a. Lasers, which provide an intense light source, are used to excite the fluorescence of latent fingerprints that have been subjected to the "superglue treatment," i.e., exposed to cyanoacrylate ester fumes (cyanoacrylate is the principal ingredient in superglue).

    b. The cyanoacrylate ester polymerizes on the fingerprint ridges, stabilizing the latent print and providing a site on which highly fluorescent dyes such as rhodamine 6G will easily adhere.

    c. The laser light passing through an optical fibre will illuminate the subject article as an examiner wearing goggles equipped with laser-light filters examines it.

    d. When a fluorescent print is located, it is photographed through the same kind of filter.

    e. Although laser examinations normally take place under laboratory conditions, portable lasers can be used at the crime scene on objects that are too large or too heavy to be moved.

    f.   Movable objects should be sent to the laboratory for examination whenever possible.

NOTE: Do not refrigerate the body prior to fingerprint examination.

C. Precautions in Collecting Evidence

1. While searching the scene, be careful not to add fingerprints to possible evidence items or destroy any prints that may be present.

2. Do not pick up objects with a handkerchief—you will only smudge prints.

3. Never assume that it is too late to have an article checked for fingerprints. On many occasions, prints that were several years old have been identified positively.

D. Developing Latent Prints

1. Before attempting to develop latent fingerprints, remove any hair, fibres, blood stains, or other material and package separately.

2. Nonporous or nonabsorbent surfaces:

    a.   Use grey or black fingerprint powders, if possible.

       (1) Other powders clump between ridges, are more difficult to photograph, and don't adhere to the surface as well.

       (2) The colour of the powder should contrast with the surface colour.

    b.   On reflective surfaces such as mirrors, glass, polished chrome, painted or varnished wood, porcelain and ceramic tile, grey powder is preferable, but any powder can be used.

    c.   If the suspected object is a firearm:

       (1) Undertake fingerprint examination before any other tests unless blood or other body fluids are present (fingerprint powders can interfere with blood group testing).

       (2) Note the position of the bullets in the weapon before beginning fingerprint examination (see "Firearms," page 144).

3. Porous or absorbent surfaces:

    a.   These surfaces will be processed chemically using iodine fuming, ninhydrin, or silver nitrate.

    b.   The use of these chemicals will prevent the identification and grouping of blood and other body fluids such as semen and saliva.

    c.   Have examinations of any stains that may be body fluids performed before attempting to develop fingerprints.

    d.   See "Documents," page 140.

4. Lasers can be used on all surfaces.

TIP: Masking tape is often used for binding victims, wrapping parcels or explosives, and for other criminal purposes. Because it has a roughened texture on one side and adhesive on the other, masking tape is not suitable for the application of standard techniques of lifting prints.

The use of Crystal Violet has, however, proven to be a simple and effective means of obtaining prints. The adhesive layer of the tape tends to retain the epidermal skin layer of a person who touches it.

When the tape is immersed in a solution of 0.15 g of Crystal Violet to 10 mL of water, the adhesive will repel the dye. Ridge separation will become apparent as the skin deposit turns violet. The tape samples can then be placed on glass sheets, photographed, and left to dry.

E. *Preservation of Latent Fingerprints Through Photographs*

1. Any camera that has a close focusing capability can be used to photograph fingerprints.

    a. Special fingerprint cameras such as the Folmer-Graflex, the Serchie fingerprint camera, and the Kodak Visual Maker are available, but of limited usefulness.

    b. The following types of cameras will produce consistently good results under most circumstances:

    (1) High-quality 35 mm camera mounted with a macro lens (preferably with a long focal length, e.g., 90 mm)

    (2) Medium- or large-format camera capable of producing an image at either 1:1 (life-size) or 1:2 (half life-size) magnification

2. To photograph a latent impression:

    a. Set your exposure according to the film and magnification used with your camera and flash combination.

    b. Ensure that your camera back (and therefore the film plane) is parallel to the plane of the impression.

    c. Hold your flash to one side and point it at the latent print at a 45-degree angle. (This will prevent reflection from bright surfaces.)

    d. Overlap your shots if the prints exceed the frame of the camera lens.

    e. Take several "protection" shots of each surface, using various exposures, i.e., "bracketing."

    f. Take a location shot to show the position of the print on the object.

g. Take another shot to show the object in relation to its surroundings, e.g., a window in a room.

h. Include an identification tag in each shot (wax pencil can be used) listing:

    (1) Date
    (2) Location
    (3) Occurrence number
    (4) Latent print number
    (5) Initials of the photographer

i. Include a scale or ruler in each shot to indicate the dimension of the fingerprints.

NOTE: If the latent print is on a transparent surface such as a window, hold a contrasting-colour card no closer than 30 cm behind the surface to provide a background for the impression.

F. *Transporting Latent Fingerprint Evidence*

1. Ensure that all items to be examined for latent fingerprints are packed so that no print-bearing surfaces come into contact with any other surface.

2. Bottles and other curved or cylindrical objects:

    a. Outline with a pencil the base and top ends of the object on two separate pieces of wood.
    b. Hammer nails around these lines to create supporting frames for each end of the object.
    c. Place the ends of the object in position on the two boards.
    d. Fasten wood strips between the ends of the two boards to create a four-sided rectangular frame.
    e. Pack this frame in a strong container with paper filler to prevent movement during shipment.

3. Mirrors, plates of glass and metal, and other flat objects should be shipped between two pieces of plywood or heavy, stiff cardboard. Leave at least 2.5 cm of clearance around the suspected areas.

G. *Dead Bodies*

1. If you wish to identify a dead body through fingerprints, take inked prints of both the fingertips and palms. A file search may confirm the identity of a named person.

2. In deaths by drowning, fire, or exposure, skin damage or decomposition may make it extremely difficult to obtain identifiable prints.

a. If the inked fingerprints you have taken are not legible, obtain the authority of the coroner to have the hands severed at the wrists by a qualified medical examiner.

NOTE: Do not allow fingers to be severed.

b. Place these exhibits in a well-protected airtight container containing alcohol or 5-percent formaldehyde solution.

c. Ship to the laboratory as quickly as possible by express, registered air mail, or personal delivery.

3. If you have any doubts or questions about proper procedure, call the laboratory before shipping.

4. Through visual examination and other techniques, identification experts can sometimes develop a 10-finger formula. This information can be used in a file search for a named person or for comparison with samples of other inked prints that you submit.

5. There is normally no need to resubmit original evidence with later comparison requests. The laboratory will retain photographs and negatives of the original submission.

V. Clothing as Evidence

A. Removal

1. During removal of any clothing for evidence purposes, do not turn the garments inside out.

2. Make notes regarding:

a. Order of removal of each item

b. How the item was worn, e.g., unbuttoned, zipper halfway down, collar point bent under, etc.

c. Any apparent damage

B. Preservation of Evidence

1. Do not shake or try to clean clothing that will be subjected to laboratory examination. Dust from trouser cuffs, pockets, gloves, and other locations can yield significant information.

2. Do not cut off any pieces of the garment for shipment to the crime lab. Send the complete article.

3. Do *not* fit any suspected weapons or instruments into holes in the clothing.

a. This action could remove microscopic evidence that would have indicated if the hole was a cut or a tear.

b. Insertion and withdrawal of an instrument could add to, or remove from, the hole important trace evidence such as blood, hairs, and fibres.

4. Attach a tag to each article of clothing containing all identifying data.

   a. Mark the garment in ink for identification purposes, preferably on the manufacturer's label.

   b. Position any marks or tags on the item as far away from stained areas as possible.

5. Wrap each article of clothing separately in paper. Intermingling of the clothing will result in contamination of *all* the articles shipped.

   a. Visible trace evidence such as hairs and fibres should be removed from the article and packaged separately, with a notation indicating where it was originally located. (If this precaution is not taken, the trace evidence could move or fall off in transit.)

   b. Wrap leather articles in paper, not plastic.

   c. Do not use large plastic garbage bags to package clothing.

6. If gunshot or powder patterns are to be examined, place a piece of clean white paper on both sides of the suspected area. Do not make folds through this area.

7. Allow wet stains to dry in a room with good ventilation.

   a. Do not use applied heat, sunlight, or any artificial method to speed up the drying process. (Fans could blow away trace evidence.)

   b. Place a paper under wet garments to collect any particles that might fall off during drying.

   (1) Place these particles in a paper folded into the druggist's fold.

   (2) Insert in a properly labelled envelope.

   (3) Ship with the garment.

8. Laboratory examination can sometimes positively identify a questioned piece of fabric with a known garment. For example, a button that has been torn off a sports jacket could be matched to the jacket if some fabric remains on the button.

11. FORENSIC SCIENCE

I. Introduction

In the preceding chapter, we dealt with some aspects of forensic science that relate directly to the examination of the crime scene. The field of forensic science is a vast one, however, and can be dealt with only briefly in a practical handbook such as this.

In this chapter, we look at other areas of forensic science that you will need to understand to conduct an effective crime investigation. Of particular assistance to today's police officer are the recent breakthroughs in DNA technology that permit investigators of major crimes to identify a drop of blood or semen or even a single hair found at a crime scene as belonging to a particular suspect. Because samples of body fluids and tissue are found more frequently at crime scenes than fingerprints, DNA profiling represents an important new resource in the investigation of serious violent crimes.

II. Documents

A. Definitions

1. Document examination: The examination and identification of handwriting, handprinting, typewriting, papers, inks, seals, watermarks, erasures, obliterated writing, and alterations in documents, using chemical, microscopic, photographic, and other techniques
2. Questioned document: Any document that is, in whole or in part, of doubtful authenticity
3. Standard: A document of known origin that an examiner can use for comparison to establish the origin of a questioned document

B. Handling Questioned Documents

1. Questioned documents such as fraudulent cheques, notes, or letters should be handled as little as possible to avoid destroying valuable fingerprint or other evidence. Place the document in an envelope or clear protector immediately.
2. Send the original suspected document to the forensic science laboratory whenever possible. Photographic or photostatic copies are useless for microscopic or other physical examinations.

3. Place identification marks on the envelope or protector. (Fingerprints and other identifying marks are usually found near the edges of the document.)

NOTE: Do not attach other papers to the document with a paper clip. You may destroy fingerprints, indented writing, or other evidence.

4. Do not attempt to repair fragile or torn documents. Place them carefully in a flat box. If possible, deliver these documents to the laboratory personally.

5. Do not make any new folds or creases in the original document.

C. Comparison Samples (Standards)

1. Collect as many comparison samples as possible. Laboratory experts can obtain positive findings in most examinations if they have a sufficient quantity of questioned documents and comparison samples to work with.

2. Possible sources of standards:

    a. Personal letters and postcards

    b. Work-related documents:

        (1) Memorandums

        (2) Timesheets

        (3) Manuscripts

    c. Financial and legal documents

        (1) Deeds

        (2) Contracts and agreements

        (3) Wills

        (4) Affidavits

        (5) Bills of sale

        (6) Leases

        (7) Bank deposit or withdrawal slips

        (8) Bank account signature cards

        (9) Cheques or cheque endorsements

      (10) Mortgage documents

    d. Application forms:

        (1) Credit cards

        (2) Employment

        (3) Social assistance

        (4) Telephone

        (5) Utilities (water, gas, electricity, etc.)

        (6) Club memberships

    (7) Passport

    (8) Bank loans

    (9) Licences—car, insurance, business

3.   When requesting a comparison, try to submit standards that are similar to the suspected document.

EXAMPLE: In a forgery investigation, ask your suspect to fill out blank cheque forms issued by the same bank on which the fraudulent cheque was drawn, using the same type of pen or other writing instrument.

D.   Handwritten or Handprinted Documents

1.   Try to identify the writing instrument that was used (e.g., felt-tipped marking pen, black lead pencil, cartridge pen, ballpoint pen, etc.) and submit it to the laboratory.

2.   Have the suspect write at least 10 comparison samples, using the same type of paper, writing instrument, and message as was used for the original document. For example, ask a suspected cheque-passer to fill out blank cheques, or a bank robber to write a sample holdup note that duplicates the words used in the questioned note.

    a.   Always dictate to the suspect; never let him copy the original document.

    b.   Don't suggest how to spell or punctuate the writing sample.

    c.   Obtain samples of the suspect's writing from letters, cancelled cheques, legal documents, diaries, etc., that were written about the same time as the suspected document.

    d.   Have the suspect use the same style of writing that appears in the original document. (If the questioned document was hand-printed in capital letters, your comparison samples should be written the same way.)

    e.   Remove each sample from the suspect's sight after it has been completed.

NOTE: Do not submit samples for fingerprint examination until after handwriting analysis has been completed to avoid blurring of the subject's writing style.

E.   Typewritten Documents

1.   If the suspected document is typewritten, submit the suspected typewriter or ribbon for laboratory examination whenever possible.

    a.   Do not type on the machine after it has been seized as evidence.

b.   If you are unable to submit the entire typewriter, remove the ribbon, roller and ball element, or printwheel. Do not rewind the typewriter ribbon.

c.   Insert a new ribbon in the typewriter to prepare:

(1)   Five typewritten samples of the questioned material
(2)   Three samples of all the letters and symbols on the keyboard in both upper and lower case

d.   Collect several samples of other documents that were typed on the machine during ordinary use.

e.   Submit the ribbon, roller, and typewritten samples to the laboratory for examination.

2.   Possible laboratory findings:

a.   Make and model of the typewriter upon which a questioned document was typed

b.   Confirmation or elimination of a specific typewriter as the machine upon which a questioned document was typed

F.   *Indented Writing*

1.   In some cases, messages that were written on a pad or stack of papers may be read even though the sheet they were written on has been removed.

2.   These messages may have indented the sheets of paper underneath, and can sometimes be rendered legible by photographing the indented sheets, using an oblique light source to create a shadow effect.

3.   Ultraviolet light can be used to bring up messages that have been covered by correction fluid.

4.   Infrared light can be used to make pencil tracings on forged documents visible.

NOTE: In the field, some officers rub a lead pencil across an indented paper surface to bring up writing. This practice should be avoided to prevent destruction of other evidence that might be obtained through forensic laboratory examination.

G.   *Charred Documents*

1.   Don't assume that a document cannot be read simply because it has been burned completely black.

2.   Often, through the use of a photographic process, the laboratory can render a burned document fully legible.

3.   Charred documents are extremely fragile; turn them over to a qualified document examiner as quickly as possible.

H. *Watermarks*

1. Some paper manufacturers change the watermarks on their products annually; you can, therefore, sometimes determine the date of production of the paper on which a questioned document was written or printed.

2. This information can be useful in shattering the credibility of a suspect who claims that a deed or contract was drawn up on a specific date. For example, the watermark could establish that the paper on which the contract was printed was not even on the market on the date that the suspect claims it was signed.

III. Firearms

A. *Definitions*

1. Firearms identification involves:

   a.   Study of microscopic marks on the surfaces of fired bullets, cartridge cases, and shotshell casings to identify them with a specific weapon

   b.   Gunshot residue and shot pattern tests to determine muzzle-to-target distances

   c.   Operational testing of weapons to determine trigger pull, possibility of accidental discharge, malfunctions, etc.

2. Ballistics is the study of projectile motion.

   a.   Interior ballistics: The study of projectile motion within the firearm

   b.   Exterior ballistics: The study of projectile motion in flight

   c.   Terminal ballistics: The study of the impact effect of the projectile

B. *Sources of Unique Microscopic Characteristics*

1. Tools used in the manufacture of the firearm
2. Handling and use of the subject firearm
3. Loading, firing, extraction, and ejection of ammunition

C. *Ammunition*

1. Cartridges fall into two major categories:

   a.   Rimfire:

      (1) The primer material is located in the rim around the head of the cartridge.

      (2) Most of the cartridges in this category are .22 calibre, but other types are also available, such the .22 Magnum.

   b. Centrefire:

     (1) The primer material is located in a self-contained primer cup in the centre of the cartridge's head end.

     (2) Example: .38 Special ammunition

2. Components of the cartridge:

   a. Bullet:

     (1) Lead, coated lead, zinc alloy, or magnesium composition

     (2) Shape will vary according to such factors as powder charge, intended use, ballistic requirements, and type of firearm

     (3) May bear cannelures (grooves that are used for manufacturer and bullet weight identification, lubrication, etc.)

   b. Cartridge case:

     (1) Rimmed—has a full rim, e.g., cylinder-loaded cartridges

     (2) Rimless—has no rim, e.g., .45 calibre Auto cartridge

Illustration 6
COMPONENTS OF A CARTRIDGE

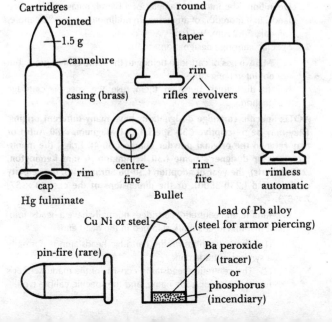

(3) Semi-rimmed—has a very slight rim, e.g., .25 calibre Auto cartridge

(4) Belted—built up or reinforced near the base or head

c. Powder charge may be:

(1) Smokeless:

    i. Single base—nitrocellulose gelatinized by a solvent

    ii. Double base—nitrocellulose and nitroglycerin

(2) Black powder—rarely used today

d. Primer mixture

e. Primer cup (except rimfire cartridges)

3. Disposal of the spent cartridge case

a. Rifle:

(1) Ejection (if autoloading)

(2) Bolt action

(3) Lever action

b. Semiautomatic firearm: ejection

c. Cylinder-loaded handgun: nonejecting

D. *Calibre*

1. Definition: The internal diameter of a barrel, measured between lands, in hundredths of an inch or in millimetres, e.g., .22 calibre, .38 cal., 7.62 mm, 9.3 mm

2. Specific cartridge designation:

a. Many types of cartridge belong to the same calibre group but are not interchangeable.

b. To distinguish between them, use the specific cartridge designation.

NOTE: Specific cartridge designations have many different origins. They may be descriptive (.38 Special, .41 Magnum, .380 Auto) or may refer to the original powder charge (.30-40 Krag), the manufacturer's or designer's name (.30 Remington, 6 mm Remington, .257 Roberts), the year of adoption (.30-06 Springfield), the velocity of the round (.250-3000), or the dimensions of the case (8 × 57, 7 × 57).

c. Rimfire and centrefire cartridges normally have a headstamp, i.e., a manufacturer's mark stamped in the head end.

(1) The .22 calibre rimfire cartridge headstamp is normally a symbol or trademark.

(2) The centrefire headstamp consists of the manufacturer's name, initials or trade name, and the specific calibre type.

E. *Common Types of Firearms*
1. Handguns (cylinder or autoloading)
2. Rifles and shotguns
    a. Autoloading
    b. Lever action
    c. Bolt action
    d. Pump action
3. Machine guns (weapons capable of fully automatic rapid fire)

TIP: In a case of apparent suicide involving a pump-action shotgun, you may sometimes see an ejected round on the floor near the victim, despite the fact that death appears to have been instantaneous. In these situations, the recoil of the weapon after firing may have unlocked the pump mechanism and allowed the slide to come back, ejecting the round. In these cases, safely secure the firearm and check the breech to see if it is empty.

It is also possible that the recoil created a "stovepipe"—a shell that is only partially ejected out of the chamber. As the weapon fell from the victim's hand after discharge, it may have struck the ground butt-first, resulting in full ejection of the cartridge.

F. *Rifling*
1. Definition: A series of spiral grooves running along the interior surface of the firearm's barrel. These grooves spin the bullet, causing it to maintain a straight course in flight, with the nose forward.
2. General rifling characteristics (GRC) vary among manufacturers in:
    a. Number of lands and grooves (4–7)
    b. Dimensions of lands and grooves
    c. Direction of the rifling twist (clockwise or anticlockwise)
3. Rifled weapons:
    a. Rifles
    b. Handguns
    c. Automatic weapons (machine guns, etc.)

G. *Firing Sequence*
1. Firing pin ignites the powder.
2. Nitrocellulose or glycerin burns, creating about 1000 mL of gas for each gram of propellant.
3. Gases propel the projectile down the barrel of the firearm.

Illustration 7
RIFLING

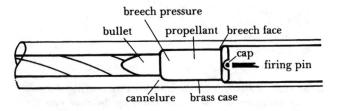

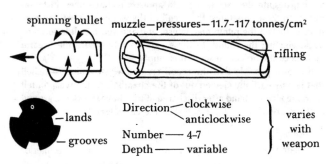

4. The case spreads out and the bullet is released from the cannelure.

5. The rifling along the barrel imparts spin to the projectile for greater accuracy.

6. As the bullet leaves the muzzle:

   a. Gases and air rush back into the barrel, creating the characteristic "bang" noise.

   b. This sudden force creates a recoil effect.

   c. The force of the recoil ejects the spent cartridge (in some weapons).

NOTE: Muzzle velocities of common centrefire firearms:

   a. Rifle 914 m/s (3000 ft./sec.) = 3219 km/h (2000 mph)

   b. Autoloading handgun 305–396 m/s (1000–3000 ft./sec.) = 1127 km/h (700 mph)

   c. Cylinder-loaded handgun ("revolver") 190 m/s (650 ft./sec.) = 644 km/h (400 mph)

H. *Shotshells*

1. Components:

    a. Shot pellets, buckshot, or slug load

    b. Shotshell casing (a cardboard or plastic tube with metal at the head end)

    c. Primer mixture

    d. Primer cup

    e. Battery cup

    f. Powder charge

    g. Wads (may be cardboard, plastic, felt, single unit polyethylene, etc.)

2. Marking may indicate:

    a. Particular shotshell loading, such as 11.7–35.4–19, where 11.7 = gram equivalents of powder, 35.4 = grams of shot, 19 = size of shot (3–1¼–7½, where 3 = dram equivalents of powder, 1¼ = ounces of shot, 7½ = size of shot)

    b. Gauge

    c. Manufacturer's name or trademark

    d. Type of shell

Illustration 8
SHOTSHELLS

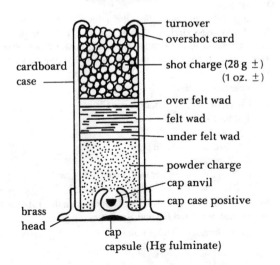

turnover
overshot card
shot charge (28 g ±) (1 oz. ±)
cardboard case
over felt wad
felt wad
under felt wad
powder charge
cap anvil
cap case positive
brass head
cap
capsule (Hg fulminate)

3. Gauge:

   a. Definition: The number of equal-sized balls that have the diameter of the shotgun barrel and can be manufactured from 0.45 kg (1 lb.) of lead. For example, a 28 g lead ball would fit the bore of a 16-gauge shotgun.

   b. If the bore is less than 1.3 cm, it is expressed as a fraction of a centimetre or inch, e.g., the .410 calibre shotgun.

   c. If the bore is greater than 1.3 cm, gauge designation is used, e.g., gauge 4, 8, 12, 16, 20.

NOTE: The smaller the gauge designation, the larger the diameter of the barrel.

I. *Common Types of Shotguns*

1. Single barrel
2. Double barrel
3. Autoloading (often called automatic)
4. Pump action
5. Bolt action
6. Lever action
7. Combination rifle and shotgun

NOTE: The adjustable choke on a shotgun is a constriction device at the muzzle end of a shotgun barrel designed to control the spread of shot pellets. The gauge of the shotgun has no effect upon the size of the pattern.

Gauge does, however, affect the percentage of pellets that will be found in a given circle at a given distance. For example, given the same choke size, a 12-gauge shell will create more holes than a 16-gauge at the same distance, a 16-gauge more than a 20-gauge, etc.

J. *Firearms Injuries*

1. Characteristics of entrance wounds:

   a. Inverted edges
   b. Black scorching
   c. Traces of metal in skin
   d. "Tattooing"
   e. Grease ring or abrasion collar
   f. Circular hole

NOTE: Wound characteristics will not indicate the distance at which the weapon was fired beyond about 1 m.

2. Characteristics of exit wounds:

    a.   Edges of the skin turned outward

    b.   Irregular shape

    c.   No scorching, tattooing, or grease rings

3.   Interpretation:

    a.   If you are able to count an equal number of entrance and exit wounds, this may indicate that no bullets remain inside the victim.

    b.   An unequal number of entrance and exit wounds indicates that a bullet may still be inside or that it has fragmented prior to exiting the body.

    c.   Exceptions:

        (1) A grazing wound could result in an unequal number of wounds although no bullets remain inside the body.

        (2) Occasionally a bullet will have a single entrance point and multiple exits because:

            i.   The bullet has fragmented upon impact.

            ii. The bullet's impact transferred energy to tooth or bone fragments that exploded out of the body.

Illustration 9
FIREARMS INJURIES

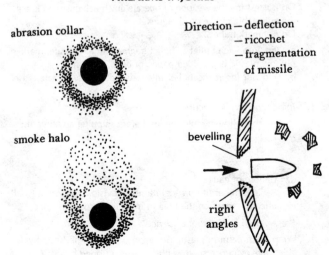

abrasion collar

smoke halo

Direction — deflection
          — ricochet
          — fragmentation
          of missile

bevelling

right angles

K. Handling Precautions

1. Assume that *all* firearms are loaded until you have confirmed that they are not.
2. Unload the suspected gun immediately upon recovery. Never submit a loaded gun to the laboratory.

    a. If you are unable to remove an unfired cartridge, contact the laboratory for further instructions.

    b. If the firearm is self-loading, remove both the magazine and the cartridge from the chamber. Preserve the bullet for future fingerprinting.

    c. Remove all cartridges from the cylinders of revolvers.

    (1) Make a note of the exact position of each cartridge, fired and unfired, in the cylinder.

    (2) Identify the position of each cartridge numerically in your notes.

    i. Record the bullet aligned with the barrel as being in the number one position.

    ii. Count upward in a clockwise direction. Looking at the cylinder of a handgun from the butt end, the round in front of the barrel is Number 1, the round to its right is Number 2, etc.

3. Do *not* test-fire the weapon or operate any mechanism on it, e.g., the adjustable choke on shotguns.
4. Do *not* mark bullets.

    a. Enclose each bullet or bullet fragment in a separate, marked pillbox, plastic bag, folded paper, or other container.

    b. Do *not* insert the bullet into a weapon prior to laboratory examination.

L. Information to be Recorded

1. Record the following information before shipping any firearm:

    a. Make

    b. Model

    c. Type

    d. Calibre or gauge

    e. Serial number (if no serial number is visible, scratch a small identification mark on the firearm in an inconspicuous place)

M. Preservation of Gunshot Evidence

1. Wrap the firearm in plastic or paper to prevent the loss of valuable trace evidence such as fibres, hairs, or dried blood.

2. Do *not* attempt to dig out bullets or fragments that are lodged in wood, plaster, or other materials.

   a. Cut out a generous section of the surface area around the bullet holes.

   b. Wrap the entire object and ship it intact to the laboratory.

3. If a bullet is lodged in the body of a murder victim, request that the pathologist performing the autopsy recover it.

   a. The bullet must be removed from the body by hand. Forceps or other hard instruments should *not* be used.

   b. Caution the doctor not to probe for the bullet.

4. Laboratory examination of clothing with suspected powder burns or shot patterns can reveal:

   a. Distance from which the shot was fired if the range is sufficiently close

   b. Direction from which the shot was fired (in some cases)

   c. Type of powder charge in the fired ammunition

5. Preparation for shipment of clothing to the laboratory:

   a. Make a note if the clothing was worn inside out or back to front.

   b. Avoid cutting or tearing clothing near a suspected bullet hole when removing clothing.

   c. Do *not* attempt to cut out the suspected area. Send the entire garment or garments to the laboratory.

   d. Pin or tape paper or plastic on each side of the area around the bullet holes.

   e. Sandwich the cloth and paper between two pieces of heavy cardboard to prevent bending or folding. This will also prevent gunshot residue from falling off.

   f. Wrap each garment separately to prevent contamination by other items enclosed in the same shipping container.

N. *Comparison and Other Tests*

1. For comparison purposes, submit:

   a. All available firearms involved

   b. All available unused ammunition (up to one full box) that may be related to the offence under investigation

2. Other examinations:

   a. Gunshot residue tests:

      (1) Microscopic examination of the area surrounding a bullet hole for gunpowder particles, residues, smudging, and singeing.

(2) Chemical processing of the area surrounding the bullet can create a graphic representation of any powder or lead residues that may be present.

(3) Comparison of these patterns with patterns produced by firing the suspect firearm at various distances may determine the distance between the muzzle and the target.

(4) Testing of both hands of the suspect for traces of lead, antimony, and barium can help establish whether or not he recently fired a weapon.

NOTE: Time is of the essence. The gunshot residue test should be performed within five hours of the suspected offence. Do not allow the suspect to wash his hands before being tested.

b. Shot pattern tests:

(1) Determine the distance at which a shotgun was fired

(2) Require test-firing of the suspect weapon at various distances using the same type of ammunition involved in the shooting under investigation

c. Parts examinations:

(1) Can determine the type of weapon that the part came from

(2) Can identify the part with a specific weapon

O. *Possible Findings*

1. Bullets:

a. Type, make, manufacturer, and specific calibre of the firearm from which the questioned bullet was fired

b. Identification of a fired bullet or cartridge case as having been fired from a specific firearm (if it can be test-fired)

NOTE: A positive identification of a firearm through microscopic examination is as reliable as fingerprint evidence.

c. Elimination of a specific firearm from involvement in the case under investigation

d. The number and type of firearms discharged during a shooting incident (if two or more bullets are recovered)

e. The distance between the muzzle of the firearm and the victim when the shooting occurred

2. Shot pellets, buckshot, or slug load:

a. The size of the shot and the gauge of the slug load.

b. Shot pellets cannot be identified with a specific firearm.

3. Fired cartridge case or shotgun casing:

    a.   Specific calibre, type, and possibly the make of the weapon from which it was fired

    b.   Positive identification with a specific firearm (if sufficient firing pin impressions, breech face marks, or chamber marks are present)

NOTE: Extractor or ejector marks can *only* identify the case as having been loaded into and extracted from a specific firearm; they cannot prove that the round was fired from the questioned firearm.

4. Fired shotshell casing:

    a.   Gauge of original factory loading

    b.   Positive identification with a specific firearm (if sufficient markings are present)

5. Wadding:

    a.   Gauge of shot

    b.   Name of the manufacturer (sometimes)

NOTE: Plastic wads that were fired from sawed-off shotguns may be marked by the jagged steel at the sawed-off end of the barrel. This can result in a positive identification of the wad as coming from a specific firearm. Always collect wads at crime scenes, especially if they are plastic.

6. Shot—size

7. Unfired cartridges or shotshells

    a.   Specific calibre or gauge of firearms involved

    b.   If the cartridge or shotshell has been loaded into or extracted from the suspect firearm

NOTE: This does not apply to cylinder-loaded handguns.

8. A comparison microscope permits direct side-by-side comparison of:

    a.   Fired evidence bullets, cartridge cases, and shotshell casings

    b.   Unfired cartridges and shotshells

IV. Toolmark Evidence

A. Identification of Toolmarks

1. All tools bear microscopic imperfections on their cutting edges or service areas. These defects are frequently reproduced to some extent on objects that the tool has scraped, punched, hit, or cut, permitting a positive identification.

2. As a general rule, when two objects come into contact, the harder object will mark the softer.

3. Examples:
   a. Knife
   b. Axe
   c. Saw
   d. Hacksaw
   e. Screwdriver
   f. Punch
   g. Chisel
   h. Bolt-cutters
   i. Pliers
   j. Drill

4. These items cannot normally be related to the marks that they produce:
   a. Saws
   b. Files
   c. Grinding wheels

5. Toolmark identification procedures are applicable to any objects that:
   a. Have been joined together under pressure for some time and then separated
   b. Were originally a single object but have been broken or cut apart
   c. Have come into contact forcefully

B. *Handling of Toolmark Evidence*

1. Do not clean, wipe, or touch the cutting edge or service area of any object that will be sent for toolmark examination.

2. Pack the tool carefully to prevent the cutting edge or service area of the tool from coming into contact with other surfaces. (Use cotton filler if necessary to keep the tool from shifting during shipment.)

3. Send the object bearing the imprint of the tool to the laboratory with the suspected tool.
   a. Wrap the articles individually to ensure that any foreign material is not lost.
   b. Pack the items separately to ensure that they are well protected from friction or contact with other surfaces.

4. If it is impossible to submit the original toolmark, send a plastic cast of the mark.

NOTE: Do not send a photograph of the toolmark for laboratory examination; it is useless for identification purposes.

5. Do not make test cuts or impressions prior to submission; send the tool to the laboratory.
6. Do *not* place the tool against the toolmark for an initial comparison.
7. Indicate the surfaces of the evidence items that you wish to be examined and those you do not.

C. *Examination of Toolmark Only*

1. Examination of the toolmark by itself can reveal:
   a. Type of tool used
   b. Size of the tool used
   c. Unusual features of the tool
   d. Individual characteristics that can positively identify the tool if and when it is located

2. Examination of impressions can indicate the type of mark produced by a perpendicular force acting against the object. Examples:
   a. Gripping tools
   b. Punch
   c. Hammer blows
   d. Number stamps

3. Scrape marks result when various types of tools are scraped laterally across the object. Examples:
   a. Screwdrivers
   b. Crowbars
   c. Pliers
   d. Wrenches

4. Shearing or pinching marks are produced when the object is caught between two opposing cutting forces. Examples:
   a. Scissors (shearing)
   b. Tin snips (shearing)
   c. Wire or bolt-cutters (pinching)

D. *Comparison of a Tool with a Toolmark*

1. Laboratory experts will compare foreign materials such as paint, metal filings, or dirt found on the tool with the questioned object.
2. Both objects will be examined for consistent class characteristics.
3. The tool will be used to make test marks and/or cuts for microscopic comparison with the questioned object.
4. If sufficient individual characteristics are discovered, this could lead to a positive identification.

E.   Other Possible Examinations

1.   Fracture:

    a.   Relates broken items with the object from which they were broken

    b.   Examples

        (1) Automobile ornaments

        (2) Knife blades or tips

        (3) Bolts and screws

2.   Wood:

    a.   Relates wooden objects with tools that marked them

    b.   Examples

        (1) Auger bit turnings

        (2) Axes

        (3) Pruning shears

        (4) Knives

3.   Possible findings:

    a.   A positive identification of the tool with the toolmark

    b.   Elimination of the tool as the source of the toolmark

    c.   Insufficient individual characteristics present on the samples to prove whether or not the tool and the toolmark are associated

V.   Blood

A.   *Importance of Analysis of Bloodstains*

1.   Bloodstains subjected to laboratory analysis may yield important information in investigations of violent crimes such as rape, murder, and assault.

2.   Photograph the stain immediately—its size, shape, location, and appearance could be important to your investigation.

3.   Investigative uses of bloodstain analysis:

    a.   Confirmation that a suspicious stain is human blood, indicating that further investigation is required

    b.   Probable location of the crime scene, through DNA analysis of human blood or its identification as being of the same group as the victim's

    c.   Identification of an object as the weapon of attack

    d.   Identification of a bloodstain as being of human or animal origin, to prove or disprove an alibi

4.   Forensic analysis of human blood can eliminate suspects by:

    a.   Establishing that the person responsible for a crime had a different blood group or DNA profile from that of the suspect

b. Indicating that a questioned stain is of the suspect's blood group or DNA, but not the victim's, e.g., to confirm a claim that he cut himself

NOTE: Secretors make up 80 percent of the population. These persons have identifiable blood group substances in their other body fluids, such as saliva, tears, perspiration, semen, and even vomitus. In fact, the quantity of blood group antigens in semen and saliva is much greater than is found in red blood cells. This means that a suspect or victim's blood group can often be detected with a very small amount of specimen, e.g., a saliva trace on a cigarette butt, a drop of semen on automobile upholstery, etc.

5. DNA profiling can be used in investigations of major crimes to conclusively identify a particular individual using a minute sample of blood, semen, hair, or other bodily fluids or tissue.

   a. Deoxyribonucleic acid (DNA) is an organic substance found primarily in the nuclei of living cells.

   b. DNA comprises the chromosomes that provide the individual genetic codes that determine such personal characteristics as colour of skin, hair, and eyes.

   c. Under appropriate laboratory conditions, a DNA profile can be developed that is extremely reliable except in extremely rare cases involving monozygotic twins, triplets, etc.

Illustration 10
BLOOD

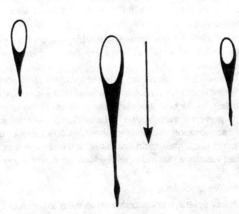

6. Not all biological samples will be suitable for DNA testing, nor will all crimes be sufficiently serious to justify the lengthy and expensive process involved in preparing a DNA profile. It is therefore important to handle all samples in a manner that permits them to be subjected to normal laboratory analysis.

B. *Bloodstained Clothing*

1. Do not cut out a section of clothing containing a suspected bloodstain; send the entire garment to the laboratory.

2. Do not wrap or ship the article while the stain is wet. Allow it to dry naturally through evaporation.

3. Do not put the garment in a draft or use a fan or artificial heat source for drying.

4. If the suspected bloodstain is still wet, apply a cotton swab or a clean blotter on the area to absorb it.

   a. Place the specimen in a clean jar or other suitable container.

   b. Refrigerate and forward to the laboratory as quickly as possible.

   c. If refrigeration is impossible, add a small amount of anticoagulant to the container.

NOTE: Many stains have the appearance of dried blood, e.g., rust, coffee grain vomitus, etc. Even in apparently obvious cases, do not assume that a suspicious stain is blood until you have received confirmation from the laboratory.

C. *Bloodstains on Floors, Walls, and Other Fixed Objects*

1. If the suspected bloodstains are on a floor, walls, or other fixed objects, flake off particles of the dried stain into a clean pillbox or plastic vial.

   a. If neither of these items is available, use a clean piece of paper, which is then folded into a druggist's fold and inserted in an envelope.

   b. If samples are taken from different locations at the scene, use a different knife for each operation. Send all the knives, wrapped separately, to the laboratory with the samples.

   c. To prevent contamination of the evidence, place the samples from each location in a different sheet of white paper or pillbox. If paper is used, make a druggist's fold and insert the sample in a marked envelope that indicates the location where it was recovered.

2. Alternative procedure:

   a. Apply several wet cotton swabs to the dried stain.

b. Allow the swabs to dry in the air.

c. Submit them for examination in plastic vials.

d. Ensure that a control sample is also taken near each location.

D. *Bloodstains on Smaller Objects*

1. If possible, remove and store the object on which the spots or stains were found as evidence for trial. The stained area should not be allowed to come into contact with any other surface.

NOTE: Do not hesitate to send an object such as a knife or axe for laboratory examination simply because its cutting surface appears to have been cleaned thoroughly. Liquid blood may have seeped into small crevices such as cracks in the handle or spaces between the blade and the handle.

2. Weapons, tools, broken glass, or other smaller objects should be sent to the laboratory intact.

NOTE: Wrap the item in paper or plastic to prevent the dislodging of hairs, fibres, and other minute foreign material.

E. *Blood on Automobile Surfaces or Large Metallic Objects*

1. If insufficient quantities of blood are present for scraping, cut out a generous section of the area on which it is located and ship to the laboratory.

2. Identify the item by scratching your mark into the metal.

3. Ensure that the item is well secured in its container through the use of wooden cleats or holding wires. (If the object is not totally immobilized within the container, the stains could be rubbed off in transit.)

F. *Blood in Dirt and Sand*

1. If the blood has become encrusted on the surface:

a. Remove the crusted areas.

b. Place them in separate pillboxes or plastic vials to prevent contamination of the evidence.

2. Because blood may have drained down below the surface:

a. Scoop out an ample amount of the sand or dirt.

b. Forward the sample to the laboratory in a circular container, e.g., a clean plastic ice-cream bucket.

G. *Liquid Blood Samples*

1. Submit blood samples from the victim and suspect, if available.

a. Collect 5 to 10 mL in a Vacutainer containing a small amount of an anticoagulant such as Heparin. (Do *not* use fluoride; it may interfere with blood group testing.)

b. Indicate if seized under a search warrant or provided voluntarily.

c. Note any history of recent blood transfusions and forward this information with the sample. (Blood samples taken from a person who has had a transfusion in the past three months may provide an inaccurate blood group reading.)

2. Ship to the laboratory by the fastest possible means.

NOTE: If you ship by air, ensure that the stopper in the vial containing the blood sample is securely sealed with tape. Air-pressure changes during the flight could cause the stopper to loosen or dislodge.

3. Any blood samples sent to the laboratory should be accompanied by the following information:

a. Any claims made by the suspect or victim as to the source of blood on the submitted objects

b. The blood group of the victim and the suspect, if known

c. Any injuries the suspect may have sustained

d. Any possibility that the blood is a mixture from different sources

e. Any possibility that animal blood may be present in the samples

H. Possible Findings of Routine Bloodstain Analysis

1. Whether the blood sample is of human or animal origin

2. If the sample is animal blood, the specific animal family of the source

3. If the blood is human, which of the four major blood groups it belongs to:

a. O (45 percent of the population)

b. A (40 percent)

c. B (10 percent)

d. AB (5 percent)

4. Depending on the age of the sample, the laboratory may also determine the blood subgroup:

a. M

b. N

c. MN

d. RH factors

e. Other factors

5. DNA analysis can identify a blood sample as coming from a specific individual.

6. Human blood samples cannot reveal the race or sex of the person they came from.
7. The age of dried bloodstains cannot be determined.

I. *Tests of Blood-Alcohol Levels*

1. Send 10 cm^3 of blood sealed in a clean glass container. (The blood specimen should completely fill the container to eliminate any air pockets.)
2. Human blood specimens should be taken only under the supervision of a qualified physician or a qualified person acting under his direction.
3. If a blood sample from a dead body is required, it must be taken before the embalming process begins.
4. Blood samples must arrive at the laboratory within five days. If this is not possible:
   a. Make a stain of the blood on a clean white cloth.
   b. Allow the stain to dry.
   c. Place it in a plastic bag.
   d. Submit it as quickly as possible.

VI. Seminal Stains

A. *Sexual Assault*

1. In the investigation of rape and other sexual offences, semen may be found on clothing, blankets, automobile upholstery, or other objects.
2. If the assailant was a secretor, laboratory examination can reveal his blood group to assist in the identification and elimination of suspects.
3. DNA analysis can match a sample to a named suspect.

B. *Preservation of Evidence*

1. Follow the drying and wrapping procedures noted earlier to protect any questioned garments or cloth articles.
2. A medical examination of the victim may recover semen samples from the vagina.

   a. If oral sex or sodomy were involved, semen may also be present in the victim's mouth or anus.
   b. If the victim is a minor, obtain the consent of the parents before requesting a physical examination.
   c. Ask the physician to look for hairs or other foreign matter during the examination.

3. All clothing worn by the victim at the time of the attack should be submitted to the laboratory.

NOTE: In a case of sexual assault, the victim may have scratched her assailant during the struggle, lodging valuable blood, fibre, or tissue evidence under her fingernails.

As part of your investigation, you should ensure that a qualified person:

1. Uses toothpicks to obtain the scrapings from under all 10 fingernails
2. Places each toothpick with its scraping in a separate envelope
3. Labels each envelope with the location from which the scraping was taken
4. Forwards this evidence to the forensic science laboratory

If you have a suspect, examine him for bodily injuries, and for foreign hairs and semen in his pubic area. Any articles of clothing that he may have worn during the attack should be submitted for laboratory examination.

Any injuries sustained by either the suspect or the victim should be photographed immediately. Photographs should be taken with and without a scale of measurement.

If the suspect has not signed an informed consent, obtain a Criminal Code search warrant prior to combing or seizing pubic and head hair, and a DNA warrant before swabbing for saliva and other bodily fluids.

VII. Blunt Trauma

A. Definition

1. Blunt trauma is a mechanical injury resulting from the application of force on a tissue causing an alteration of the normal anatomic pattern of the tissue.
2. The characteristics and severity of a wound depend primarily upon the amount of kinetic energy that is released in the tissue.

   a. The more kinetic energy involved, the more severe the wound.

   b. Factors include:

   (1) The velocity of the object and the tissue that has been impacted.

   (2) The plasticity of the object and the tissue being struck. For example, the impact of a rubber hose on a soft buttock will be less severe than the impact of a lead pipe on an unprotected skull.

   (3) Area of impact: Destructiveness will increase if a fixed amount of kinetic energy is dispersed in a smaller area. For example, a person who is stabbed with a knife will be more

severely injured than if he had been struck by the flat side of the blade with the same force.

B. *Abrasions*

1. Abrasions result from the forceful impact of a blunt surface or object upon tissue.
2. They may result from a moving object striking fixed tissue or a fixed object being struck by moving tissue.
3. They are important evidence in establishing points of impact.
4. Types:

    a. Sliding abrasion—This injury occurs when the force vector, acting parallel to the surface area, is greater than the inward directed force vector, with a sliding component, e.g., the common scratch.

    b. Pressure abrasion—This injury results from an inward directed force vector with a slight sliding component, e.g., the marks on an air crash victim made by his seat belt.

    c. Patterned pressure abrasion—This injury is an abrasion whose characteristics suggest the causative agent, e.g., an indentation in the skin that matches a protrusion on the surface of a tool, a geometric pattern of marks on an automobile accident victim that matches the headlight pattern of a suspect vehicle.

    d. Postmortem abrasions—Abrasions that occur after death tend to be yellowish-orange. However, medical experts are often unable to state with certainty whether a specific abrasion occurred before or after death.

C. *Bruises*

1. Bruise marks cannot indicate the point of impact.
2. Bruises are impossible to date. (Their colour is not a reliable indicator; it can vary considerably among individuals and have no relation to the time when the injury occurred.)
3. Bruises can be inflicted after death, but it is extremely difficult to determine whether a bruise occurred post- or antemortem.
4. Significant trauma does not always produce significant bruising.

    a. The amount of force that was used to create an injury cannot be determined from the amount of bruising because of the many variables involved.

    b. Examples of persons who bruise more easily than healthy adults:

    (1) Persons who take aspirin regularly
    (2) Elderly persons

  (3) Infants

  (4) Persons suffering from scurvy or leukemia and other blood disorders

  (5) Persons taking certain types of medicines

TIP: If you encounter an alleged assault victim who claims to have been severely beaten but shows no signs of bruising, check with him again in a day or two. His bruises may simply take longer to appear than those of the average person.

D. *Lacerations*

1. Definition: The tearing of the skin as a result of the application of blunt trauma

2. Common locations:

 a. Forehead

 b. Scalp

 c. Other locations on the body where the skin cannot stretch

3. Characteristics:

 a. Irregular margins

 b. Associated bruising

 c. Bridging of tissue

 d. Debris in the wound (can sometimes be related to the striking object)

VIII. Hairs and Fibres

A. *Hairs and Fibres as Evidence*

1. Although a laboratory examination of fibres has only limited value in making an identification, it may provide important corroborative evidence.

 a. The mixing of hairs and fibres between the clothing of the victim and that of the suspect can establish that they have been in contact with each other.

 b. Hairs and fibres left by the suspect help to place him at the crime scene.

 c. The presence of these items on an object can indicate that it was a weapon of attack.

 d. They can sometimes identify a hit-and-run vehicle.

2. DNA profiling can be used to match a single hair sheath with a particular individual.

3. Possible locations:

 a. In the grasp of the victim

 b. On clothing

    c. On the attack weapon

    d. Under fingernails

    e. In hats

    f. On the damaged area of a suspect vehicle

    g. On bedsheets or blankets

B. *Handling*

1. Handle suspected hair specimens with tweezers, combs, or clean instruments.

    a. Do not handle with your fingers; you could transfer oil, grease, or other substances on your hands to the sample.

    b. Place the hairs on a clean sheet of white paper.

    c. Fold using the druggist's fold.

    d. Insert the sample in a labelled envelope for transport to the laboratory.

2. If hair samples are found on a weapon such as a gun, hammer, club, or axe, do not disturb them. Wrap the weapon in plastic or paper carefully and ship it to the laboratory.

3. When you submit hair evidence, include at least 12 full-length hairs from different areas of the head, and an additional 12 hairs from the pubic area in cases of sexual assault.

    a. Collect hair from both the victim and the suspect, if available, for comparison purposes.

    b. To remove, ask the suspect or victim to pull the hairs out to preserve the root sheath for DNA comparison. If hairs must be cut, clip them as close to the skin as possible.

    c. In rape cases, obtain pubic hair combings before taking other samples.

    d. Wrap the known samples separately and label them clearly to avoid contamination with other evidence.

C. *Possible Findings*

1. Hair samples can be examined to determine whether the hair is of human or animal origin.

    a. If the sample is animal hair, the species of animal can be identified, e.g., cat, dog, horse, deer, etc.

    b. If the sample is human, microscopic examination can determine:

        (1) Race of the person it came from (Caucasian, Negroid, Mongoloid, or a mixture of two or more)

        (2) Whether the hair fell out naturally or was pulled out

(3) Body area in which the hair was located (head, pubic, limb, chest)

(4) Cause of any hair damage (cutting, crushing, burning, etc.)

(5) If the hair has been bleached, dyed, or otherwise artificially altered

(6) If the hair is naturally or artificially waved

2. Hair samples do not reveal age or sex, but microscopic comparisons of unidentified hairs with known hair samples can prove that the questioned sample either:

   a. Came from the same individual, or

   b. Came from an individual of the same race as the originator with identical microscopic hair characteristics

3. The results of hair comparisons may be inconclusive.

4. Fibres may provide evidence through identification of the origin of the fibre:

   a. Animal (wool)

   b. Vegetable (cotton)

   c. Synthetic (nylon, Dacron, polyester, etc.)

   d. Mineral (glass)

5. Tests can also determine whether the questioned fibres and the suspected article of clothing share the same

   a. Origin

   b. Colour

   c. Microscopic characteristics

NOTE: Such factors as wear and fading may result in inconclusive findings even if the fibres are from the suspected garment.

IX. Soils and Plant Materials

A. Soils as Evidence

1. Soils adhering to shoes, tires, fenders, and other objects may assist you in tracing the movements of a suspect.

2. Soil found on the clothing of a suspect can be examined for similarities with:

   a. Soil on the clothing of the victim

   b. Soil samples from the crime scene

3. Soil at an arson site can help to identify the accelerant used.

NOTE: Although such comparisons are not conclusive, they can make a significant contribution to building a strong body of circumstantial evidence for or against the accused.

4. Clothing containing questioned soil materials should be wrapped and sealed in paper.

B. *Handling Soils*

1. Collect samples from several likely locations at the crime scene, using a clean teaspoon.
2. Place each sample in a clean leakproof container such as a glass jar.
3. Label the container properly for later identification, noting the location from which it was taken.
4. If the suspected soil materials are on a small, movable object, send the entire object to the laboratory.
5. If the object bearing the suspected soil materials cannot be sent to the laboratory:
   a. Flake off suitable samples.
   b. Place them in a clean glass jar.
   c. Seal, label, and ship.
6. Also collect comparison samples at distances of between 30 and 90 m of the crime scene, covering all directions. (These samples will help to delineate the soil areas around the crime scene.)

NOTE: Gather samples only from the surface of the top layer of soil; do not dig into the ground. (For Blood in Dirt and Sand, see page 161.)

C. *Plants*

1. Plant materials such as seeds, pollen, or flower particles may be important to your case.
2. Submit plants known to be from suspected areas with your other soil samples for comparison.

X. Metals

A. *Testing Procedures*

1. Toolmark identification (see page 155)
2. Physical tests (measurements, appearance)
3. Mechanical tests (tensile, strength, hardness)

B. *Serial Number Restoration*

1. Obliterated serial numbers can sometimes be restored if only the visible markings have been removed, and the underlying disturbed area has not been seriously affected.

   a. Metal stamping, electric needle, and engraving procedures disturb the molecular structure of the metal beneath the serial numbers.

        (1) This physical change causes associated chemical and magnetic changes in the metal.

        (2) Restoration techniques use these changes to render the obliterated serial number legible.

    b. The depth of the disturbed area varies according to:

        (1) Amount of force used in applying the serial number

        (2) Strength of metal

2. Methods of inscribing numbers on metal:

    a. Stamping:

        (1) Most commonly used method of creating serial numbers

        (2) Most easily restored of all methods of metal inscription

    b. Electric needle marking:

        (1) Frequently used to mark tools, electronic equipment, and other valuable property for identification

        (2) More difficult to restore than stamping because the disturbed layer in the metal is not as deep

    c. Engraving:

        (1) Very difficult to restore

        (2) Number has been cut or scooped out, resulting in only minor metal deformation

    d. Moulded markings:

        (1) Usually used for part or pattern numbers

        (2) Numbers are formed during the casting of the object, resulting in no deformation of the metal

        (3) Can sometimes be restored if differences in cooling rates caused the grain structure of the metal in the numbered area to differ significantly from the rest of the object

        (4) Are of little value for identification purposes, since they identify only the type of part

3. The critical factor in restoring a number is the extent of the internal metal damage caused by the obliteration attempt.

    a. If only the visible markings have been removed, the number can usually be restored.

    b. If the underlying disturbed area in the metal was also affected, number restoration is usually impossible.

C. *Other Types of Metal Examination*

1. Wires used to bind victims may be examined to determine:

    a. Possible sources

    b.   Similarities with wire in the suspect's possession

2. Metal fragments from a bomb timing device may reveal:

    a.   Type of mechanism

    b.   Manufacturer and date of manufacture

    c.   Specific clock model used

3. Wristwatches may be examined for jeweller's identification scratches to determine ownership.

4. Metal auto trim found at hit-and-run accidents can reveal:

    a.   Make of the vehicle

    b.   Specific vehicle involved (if located for comparison with the sample)

5. Lamp bulbs from vehicles that have been in accidents can reveal:

    a.   If the lights were on or off at the time of the collision

    b.   Whether the brakes were applied at the time of the impact

6. A metal piece cut from a safe door can indicate:

    a.   Type of equipment used

    b.   Level of expertise of the person who attacked it

NOTE: In collecting metal samples, be sure not to use heat or bending to remove the specimens from the crime scene. These actions could result in physical or chemical changes that would destroy the sample's evidentiary value. Mark the item to maintain the chain of custody.

XI. Wood

A. Handling

1. Handle clothing, tools, weapons, and other objects carefully to avoid dislodging wood particles that may be present.

2. Submit fairly large wood samples for examination to permit drilling, cutting, and other tests for comparison with the questioned sample.

3. Mark each questioned sample, if possible.

4. Wrap to prevent contamination with other evidence or loss of minute particles.

B. Possible Findings

1. Sawdust-sized samples can be identified as to species, e.g., spruce, oak, maple, pine, but cannot be associated with a specific source.

2. Larger samples, such as tree trunks, tool handles, fence posts, and branches, can sometimes be matched with the specific source from which they were cut.

3. Wood fragments, such as chips or small pieces that have broken off, can sometimes be fitted into the parent wood for a specific source identification. For example, a splinter from a baseball bat that was used in a violent assault could be matched with the bat.

4. Wood specimens that have been cut with a tool such as an axe, shears, or an auger bit can sometimes be matched with the specific cutting tool, if sufficient microscopic toolmarks are present.

XII. Paint

A. Paint Traces as Evidence

Analysis of the composition of trace amounts of paint, especially if the sample is multilayered, can help to identify a suspected vehicle, tool, weapon, or person.

B. Handling

1. Use a small, clean knife or other instrument to chip off paint samples.

NOTE: Do *not* scrape paint off. By chipping off the paint sample, you will preserve its layer structure intact. This can be important in linking an object to the case under investigation. In a hit-and-run, for example, your paint sample could reveal that the suspect vehicle has been repainted three times and indicate the colour of each coat of paint. You now have strong evidence to use in identifying the vehicle.

2. Photograph the area from which the sample was taken.
3. Never use the same knife to remove samples from two different sources.
4. Place each specimen of paint chips on a separate sheet of paper.
   a. Fold using the druggist's fold.
   b. Insert in an envelope.
   c. Forward to the forensic science laboratory for analysis.
5. If paint specimens have been removed from two or more different locations:
   a. Package each specimen separately.
   b. Note the following on the envelope:
      (1) Location from which the specimen was taken
      (2) Date and time
      (3) Your initials

NOTE: Do not stick particles of paint on cellophane tape or place them in cotton.

6. Tools and other instruments that may bear paint traces should be sent to the laboratory intact.
7. If your suspect has a suspicious stain on his hands or clothing:
    a. Ask him where it came from.
    b. Obtain a sample from the named source.
    c. Forward it to the laboratory with the original sample for comparison.

XIII. Glass

A. Matching Fragments

Glass fragments can often be matched with comparison samples to make a positive identification.

B. Handling

1. Wrap all glass specimens separately in cotton to prevent breakage.
2. Carefully mark on the container the location from which the samples were taken.

C. Direction Analysis

1. Bullet impact:
    a. A bullet passing through glass creates a cone-shaped hole that is larger on the exit side of the glass.
    b. If the impact force of the bullet blows out the cone shape of the hole, the direction of flight can be established by stress-line configuration.

        (1) A series of radial and concentric cracks appears in glass that has been broken by an external force.
        (2) Radial cracks radiate from the point of impact.
        (3) Concentric cracks form rough circles around the point of impact.
        (4) The result is a pie shape.

2. Other impacts:
    a. A series of stress lines that tend to be parallel on one face of the glass and perpendicular to the other is created on the fractured edges of glass pieces.
    b. On a radial crack edge these stress lines will be at right angles to the rear surface (the face of the glass opposite to the one struck).
    c. You must establish which cracks are radial and which are concentric.
    d. For this reason, all available pieces of glass must be used for examination.

NOTE: If you wish the laboratory to establish the direction of the blow that struck a window, send the remaining glass (in its frame, if possible) with labels that clearly indicate "inside" and "outside."

D. Possible Findings

1. Direction of bullet or blow that struck the glass sample
2. If the glass fragment is large enough, positive match with a specific source, e.g., beer bottle, window pane, etc.
3. In hit-and-run accidents:

    a. Year and make of car (if sample from parking lights or tail-lights)

    b. Type and manufacture (if headlight only)

    c. Positive match with the suspect vehicle, when located

Illustration 11
BULLET DIRECTION

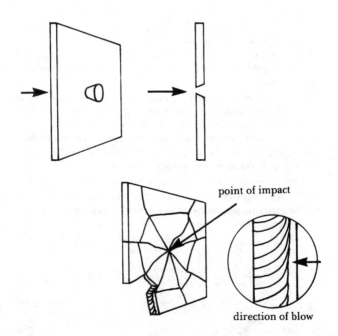

point of impact

direction of blow

NOTE: In hit-and-run investigations, damaged headlights from the suspect vehicle should be dismounted, packed separately, sealed, labelled, and sent to the laboratory with lens fragments collected at the scene.

XIV. Drugs and Poisons

A. *Suspected Poisonings and Drug Overdoses*

1. In these cases, the laboratory will examine foods, liquids, body fluids, and other materials to determine if poisons or drugs are present.
2. Blood analysis can reveal the presence of carbon monoxide.
3. Bile should be collected if narcotics are suspected.
4. Urine samples should also be collected for analysis for the presence of alcohol, drugs, or poison.

NOTE: All blood exhibits should be refrigerated immediately after being collected.

B. *Preservation of Evidence*

1. In cases requiring drug or poison analysis, urine should be collected in watertight vials or plastic specimen jars.
   a. Seal it with a tight-fitting stopper or screw top.
   b. Pack it securely in a suitable container.
   c. Send it to the laboratory.
2. Record on the container any prescription numbers and other information.
   a. Question the pharmacist who prepared the prescription.
   b. Send this information with the sample to the laboratory.

NOTE: Don't add chemical preservatives to suspect poison samples. Refrigerate the sample by placing dry ice around the container and deliver it to the laboratory as quickly as possible.

3. Take every precaution while packaging the sample to prevent leakage or breakage.

XV. Shoe Prints and Tire Treads

A. *Photographs*

1. Photograph tire treads and shoe prints found at a scene using a tripod-mounted camera.
2. Include a ruler and an identification label in each shot.
3. Set the camera directly over the impression and focus it so that the impression fills the frame.
4. Hold the flash gun low and to one side.

5. Take a second exposure with the light source rotated through 90 degrees horizontally.

B. Casts

1. Always make casts if possible.
2. Materials required:
   a. Plaster of Paris
   b. Mixing container
   c. Wire to reinforce the cast
   d. Stirring paddle
   e. Metal or wood strips to build a frame around the impression
   f. Spray gun or similar device if the impression is in a difficult substance such as loose dirt or sand
   g. Flowers of sulphur, if the impression is in snow (this material is very brittle and should be backed with a stronger material such as plaster of Paris)
      (1) Heat the crystals in a double boiler until they liquefy.
      (2) Let the liquid cool until a film appears on the surface.
      (3) Pour the liquid gently into the impression.

TIP: Preparing impressions and taking casts requires a practised hand. Remember that casts and lifts will destroy the impression when they are moved. Experiment with these procedures thoroughly before using them during a real investigation.

3. Preparation of impression:
   a. Clean out loose material only, using extreme care not to disturb the impression.
   b. Plastic spray or hair spray may be used to fix problem impressions, e.g., sand, loose dirt.

NOTE: If improperly applied to the impression, sprays may cause a loss of the detail that is necessary for minute comparisons.

   c. Fine water spray may be used to fix sand impressions, but use extreme care.
   d. Place forms around the impressions to hold in the plaster.

4. Preparation of plaster of Paris:
   a. Pour the amount of water required to fill the impression into a pail or bucket.
   b. Sprinkle plaster into the water, stirring continuously until the mixture has the consistency of pancake batter.
   c. Gently (and immediately) pour the mixture into the impression, taking care not to wash away the impression.

d. When the solution is about 1.3 cm thick, place reinforcing wires or sticks into the liquid.

e. Continue pouring until the cast is about 2.5 cm thick.

f. Scratch your initials, the date, and other identifying information into the cast while it is still soft.

g. Remove only loose material from the face of the cast when it is lifted.

NOTE: Improper cleaning of the face of the cast before it has dried can damage the detail on the surface impression.

h. Handle the cast carefully—it is *extremely* fragile.

i. Allow the cast to dry thoroughly before attempting to transport it.

j. Wrap to avoid breakage.

k. Do *not* place casts in plastic bags.

C. *Impressions on Firm Surfaces*

1. If possible, darken the area to eliminate ambient lighting.

2. Direct the beam of a flashlight light parallel to the suspected surfaces to locate impressions.

3. To photograph the impression, hold the light source (flashlight, floodlight, etc.) as close to the floor or ground as possible to achieve a side-lighting effect.

4. If possible, retain the original evidence for laboratory examination.

5. Protect impressions so they will not rub off during handling.

6. Lift impressions if the original evidence cannot be retained.

a. Apply large pieces of fingerprint lifting tape to the impression.

NOTE: Do not dust or otherwise treat the impression.

b. Start the tape at one edge and roll over the impression smoothly and firmly to keep out air bubbles.

7. Moistened gelatin applied to photographic film creates an excellent surface for lifting impressions.

a. Clear film can be made by fixing and washing.

b. Black film can be made by exposing, developing, fixing, and washing.

c. Film should be placed in water, wiped off, and dried until tacky.

d. The tacky film should be applied to the impression with a squeegee, scraper, or roller from edge to edge, taking care to avoid air bubbles.

e.   Protect the lifted impressions so they will not be destroyed or erased during handling or shipping.

8.   A positive identification can be made if:

a.   Sufficient detail has been reproduced from the original impression

b.   Sufficient identifying marks have been created by wear to associate the sample with the impression

XVI. Fire Accelerants

A.   *Suspected Arson*

1.   In your investigation of suspected arson, always consider the possibility that the fire may be related to another crime, e.g., attempted murder, break and enter, etc.

2.   The source of ignition may have left detectable traces in the fire residue, e.g.:

a.   Candles
b.   Inflammable liquids
c.   Matches
d.   Cigarettes
e.   Wick fragments
f.   Containers
g.   Twines
h.   Fuses
i.   Clockwork mechanisms
j.   Phosphorus

3.   Be alert to unusual odours that may indicate the use of an inflammable liquid.

a.   If a liquid is recovered, it can usually be identified even if it has badly evaporated.

b.   If no liquid is recovered, it can still often be identified from its vapours.

B.   *Collecting Physical Evidence*

1.   Try to establish the fire's point of origin as precisely as possible:

a.   Locate any inflammable materials that may have been deliberately placed at the scene to spread the fire.

b.   Carefully collect these materials, including charred fragments, ash, mechanical devices, the stubs of matches, and other items.

c.   Collect any debris that is giving off an odour.

d.   Include a sample of soil from the arson site.

2. Place all such evidence in jars that can be closed with a screw cap or tight-fitting stopper. If large quantities are involved, use clean unlined metal cans direct from the supplier.

   a.   Do not use a rubber stopper for a jar containing inflammable liquid. It may deteriorate, causing spillage.

   b.   Submit only a small sample of liquid (about 10 mL) and retain the rest in safe storage in case further testing is needed.

   c.   Do not submit gas or other petroleum products in plastic containers.

   d.   Do not submit bulky items. Cut off a small portion and submit in a jar.

   e.   Submit to the laboratory with full details.

3. Collect samples of rags, clothing etc., from suspect and send to the laboratory for comparison.

4. Collect samples of synthetic materials such as carpeting and padding that have not been touched by the fire and submit for comparison.

TIP: Ask a witness or someone familiar with the site of the fire to accompany you on your search to assist in identifying containers or other items that are foreign to the location.

5. Store all arson debris in a freezer until it is submitted to the forensic science laboratory.

6. Follow the requirements of the Transportation of Dangerous Goods Act in sending samples to the laboratory.

12. MAJOR CASE MANAGEMENT

I. Introduction

Serious crimes such as homicide, kidnapping, and bombings often result in lengthy, exhaustive, and highly complex criminal investigations. During one double rape-murder investigation, for example, our officers interviewed more than 3000 persons before a suspect was eventually arrested.

If you are assigned to this type of investigation, your major challenge will be to maintain control, both of the staff working with you and of the information that is received. A team of detectives working around the clock can, within a very few days, amass thousands of scraps of information, any one of which could prove to be the vital clue needed to solve the crime. The "essential of control" in these cases is continuous feedback that offers you a clear understanding of the investigation's progress on a virtually minute-by-minute basis.

The procedure outlined in this chapter is recommended as an effective way of managing a complex investigation. While it is by no means the only way, it may offer a few ideas that you can adapt to assist you in conducting complex investigations.

II. Characteristics of a Major Case

1. Accidents or disasters involving multiple victims
2. Serial crimes involving property losses or violence against persons.
3. Homicides
4. Sexual assaults involving multiple victims
5. Institutional abuse of children
6. White-collar crime involving large amounts of money, well-known suspects or victims, and large-scale media attention
7. Public inquiries
8. Death of police officers

III. Principal Goals of Major Case Investigations

1. Identification and arrest of suspects
2. Protection of victims, both actual and potential
3. Suppression of criminal activity

4. Evidence collection and documentation
5. Event reconstruction
6. Successful prosecution and conviction of the person or persons responsible
7. Providing information that assists the court in making an appropriate sentencing decision

IV. Controlling the Investigation

A. Investigation Operations Plan

1. Immediately upon assignment to a case that will require a heavy allocation of manpower, draw up an Investigation Operations Plan.
2. The plan should indicate the following:
    a. Command posts
        (1) Location, e.g., police station, mobile command trailer, temporary takeover of civilian office, etc.
        (2) Facilities available:
            i. Telephones
            ii. Desks
            iii. Laptop computers for all investigative teams
            iv. Communications link to dispatcher
            v. Interview rooms
            vi. Cells
            vii. Meeting rooms (location and capacity)
            viii. Computer equipped with CASEFILE® software or similar programs
            ix. Facsimile machine
        (3) Facilities required
    b. Personnel assignments:
        (1) *Officer in charge*
            i. Directs all aspects of the investigation
            ii. Evaluates all incoming information
            iii. Maintains custody of all files, reports, and other materials
            iv. Assigns investigation teams to specific tasks
            v. Approves all statements to the media
            vi. Reports to senior officers
            vii. Maintains liaison with other police departments or agencies
            viii. Chairs meetings of investigators assigned to the case

NOTE: By maintaining a checklist of the primary tasks being performed during the investigation, the team commander should always have an up-to-date knowledge of the following:

1. **How many suspects have been investigated**
2. **Important leads currently under investigation**
3. **Results of laboratory reports**
4. **All unassigned leads**
5. **Results of all significant interviews**
6. **Names of all identified persons**
7. **Whereabouts of all investigators and assignments**

   (2) *Coordinator*

      i. Ensures that computer records are updated as soon as information becomes available

      ii. Assists the officer in charge as required

   (3) *Reader* (could be the officer in charge in some investigations)

      i. Reads and provides initial evaluation of all incoming information to officer in charge

      ii. Details field investigators to assignments

      iii. Performs other administrative duties as assigned by the officer in charge

   (4) *Field investigators*

      i. Investigate incoming leads and develops new sources of information

      ii. Keep the team commander informed of vital case details throughout the investigation

B. *Field Investigation*

1. Field investigators may be assigned to such specific details as:

   a. Making door-to-door checks of the neighbourhood in which the crime occurred

   b. Checking out relatives, suspects, victims, known associates of the suspect or victim, etc.

   c. Investigating suspects

2. Officers assigned to field investigation may also:

   a. Identify vehicles and licence numbers

   b. Maintain custody of all seized exhibits

   c. Develop and maintain computer records

V. Information Control

1. It is crucial to the success of any long-term investigation that supervisors establish an effective system for controlling case files.
2. The massive amounts of information received during a major investigation can be effectively controlled through an Investigative Action File, whose contents can be loaded into a computer.
3. Cases that generate fewer than 300 leads can probably be managed by using hard-copy lead sheets and indices.
4. Supervisors should make use of computer software programs, such as CASEFILE®, to catalogue and analyze information in cases that have the potential to generate a great number of leads.
5. To ensure that good leads are recognized quickly, no reports should be put into the file until the officer in charge and the coordinator have read and initialled them.

A. The Investigative Action Form

1. All information received from external sources, such as members of the public, regular informants, or phone calls from other police agencies, should be recorded on an Investigative Action Form.
2. Contents of the Investigative Action Form:
   a. Name of the officer receiving the call or tip
   b. Occurrence number of the crime under investigation
   c. Date and time of call
   d. Name, address, and phone number of the informant
   e. Synopsis of the information received
   f. Officer to whom the information has been assigned
   g. Time and date of assignment
   h. Time and date of interview
   i. Whether or not a formal statement was taken

NOTE: These forms should be supplied to all stations at the outset of your investigation so that any information received can be immediately recorded and forwarded to the officer in charge.

3. Upon receipt of the Investigative Action Form, the officer in charge will evaluate the information and ensure that it is added to the CASEFILE® or other program.

   a. If the information is important, he will assign it to an investigation team for immediate action.
   b. If the information has a low priority, he may

      (1) File the information temporarily for follow-up after more promising leads have been investigated.

(2) Assign the information to another unit for investigation, if appropriate.

(3) File the information as "unfounded." (Even the most bizarre leads should never be discarded; they may eventually prove to contain a valuable nugget of information or assist in the investigation of unrelated crimes.)

4. All assignments made by the officer in charge and the reader should be recorded in a computerized or hard-copy Assignment Log that lists:

   a. Names of assigned officers
   b. Date and time of assignment
   c. Investigative Action Form number

5. A quick check of the Assignment Log will reveal if any investigative teams have not reported in within a reasonable period of time.

B. *Special Reports*

1. The officer in charge may also be required to prepare special reports to senior officers on a regular basis:

   a. To keep them informed of the progress of the investigation
   b. To request additional manpower and resources
   c. To ensure accurate statements to the media that do not harm the investigation

2. Such reports should normally be in the form of a brief synopsis or meeting, with computer printouts of information as required.

VI. Sources of Information

A. *Government*

 1. National police computer records (CPIC, NCIC, INTERPOL)
 2. Other police departments, including railway and university police
 3. Bylaw enforcement officers
 4. Court records
 5. Immigration officers
 6. Defence department records
 7. Postal investigators
 8. Welfare
 9. Other social service agencies
10. Port authorities
11. Employment counsellors
12. Public schools and universities

13. Libraries
14. Voter registration lists
15. Public utilities
16. Parole and probation officers
17. Prisons and custodial institutions
18. Motor vehicle registrar

B. Private

1. Banks

NOTE: Contact banks and other financial institutions through your fraud bureau, which probably has a working relationship with internal security investigators. You will need a search warrant to examine documentation in their files.

2. Private educational institutions (trade schools, privately funded schools and colleges, etc.)
3. Hospitals
4. Hotels and motels
5. Real-estate brokers
6. Airlines
7. Credit bureaus
8. Taxi companies
9. City directory
10. Telephone company
11. Finance companies
12. Newspaper files
13. Private investigators
14. Churches
15. Drug stores
16. Automobile dealers
17. Insurance companies
18. Labour organizations
19. Physicians (search warrant required)
20. Dentists (search warrant required)
21. Moving companies
22. Family members
23. Ex-spouses
24. Fellow employees
25. Neighbours
26. Youth organizations, e.g., Scouts, YMCA
27. Fitness clubs
28. Professional associations

29. Current and former employers
30. Video stores
31. Service clubs
32. Canada Directory (computer program that lists in a computerized directory telephone numbers and street addresses across Canada)

VII. External Communications

A. *Other Police Services*

1. Supervisors can enhance investigations greatly by fostering communication with other law enforcement agencies.
2. You may wish to contact other police agencies to determine whether they have investigated similar crimes by issuing a zone, provincial, or Canada-wide alert on CPIC.
3. Keep a permanent record of the names of any officers who respond to your alert.
4. Cooperation and mutual assistance are the key factors in encouraging other departments to devote time and manpower to your requests for information.

B. *Relatives*

1. During lengthy investigations, particularly those involving homicide or child disappearances, keep the victim's relatives up to date on the progress of your investigation.
2. Their cooperation and support can be invaluable during the course of a lengthy, difficult investigation.
3. If the relatives feel they are being ignored or "kept in the dark" deliberately, they may take their case to the media, resulting in adverse publicity for your department.

C. *Citizens*

1. Citizens who provide information should be called back when possible and advised of the outcome of your inquiries.
2. This practice may be time-consuming, but it is also good public relations and will encourage future assistance and support.

D. *News Media*

1. The media can be an indispensable asset in disseminating potentially helpful information to the general public—information that can produce valuable leads in a stalled case.
2. Many complex investigations involve sensational crimes that are the subject of intense media interest.
3. The frequent calls you will receive from newspaper, radio, and television reporters can disrupt your investigation by tying up phone lines as well as the time of your investigators.

4. In such cases, the officer in charge should establish a procedure for distributing information to the media that does not involve himself or his personnel.

   a. All calls should be referred to one appointed media relations officer.

   b. The media relations officer should not use a telephone line assigned to the investigation.

   c. During the first few days after the crime, the media relations officer should meet regularly with the officer in charge for a quick update on the investigation.

      (1) These meetings should be initiated by the media relations officer; the officer in charge will have other matters on his mind.

      (2) The officer in charge should give the media relations officer a full briefing on the investigation, withholding nothing.

      (3) The officer in charge should specify all details that are not to be released because they could prejudice his investigation.

      (4) The media relations officer should forward copies of all written news releases to the officer in charge for approval before distribution.

5. In some investigations, you may wish to direct the media relations officer to circulate a description or sketch of the suspect to the news media, e.g., via a news conference, or a release to a newswire service.

NOTE: If your case has been highly publicized and your leads are few, set up a hot-line number that members of the public can call to offer information, anonymously if they prefer. An experienced, diplomatic, and patient officer should be assigned to this detail to ensure that good community relations are maintained, and that the information received is screened effectively. If the phone is not being manned 24 hours a day, arrange for voice mail to be put on that line or extension.

E. The Prosecutor's Office

1. Maintain a close liaison with the prosecutor's office during the course of your investigation.

2. The prosecutor will need to be kept up to date in order to:

   a. Plan allocations of legal staff to the case

    b.   Develop a fuller understanding of the case than would be possible if the arrest came unexpectedly

    c.   Assist with wiretap and search warrant applications

3.   When officers keep the prosecutors informed from the beginning of an investigation, they eliminate the untimely delays that occur when prosecutors must review bulky case files to familiarize themselves with an investigation after it has been conducted.

VIII. Identification of Suspects

A. *Photographs*

1.   The courts have ruled that a person who has previously identified a suspect from a single photograph is usually no longer useful as a witness in identifying him by other means.

    a.   This conclusion is based upon the belief that the person will remember the suspect's photograph in other identification procedures, and use it, rather than his memory of the actual event, to make the identification.

    b.   The person may still be called as a witness at trial, but the court must rule whether or not the identification was adequate.

    c.   In the absence of other more conclusive evidence, a court will generally rule that the accused was not properly or positively identified, and the prosecution will fail.

2.   Use at least 12 photographs of persons similar in appearance to the suspect.

    a.   Record the file numbers of all photos used.

    b.   Retain all these photographs in your possession until the prosecution has concluded.

3.   Save your most reliable witnesses for a photographic lineup identification.

4.   Do not allow more than one person at a time to look at suspect photographs—they may influence each other.

5.   Once you have an identification, GO NO FURTHER; do not show the same photograph to any other witnesses. Prepare a fresh photo lineup for other witnesses.

6.   Have the witness initial any photographs he selects. This will mean that the identification can be used at trial even if the witness cannot remember by the time the proceedings take place.

NOTE: *Never* **show a single photograph of a suspect to a witness; this will lead the court to conclude that he was directed to a specific suspect.**

Illustration 12
PHOTOGRAPHIC LINEUP INTERVIEW FORM

LINEUP TITLE: _____   OFFENCE TYPE: _____

DATE OF VIEWING __ / __ / __   TIME: _____ OCC. #: _____
                  YY   MM   DD

VIEWING LOCATION: _____

INSTRUCTIONS TO PERSON VIEWING LINEUP:

Before you view these photographs, I would like you to be aware of the following information:

(1) The person who committed the offence may or may not be in the selection of photographs you are about to view.

(2) You are in no way obliged to select any of the photographs if you do not recognize the individual as being involved in the case under investigation.

(3) Study each photograph carefully before making any comments.

(4) Be advised that the individuals may have somewhat changed their appearance since these photographs were taken. For example, their hairstyle or colour may have changed, or facial hair may have been added or removed.

(5) Additional Instructions: _____
_____

I DECLARE THAT NO OTHER INSTRUCTIONS CONCERNING THE PHOTOGRAPHS OR THE SUSPECTS HAVE BEEN GIVEN TO ME.

_____   _____
Signature of Person Viewing Lineup   Signature of Officer Conducting Viewing

===

PERSON SELECTED (IF ANY)

Photo Number: _____

_____   _____
Signature of Witness   Signature of Officer

Comments: _____
_____

IX. Modus Operandi Analysis

A. Definition

1. Modus operandi analysis in a complex investigation provides an operational profile of the suspect based upon his established behaviour patterns.

   a. To increase their sense of security, criminals tend to develop unique and identifiable habits and techniques that they use in the commission of crimes.

   b. These operational characteristics will be repeated consistently throughout their criminal careers.

EXAMPLE: A burglar will often use the same method to break into homes, in the same types of neighbourhoods, at the same time of night, even after he has been arrested and become known to police. A rapist will choose the same type of victim, use the same threats, and attack in the same types of locations repeatedly.

On several occasions, the first indication I had that a criminal had been released on parole was a crime report that detailed his modus operandi. Many criminals cannot deviate from their M.O. even when they know that it will lead the police directly to them.

B. Characteristics of the Modus Operandi

1. Type of crime: e.g., burglars rarely become bank robbers, con men rarely become shoplifters.

2. Persons attacked:

   a. Age
   b. Sex
   c. Physical appearance
   d. Occupation
   e. Race

3. Property attacked:

   a. Banks
   b. Type of business (convenience stores, liquor stores, etc.)
   c. Chain store
   d. Apartments
   e. Detached homes
   f. Doctors' offices
   g. Private clubs

4. How attacked:

   a. Break and enter—through milk chute, broke basement window, slipped lock with credit card, etc.

b. Rape—threatened with knife, pulled hair, twisted arm, asked for lighter, shoved into car, etc.

c. Robbery—displayed handgun, threatened with baseball bat, used holdup note, etc.

5. Means of attack:

   a. Break and enter—tools used
   b. Robbery—description of weapon used
   c. Theft—false-bottomed "booster" box, etc.

6. Time of attack:

   a. Time reported
   b. Time committed
   c. Consistent days, weeks, or months of the year

7. Object of attack:

   a. Burglary—money (may overlook valuable jewellery or silverware)
   b. Fraud—insurance plot
   c. Attempt murder—revenge

8. Trademark:

   a. Unique behaviour common to all the suspect's crimes
   b. Examples:

      (1) Robbery—always carries sawed-off shotgun, never speaks, always lights a cigarette, always escapes in a waiting cab
      (2) Burglary—always defecates on rug, rearranges furniture, pours himself a glass of milk, writes on bedroom mirror with lipstick
      (3) Rape—always wears a ski mask, asks for victim's phone number, apologizes afterward, offers victim money after attack, claims to be meter-reader

NOTE: The more unusual the trademark is, the greater its value in identifying your suspect.

C. The Modus Operandi File

1. In complex investigations, you may wish to build a modus operandi file to assist you in identifying suspects.

2. Use the headings listed above to check police computer records or to build an M.O. subfile as part of your Investigative Action File.

X. Psychological Profiling

A. Definition

1. An investigative process that attempts to identify an unknown subject by determining his unique personality traits, behavioural patterns, and other psychological characteristics.

2. Psychological profiling is particularly useful in investigations of psychopathological crimes, e.g., sadistic rapes, ritual murders, motiveless arsons, mutilations, and other crimes that by their nature suggest the offender suffers from severe mental or emotional difficulties.

B. Characteristics That May Be Suggested by a Psychological Profile

1. Age
2. Sex
3. Race
4. Marital status
5. Appearance
6. Grooming
7. Employment history
8. Work habits and standards
9. Proximity of personal residence to crime scene
10. Lifestyle
11. Childhood environment
12. Intelligence level
13. Educational level
14. Personality traits
15. Criminal record
16. Sexual orientation
17. Emotional well-being
18. Mental condition

NOTE: Upon request, the Royal Canadian Mounted Police and the Ontario Provincial Police will provide detailed psychological profiling of suspects wanted for major crimes using VICLAS, the Violent Crime Linkage Analysis System. The system was created to help ensure that dangerous serial offenders do not elude capture by simply moving between the jurisdictions of municipal police services as they commit their crimes.

13. RAIDS AND SEARCHES

I. Planning a Raid

A. Factors to Consider

1. Surprise
2. Simplicity
3. Speed
4. Available manpower
5. Possible effect on other investigations
6. Amount of evidence (drugs, stolen property, etc.) in the suspect's possession
7. Search warrants or other legal justification
8. Specialized personnel required, e.g., female officers or medical practitioners to conduct body searches of female suspects
9. Use of tactical/rescue officers for forced entry
10. Availability of police dogs trained to sniff out narcotics

NOTE: The right of police officers to conduct searches has come under intense judicial scrutiny in recent years, and this trend will certainly continue.

It is therefore vitally important that all officers who undertake a search be fully aware of all aspects of the law relating to that search, including the preparation of the warrant, the authorization required, the nature of the alleged offence, and, most important, the limitations that the law places on their right to search.

Nothing can be more futile than to conduct a search in a manner that renders inadmissible the evidence the search reveals.

B. Preparation

1. Determine the exact layout of the area to be raided, through interviews with the landlord, former tenants, visiting social workers, floor plans, or other sources.
2. Develop a knowledge of the neighbourhood around the suspect residence, e.g., one-way streets, alleys, stoplights, possible escape routes, etc.
3. Appoint an exhibit officer to retain custody of all the evidence recovered during the raid and one or more officers to act as prisoner escorts.

4. Ensure that pretyped forms for exhibits are completed prior to the raid.
5. Acquire any tools that may be needed, such as:
   a. Sledge hammer
   b. Prybar
   c. Bolt-cutters
6. Arrange for a police photographer to accompany you on the raid to take evidence photographs.
7. Brief all officers involved on:
   a. The suspects who may be present
   b. Whether they are likely to be armed
   c. What kind of evidence you are looking for
   d. Layout of the premises
   e. Legal considerations relating to the search
8. Assign each officer a specific area that he is to go to immediately after entry.

II. Conducting the Raid

A. Precautions

1. Before going in, ensure that adequate radio communications are established by checking all equipment.
2. If possible, secure a key to the residence from the building superintendent or landlord.
3. If suspects are believed to be armed, consider a tactical entry.

B. Procedure

1. Move in as quickly as possible, using the element of surprise.
2. Immobilize all persons present immediately.
3. Conduct body searches for concealed weapons before making any attempt to locate evidence.
4. Ensure that all detained persons are informed of their rights to legal counsel.
5. Turn over the prisoners to the prisoner escort officers and remove them from the premises.
6. Begin a thorough search for evidence.

III. Evidence: Possible Places of Concealment

A. On the Person

1. Belt buckles
2. Lipstick case
3. Cigarette lighters and open cigarette packs
4. Behind lapels

5. Under breasts or brassieres
6. In hairdo
7. Beneath bandages or plasters
8. Hair clasp or clip
9. Inside luggage lining
10. Nose
11. Glasses, hearing aids, cases
12. Ears (inside and behind)
13. Mouth (swallowed, held in mouth with string)
14. Cheeks of buttocks
15. Feet (taped on bottoms or between toes)
16. Collar of shirts, jackets, etc.
17. Tie knots
18. Handkerchiefs
19. Inside jewellery—lockets, watches, bracelets, etc.
20. Wallet
21. Cuffs and bands of slacks or skirts
22. Inside pens
23. Pockets
24. Tobacco tins or pouches
25. Socks and shoes (heels, soles, toes, inside lining)
26. Pillboxes or bottles
27. Inside sanitary napkins or tampons
28. Inside flytrap of pants
29. Battery boxes, hearing aids, etc.
30. Hat band
31. Cigarette filters, cigar tips
32. Makeup compact
33. Money belt
34. Plaster casts
35. Crutches or canes (may be hollowed out)
36. Inner linings of coats, purses, etc.
37. Under or in false teeth
38. Slit or zippered belts
39. Rings, necklaces, earrings, etc.

NOTE: Although drug investigations frequently require rectal or vaginal searches, these actions should be undertaken only by medical personnel or other persons who have clear authority under the law to undertake such procedures. An insensitive approach to this type of search can result in both community and judicial outrage, which may lead to further curtailment of police powers to search.

B. *In the Residence*

1. Telephone receiver
2. Under washbasin, sink, or tub
3. Base of lamp
4. Clothing inside closets
5. Flowerpots and window boxes
6. Rolled up in window shades
7. Mailbox
8. Light fixtures
9. Inside knife handles
10. Behind wall phones
11. Mattresses
12. Behind wall pictures, posters, and mirrors
13. Inside flashlights
14. Air conditioner registers, heat vents, etc.
15. Sink traps
16. Dog collars
17. Light switches
18. Baseboards
19. Hollowed-out doors with removable tops
20. Refrigerator and containers inside
21. Inside toilet tanks
22. Magazines and books
23. Bedposts
24. Attic insulation
25. Inside footstools
26. False-bottomed radiator covers
27. Inside kitchen canisters or jars
28. In tool boxes and sewing kits
29. Inside envelopes
30. Behind drapes
31. Inside television and radio sets
32. Inside vacuum cleaners and utensils
33. Inside room dividers
34. Inside seasonal decorations
35. Dog houses
36. Under rugs and mats
37. Inside hollow curtain, shower, and closet rods
38. Wires from fuse boxes
39. Clothes hamper
40. Gutters and drain spouts

41. Air ducts
42. Shoe polish container
43. Razor blade holder
44. Stovepipes
45. Furnace
46. Ceiling tiles
47. Dolls and other toys
48. TV rabbit ears
49. Bird cage
50. Leg of bathtub
51. Plastic baking utensils (rolling pins, etc.)
52. Shower head
53. Hair dryer
54. Clocks
55. Behind and inside medicine chests
56. All drains with strings attached
57. Behind door frames
58. Wall sockets
59. Gun barrels
60. In sand on the top of an "octopus-type" furnace
61. Taped under drawers
62. In garbage
63. Chimney flues
64. Hollowed-out books
65. In used oil cans
66. In light bulbs
67. Inside cassettes, videotapes, CD jewel cases
68. In corners of empty beer cases
69. In hallway fire extinguishers

Illustration 13
COMMONLY USED DRUGS CHART

Cocaine

Source
Extracted from leaves of coca bush.

Appearance
Usually white, odourless, fluffy powder resembling crystalline snow, but may be in flake or rock form. Snorted through nose, taken orally, or injected.

Effects

Short term: increased pulse and breathing rate, excitement, sense of euphoria, loss of appetite.

Long term: insomnia, lethargy, hallucinations, maniacal sense of excitation, possible deterioration of membrane between nostrils if powder inhaled through nose.

Crack Cocaine

Source

Processed from cocaine hydrochloride.

Appearance

White crystalline pebbles ("rocks") that are smoked, resulting in an almost pure, highly concentrated vapour coming into immediate contact with the entire surface area of the user's lungs. Crack reaches the brain in less than 10 seconds after inhalation.

Effects

Instant "high" of three to seven minutes, followed by severe depression, paranoia, rapid heart rate, anxiety, possible hallucinations; users become addicted faster than from any other drug; chronic users sometimes see "snow lights," i.e., flashes of light or halos, when they try to focus on a person or object.

Heroin

Source

An alkaloid derived from morphine (chemical name: diacetylmorphine).

Appearance

Colour ranges from white to off-white, or tan to brown. Usually a powder, but may be in pill form. Can be smoked, injected, or sniffed.

Effects

Euphoria, extreme calm, serious addiction, coma, possible death.

Marijuana

Source

Obtained from the hemp plant (*Cannabis sativa*). Major mind-altering ingredient is tetrahydrocannabinol (THC). THC is usually 3 percent pure when grown outdoors. Marijuana can also be grown hydroponically in laboratories. When grown indoors in this way, the THC level can be as high as 20 percent, making the resulting drug a hallucinogen. The grower can obtain more than 100 g per plant, with a crop coming in every 60 days.

Appearance
Colour ranges from a greyish green to greenish brown. Looks like oregano. Consists of the flowering tops and leaves of the hemp plant. Frequently contains seeds. Usually smoked in pipes or homemade cigarettes.

Effects
Low dose: increased pulse rate, eyes redden, tendency to talk and laugh more excitedly than normal.

Long term, frequent use: lethargy, slow and disjointed thinking, distorted perception of time and space, weight loss, cramps, diarrhea.

Hashish
Source
Resin from the tops and leaves of *Cannabis sativa* plant.

Appearance
Colour varies, ranging from light brown to dark brown, dark green and black. May be in liquid or solid form (often dried and baked into bricks or cakes). Usually smoked in pipe or cigarette (small solid piece inserted in end, or liquid drop smeared along side).

Effects
See "Marijuana."

LSD
Source
A semisynthetic drug (chemical name: lysergic acid diethylamide). Derived from lysergic acid, an alkaloid found in ergot (a fungus that grows on rye and other grains).

Appearance
In pure form, white, odourless, and crystalline. May be mixed with coloured substances or with sugar. Sold as powder, liquid, tablet, capsule, and pill. Often found in blotting paper or gelatin sheets. Usually ingested orally, but may be sniffed or injected.

Effects
Hallucinations, nausea, increased heart rate, hyperventilation, impaired motor ability, poor physical coordination, dilated pupils, increased blood pressure, sense of exhilaration or depression,

possible psychotic behaviour, altered perceptions (user may claim to smell or hear colours, believe he can fly, etc.). Former heavy user may experience spontaneous recurrence of hallucinatory state weeks or months after ceasing to take the drug.

MDA

Source

Chemically related to mescaline and amphetamines (chemical name: methylenedioxamphetamine).

Appearance

Colour ranges from white to light brown. Usually powder, but may be an amber liquid. Normally swallowed, but may be sniffed or injected.

Effects

Low dose: heightened feelings of well-being and tactile sensation, increased blood pressure, dryness in nose and throat, dilated pupils.

High dose: similar to LSD.

Mescaline

Source

Heads of peyote cactus are dried, then sliced, ground, or chopped.

Appearance

Powder, frequently in capsules or tablets. Usually taken orally. Peyote heads (buttons) may be ground up and smoked.

Effects

Heightened sensory perception, disrupted or illogical patterns of thought, headaches, lowered respiratory rate, lowered blood pressure.

Psilocybin

Source

Active ingredient in *Psilocybe mexicana* (common name: "magic mushroom").

Appearance

In pure form, a white crystalline material. Often found in powdered material or crude mushroom preparations.

Effects
Low dose: fatigue, altered perceptions, change of mood, sense of detachment from reality.

High dose: similar to LSD, also anxiety, dizziness, lightheadedness, nausea.

PCP
Source
A general anaesthetic that has hallucinogenic properties.

Appearance
Crystals or chunks; may be white or coloured. As a powder, sometimes found in tablets and capsules or mixed with leaves or seeds. Usually injected or taken orally, but may be smoked or sniffed.

Effects
Low dose: similar to drunkenness, possible nausea or vomiting.

High dose: blurred vision, apathy, distorted perception, possible death.

PMA
Source
Chemical hallucinogen and stimulant of central nervous system (chemical name: paramethoxyamphetamine).

Appearance
White, pink, or beige powder. Usually found in pink or colourless capsules that are taken orally.

Effects
Significantly increased heart rate and blood pressure, increased and laboured respiration, high body temperature, erratic eye movements, vomiting, muscle spasms. May lead to convulsions, coma, and death.

DMT
Source
A synthetic chemical similar to psilocybin (chemical name: dimethyltryptamine.)

Appearance
Usually absorbed into parsley, which is then dried. May be injected, smoked in pipe or cigarette, or made into a tea.

Effects
Similar to LSD, but begin immediately and usually are of short duration (30 to 60 minutes).

STP (DOM)

Source
Chemically related to amphetamine and mescaline.

Appearance
Usually taken orally.

Effects
Confusion, delirium, heightened sense of excitement, flushed skin, shaking, dry mouth, nausea, blurred vision, sweating, insomnia, possible convulsions. Can last up to 24 hours.

NOTE: *Amphetamine* and its related drugs (known collectively as amphetamines) are nervous-system stimulants that were once widely used in the field of medicine to treat obesity, depression, and other conditions, under such trade names as Benzedrine, Dexedrine, and Ritalin. Because of their serious side effects, medical use of these drugs has been significantly reduced, although they continue to be used to treat such relatively uncommon conditions as minimal brain dysfunction, hyperactivity, and narcolepsy.

Under the street name "speed," amphetamines are widely used illegally for their mood- and perception-altering qualities. They often appear on the street in the form of yellowish crystals and are frequently mixed with nondrug fillers that can contribute to negative physical reactions. Among their short-term effects are dilated pupils, loss of appetite, increased respiratory and heart rates, and elevated blood-pressure levels. In the long term, they can lead to a serious chemical dependency and such conditions as malnutrition, multiple addiction, blockage of blood vessels, and an increased susceptibility to disease.

Barbiturates are sedatives that are normally sold by prescription as liquid preparations or as capsules and tablets in a range of colours and sizes. They include amobarbital (Amytal), pentobarbital (Nembutal), phenobarbital (Seconal), and amobarbital and secobarbital (Tuinal). They tend to inhibit or slow down the rate of many normal body functions and can create one of the most dangerous physical dependencies on chemicals.

14. SURVEILLANCE

I. Introduction

The purpose of police surveillance is to observe persons, places, objects, or vehicles in order to obtain information about criminal activity and evidence for court. Surveillence can be a useful tool in locating suspects (e.g., by watching their hangouts or their friends), verifying information received by informants, establishing personal connections between a number of suspects in complex crimes or conspiracies, and helping to locate stolen property or contraband. In some cases, surveillance can even prevent the completion of serious crimes, such as armed robbery, by placing officers in a position to arrest suspects during their commission.

II. Preparation for a Surveillance

A. Briefing File

Compile for all surveillance team members a briefing file that includes the following information:

1. Subject(s):
   a. Names and aliases
   b. Photos, if available
   c. Descriptions, including:
      (1) Distinguishing physical characteristics
      (2) Mannerisms
   d. Known or suspected associations:
      (1) Names
      (2) Addresses
      (3) Physical descriptions
   e. Routine activities, indicating:
      (1) Day of the week
      (2) Time
      (3) Location
      (4) Duration
      (5) Persons frequently encountered

    f.   Other background information such as where the subject works, banks, socializes, etc.

2. Crime or activity under investigation:

    a.   Occurrence reports

    b.   Follow-up reports

    c.   Witness statements

    d.   Tips from informants

3. Vehicles involved:

    a.   Suspect vehicles

        (1) Licence numbers

        (2) Description

        (3) Probable driver and occupants

    b.   Police vehicles

        (1) Licence numbers

        (2) Description

        (3) Driver and occupants

        (4) Radio call number or frequency

4. Area of operation:

    a.   Neighbourhood classification, e.g., suburb, industrial zone, high-rises, etc.

    b.   Character of neighbourhood

        (1) Income level

        (2) Typical dress

        (3) Ethnic groups—languages, dialects, visible minorities

    c.   Street layout

        (1) Major arterial roads

        (2) Dead-end streets

        (3) Road construction

        (4) Roads closed

        (5) Parking areas—lots, meters, on street

    d.   Potential observation points

        (1) Building roofs

        (2) Parking lots

        (3) Vacant offices or apartments

        (4) Other inconspicuous locations

B. *Surveillance Checklist*

1. Appearance:

a. Appropriate to the area of operation, e.g., no expensive suits in low-income neighbourhoods, no beards and sandals in the financial district

b. No bulging of concealed weapons or portable radios

c. No conspicuous jewellery or clothing

2. Operating funds, including:

a. Cash reserve for emergency use

b. Small change for pay telephones

3. Communications:

a. Agreed system of hand signals and radio codes to thwart anyone attempting to monitor team communications

b. Radio equipment in working order

4. Assignment:

a. Which suspect is assigned to you

b. How long to maintain surveillance

c. Who will relieve you and when

d. What backup you have

e. What to do if you "lose" the suspect

f. Who's in charge

III. Types of Foot Surveillance

A. One-Person Surveillance

1. Avoid one-person surveillance whenever possible.

a. An officer working alone will have to operate so close to the target that he will be easily spotted.

b. There is a greater likelihood of losing the target because of crowd congestion, unexpected actions, or deliberate evasion.

2. If one-person surveillance is unavoidable, always walk abreast of the subject, on the other side of the street.

B. Two-Person Surveillance

1. The employment of two officers in a surveillance team decreases the likelihood of detection and loss of the target.

2. Both officers should follow the target on the same side of the street.

a. One officer should follow the target.

b. The second officer should follow the first officer.

3. To reduce their risk of being seen, the officers should alternate positions frequently.

4. Occasionally, the second officer may choose to "leapfrog" ahead of the first officer.

Illustration 14
ONE-PERSON SURVEILLANCE

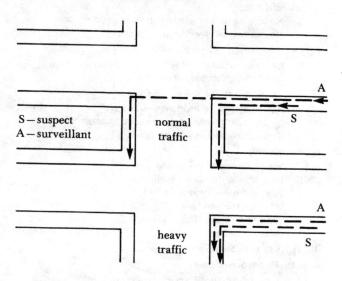

S — suspect
A — surveillant

normal traffic

heavy traffic

a. This tactic can prove useful if the target is approaching a congested area that offers many possible exits.

b. The leapfrogging officer can position himself at a vantage point ahead of the target that offers a view of all of the exits.

C. *Three-Person Surveillance (The "ABC" Tactic)*

1. Three-person teams have proven highly effective in maintaining surveillance of a target.

2. Method:

   a. Officer A follows the subject.

   b. Officer B follows Officer A.

   c. Officer C keeps abreast of the subject, on the other side of the street.

   d. B and C switch with A periodically to reduce the chance of his detection.

   e. All officers attempt to keep the suspect in sight at all times.

3. In the event the target is lost, B and C can make a quick search of the area, while A remains at the position at which the target was last seen in case he attempts to backtrack.

Illustration 15
THREE-PERSON SURVEILLANCE

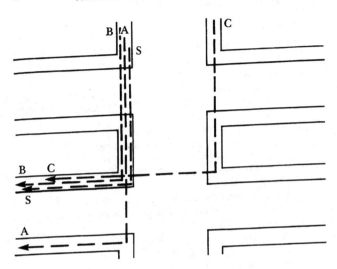

IV. Surveillance Tactics

A. General Procedures

1. Stay out of bright lights at night.
2. To avoid ambush, use caution in going through open doorways and around corners.
3. Be prepared to perform some natural activity such as reading a newspaper, lighting a cigarette, or window-shopping if you happen to fall within the target's field of vision.
4. Use mirrors or store windows to observe the subject by reflection whenever possible.

NOTE: Do *not* assume that you have been detected because the target has glanced at you a few times. Many inexperienced officers assume the worst when this happens, when, in fact, they themselves look directly at many persons on the street without becoming alarmed or suspicious. Unless you give your target some reason to believe that you are a police officer, he will rarely take notice of you, even after two or three apparent sightings.

5. If the target contacts another person:

    a.   Record a complete description of the person at the first opportunity, noting also:

        (1) Time

        (2) Location

        (3) Attitude of the subjects toward each other

    b.   Try to overhear the conversation if you can do so safely.

6. Never allow your eyes to meet those of the target.

7. If you believe the target has identified you, do *not* go to the police station or your home. He may follow *you* to confirm his suspicions.

8. Never peek from doorways or engage in other obvious actions.

9. Have a story prepared in case the target confronts you and demands an explanation for your behaviour.

10. If the target stops suddenly on the street, stop someone yourself and begin asking questions.

    a.   The target may assume you are meeting a friend.

    b.   Your backup officer should move in immediately to take over.

11. Walk close to buildings to avoid creating a reflection in store windows that the target can see.

12. Carry glasses, a hat, a spare jacket, or other items that can help you to change your appearance quickly.

13. Make detailed notes as soon and as accurately as possible, paying particular attention to:

    a.   Names

    b.   Street addresses

    c.   Physical descriptions

        (1) Habits

        (2) Mannerisms

    d.   Automobile licence numbers

    e.   Unusual behaviour

  B.   Street Tactics

1. Cabs:

    a.   If the suspect enters a cab and you are unable to follow, note quickly:

        (1) Cab company

        (2) Cab or licence plate number

        (3) Location

        (4) Time

b. Check with the dispatcher or driver to determine the target's whereabouts.

2. Telephone booths:

a. If the subject uses a pay telephone, try to overhear the conversation from an adjoining booth or other inconspicuous location.

b. If the subject writes anything down, pay close attention to what kind of notepad or paper he is using and where he puts it after the conversation is concluded.

c. If possible, try to determine the number dialled. Be familiar with the tones of the telephone keypad.

3. Restaurants:

a. If the suspect enters a restaurant, follow him inside and order a coffee or meal that can be quickly prepared.

b. Ask for the bill immediately so you are ready if the target suddenly leaves.

4. Buses and streetcars:

a. Take a seat to the rear of the subject.

b. Sit fairly close to the subject in case he tries to bolt out of the vehicle suddenly at a stop.

5. Ticket counters:

a. If the target appears about to take a trip on an airplane, boat, train, or bus, contact your supervisor immediately for further instructions.

b. Try to learn the target's destination by:

   (1) Overhearing his ticket purchase
   (2) Questioning the ticket agent
   (3) Questioning other employees such as the driver or conductor (you may be able to get him to check the target's ticket for you)
   (4) Checking the destination tags on the target's luggage

c. If you commit yourself to following the target on a long trip, be sure to keep him in sight at all times.

   (1) He may not actually board the aircraft or vehicle.
   (2) He may remain behind at a stopover.
   (3) He may board a vehicle other than the one for which he purchased a ticket.
   (4) He may leave the vehicle from another exit before departure.

6. Hotels:

   a. If the target checks into a hotel, obtain his room number by:

      (1) Listening in on his conversation during registration

      (2) Asking the front desk clerk or manager

   b. If the target appears to be staying for more than a day, take a room for surveillance use.

   c. You may be able to have the phone number and duration of the target's outgoing phone calls recorded for you at the hotel switchboard. (A warrant will be required if you intend to use this information in court.)

   d. Review the entries in the hotel register for other criminal associates who may be staying there as well.

   e. Check for method of payment, such as credit card or personal cheque.

C. *Attempts to Detect Surveillance*

1. The target may make attempts to detect surveillance by:

   a. Casually looking around at frequent intervals

   b. Dropping a piece of paper deliberately to see if someone picks it up

   c. Speeding up and slowing down while walking

   d. Stopping abruptly and looking behind

   e. Reversing direction suddenly and retracing his steps

   f. Leaving a public area such as a restaurant or lobby quickly, then waiting outside to see if anyone follows

2. To combat such efforts, you should:

   a. Act normally, continuing whatever you were doing when the target took action

   b. Have another officer take over surveillance if you believe you have been spotted

   c. Abandon the search (or make an arrest if you have sufficient grounds) if your concealment was essential to the success of the surveillance

D. *Attempts to Elude Surveillance*

1. The target may try to elude surveillance by:

   a. Plunging into a dense crowd

   b. Changing clothing

   c. Pointing you out to a police officer, who will stop you and demand an explanation

    d.   Entering a building and leaving immediately through a side or rear exit

2. If you lose the target, take the following action immediately:

    a.   Contact the officer in charge of the surveillance.

    b.   Check the target's known hangouts.

    c.   Set up observation on the residences of the target and his friends and associates.

    d.   Stake out the location where he was last seen; he may reappear.

    e.   Phone his home and known haunts and, using a false name, inquire as to his whereabouts.

V. Automobile Surveillance

A. *Equipment Required*

1. Automobiles—preferably used, two-tone, sports or other models that don't look like unmarked police cars

2. Radios—vehicle and portable

3. Two occupants for each vehicle (escort can continue surveillance on foot if the target leaves his vehicle)

4. Switch for darkening headlights and taillights

5. Equipment checklist:

    a.   Raincoats

    b.   Warm outerwear

    c.   Flares

    d.   Emergency red light

    e.   First aid kits

    f.   Heavy weapons

    g.   Sleeping bags and blankets for operations in cold weather when vehicle is switched off

    h.   Toilet facilities, if required

    i.   Binoculars

    j.   Cameras

    k.   Tape recorders

    l.   Mobile radios and hand-held units

    m.   Bumper beepers

    n.   Audio and video transmitters

    o.   Nightscopes

B. *Tactics*

1. A minimum of four cars should be assigned to an automobile surveillance.

2. The primary surveillance vehicle should be positioned:

   a. Behind the target vehicle
   b. At varying distances
   c. Not more than two vehicles behind in city traffic
   d. Off the right rear of the target vehicle

3. In rural areas, allow the target vehicle a good lead on sections of road that you know to be distant from intersections or possible exits.

4. All cars should remain behind the target vehicle during daylight.

5. Four vehicles offer greater opportunity to use parallel routes during the surveillance and lessen the chance of detection.

6. The surveillance team can use a modified ABCD approach to change positions.

7. On occasion, a police vehicle may move ahead of the target if the officers are able to keep him in sight in their rear-view mirror.

C. *Picket Surveillance*

1. This tactic involves positioning surveillance vehicles at intervals along a route that you know the target vehicle will travel.

2. As the target vehicle passes it, each surveillance vehicle:

   a. Moves into traffic behind the target
   b. Passes the target
   c. Takes up a new position further down the route

3. Picket surveillance is valuable in:

   a. Following highly suspicious targets who may be watching for police.

   b. Locating counterfeiting plants, stills, chemical laboratories, fugitive hideouts, and other sites of criminal activity that may be in isolated locations. For example, the picket tactic is highly effective on highways and rural roads with few intersections.

D. *Attempts to Detect or Elude Automobile Surveillance*

1. In an effort to detect automobile surveillance, the target may:

   a. Drive erratically to see if you follow, e.g.:

       (1) Make U-turns
       (2) Drive the wrong way down one-way streets
       (3) Run red lights

   b. Alternate between extremely fast and slow driving
   c. Make frequent stops
   d. Stop around curves or corners and over the crest of hills
   e. Drive into dead-end streets
   f. Pull into parking lots or driveways

2. To elude automobile surveillance, the target may:
   a. Deliberately drive through highly congested traffic areas
   b. Jump out of a hired vehicle such as a taxi or limousine after instructing the driver to continue on
   c. Cut through parking lots
   d. Enter an indoor parking area that has multiple exits
   e. Speed, U-turn abruptly, or take other aggressive action

VI. Fixed Surveillance

A. *General Procedures*

1. Locate a "plant" (hotel room, house, apartment, etc.) that offers:
   a. Good view of all entrances and exits of the target location
   b. Concealed entrances for officers during shift changes
   c. Access to toilet facilities
   d. Backup communications—wireless telephones, extra radios, etc.
2. Maintain a chronological log that indicates:
   a. All persons entering and leaving target location
   b. Any other incidents that may be relevant
3. Check local sources of information, e.g., merchants, janitor in target building, etc.

B. *Visual Records*

1. Still photos, videotapes, and films of a suspect's behaviour provide powerful evidence in court that is virtually impossible to refute.
2. Use a telephoto lens if available, mounted on a tripod or other fixed support.
3. Ensure that the location in which you choose to place your equipment is well concealed and offers a full, unobstructed view of the target's activities.
4. Test your equipment regularly and check that you have ample supplies of film and tape.

15. INTERNAL THEFT INVESTIGATION

I. Introduction

A. Motivations for Employee Theft

1. An employee may be disgruntled with his employer and commit theft to get even.
2. He may mentally justify his actions by:
    a. Believing he is underpaid
    b. Telling himself he needs the money or stolen property more than the company does
    c. Believing that the company steals from its customers, so he has the right to steal from the company
3. He may feel that the risk is worth the payoff because:
    a. Valuable property is easily accessible
    b. Chance of detection is small
4. He may steal to fulfil what he considers legitimate needs:
    a. Enjoyment of risk-taking
    b. Improved lifestyle
    c. Pure greed
    d. Revenge

B. Suspicious Circumstances

1. On the premises:
    a. The wiring of an alarm system is found to have been broken, jumped, or otherwise altered.
    b. Beaten pathways have been made to remote areas where fences have been bent, cut, or rigged to allow a person to slide under them.
    c. Truck seals are missing.
    d. Windows are found to be unlocked or broken.
    e. Emergency exit locks are open or broken.
    f. Broken locks or signs of tampering are found on cabinets or desk drawers.
    g. Spare keys are missing.
    h. External perimeter lights are broken or inoperative.

i.   Ladders, fixtures, or piles of boxes appear to be deliberately positioned to give access to windows.

j.   Extra merchandise is found in a receiving or shipping area near an exit.

k.   Merchandise, labels, or wrappings are found in trash bins or hidden in the washroom.

l.   Partially empty cartons are found where only full cartons are supposed to be kept.

2. Documents:

   a.   Control documents such as numbered invoices or purchase requisitions are found in the trash.

   b.   Computer-generated documents are found that were used to order goods whose purchase was not authorized by appropriate company officials.

   c.   Authorization stamps or documents are found in the possession of an unauthorized employee.

   d.   Discrepancies between inventory records and physical counts are identified.

   e.   Figures on original copies of documents differ from those on carbon copies.

   f.   Employment application forms have lengthy gaps in personal history that cannot be explained.

3. Employees:

   a.   Certain employees continually accept and approve bad cheques.

   b.   Employees, when questioned about the same incident or facts, give inconsistent explanations.

   c.   Employees are suspected to be:

   (1)   Heavily in debt
   (2)   Addicted to drugs, alcohol, or gambling
   (3)   Experiencing extreme marital difficulties

   d.   Employees freely admit to theft from a previous employer, or to a very minor theft from the current employer, in an apparent attempt to demonstrate their honesty.

   e.   Employees are overly friendly with security personnel or outside service persons.

   f.   Employees offer to become informers against other employees they claim are stealing from the company.

   g.   Employees take packages to their personal vehicles during work or lunch breaks.

h. Employees sell items available from company inventory, or on company premises, to other employees or friends at unrealistically low prices.

i. Employees are constantly identified as being present near the scene of thefts from the personal belongings of other employees.

j. Employees are frequently discovered in off-limits areas for no apparent reason.

II. Investigation of Internal Thefts

A. Security Personnel

1. Determine if the suspect has been interviewed by security personnel prior to your arrival. If he has been questioned, find out:

   a. How long they held the employee in their custody
   b. Where the interview took place
   c. How long the actual interview took
   d. Who was present at the interview
   e. If any force was used to apprehend or detain the suspect
   f. If the suspect was searched
   g. Whether the suspect was cautioned and given access to a telephone to contact legal counsel

2. Before the court date, ensure that any inexperienced security personnel involved in the case have sufficient knowledge of courtroom procedure to be effective witnesses.

NOTE: During the course of your investigation, never discount the possibility that management or security personnel may be involved in a theft conspiracy with the suspected employee.

Several years ago, I directed an investigation into the theft of more than $2 million worth of automobile parts from a warehouse in Mississauga, Ontario. Our officers spent over six months of intensive investigation on the case, which included electronic and personal surveillance of the suspects.

The case concluded with a series of raids at homes and small auto parts retailers involving 105 police officers. Using five trucks, we recovered $1.8 million worth of stolen auto parts. Eleven persons were arrested, including the company's warehouse manager, the shift supervisor, and a security guard.

B. Questioning Employees

1. Always ask a suspected employee if he is willing to take a polygraph test.
2. Check any suspected employees for prior criminal records.

3. When questioning the employee, watch for nonverbal clues (see "Nonverbal Communication," page 112).
4. In cases where drug or alcohol addiction may have been a factor in the commission of the offence, the employee should be asked to submit to blood and urine tests.

III. Prevention Techniques

A. Documents

1. Computerized management of purchase requisitions, invoices, cheques, and other financial documents, with password-protected access
2. Numbered receiving documents that include one nonremovable permanent copy
3. Invoices and receiving documents that must be joined together before any payment is made
4. Records and bookkeeping functions separated from the handling of cash
5. Verification of cash refunds through returned receipts or other procedures
6. Written procedure for handling damaged or short orders, with supporting documents
7. All invoices to include unit description, quantity, and method of payment
8. Sales invoices to include a nonaccessible file copy for all items above a given amount
9. Policy prohibiting payment of supplier invoices without an accompanying purchase order
10. Prohibition against any direct payments of commissions or gifts from a supplier to an employee

B. Cash

1. Surprise cash counts
2. Limit cash held in register, with excess to be stored in a safe
3. One employee working at each cash register
4. Instruction on techniques of short-change artists
5. Safe accessible only through double combination lock or two keys held in joint custody
6. Bank deposits made throughout the day, at unpredictable times
7. Established "No Sale" policy for opening cash registers
8. Spot-check cash register tapes for variance between amounts listed and known unit price

9. Undercover operators posing as shoppers to make purchases from a suspected employee handling cash
10. Use of ultraviolet-sensitive marker pens to identify large bills

C. Premises

1. Spot-check of receiving area to investigate possible collusion of employees with delivery personnel
2. Restriction of suppliers and customers to specified, easily controlled areas
3. Locked display cases for expensive, easily concealed merchandise
4. Spot-check of price tags in the sales area
5. Reasonable restrictions on amount of merchandise in the sales area
6. No access to premises through entrances that are not controlled by staff or alarm devices
7. Limited access of salespersons to inventory
8. Prohibition of movement of stock from inventory to shipping area or sales floor prior to a physical check of the goods for quantity and condition
9. Identified, secure storage areas for valuable articles to which employees have only restricted access
10. Frequent patrol of premises at irregular intervals, which includes checking locks and reporting any security hazards
11. Detailed survey of premises every three months to identify new areas of vulnerability that may have developed

16. CRIME BY COMPUTER

I. Introduction

Most of the techniques described within these pages have proven effective in combating such age-old crimes as murder, rape, theft, and fraud. However, today's criminal investigator is increasingly being confronted with a new, highly sophisticated form of criminal activity born of our high-technology society: crime by computer.

As computers play an ever-growing role in transferring funds, recording transactions, and communicating information, they will also increasingly become the targets of criminal attention. The deeply entrenched human traits of greed and avarice will remain unaffected by the technological revolution, and will serve only to make increasing demands upon the skills and ingenuity of the police investigator.

The staggering rewards that computer crime can offer will ensure that it remains a growth industry.

EXAMPLE: The largest fraud in U.S. history, involving over $2 billion, was made possible through highly sophisticated use of computer data. In 1973, the major stockholders of Equity Funding Corporation—which included the Ford Foundation, the National City Bank of New York, and Bankers Trust and Morgan Guaranty—were shocked to discover that of the approximately 90,000 insurance policies listed on the corporation's computer records, more than 60,000 were nonexistent.

Executives of Equity Funding, including its chairman of the board and president, had engaged in a massive fraud scheme to sell these policies to other insurance companies under a common industry practice known as reinsurance. This practice involves an insurer's selling large blocks of policies it has underwritten to other insurance companies to spread the risk. In the case of Equity Funding, funds were received for policies that existed only in the memory banks of the corporation's computers.

When the corporation was asked for a listing of its policies, printouts were quickly provided. If Equity Funding was asked for additional evidence, management officials would stall for time and scurry about forging documents to support their computer records.

Although it was apparently common knowledge on Wall Street that the corporation had been putting fraudulent entries through the books for several years, the scheme fell apart only after an outside security analyst went public with the results of his own private investigation. None of the many false financial statements that the corporation had filed with federal and state authorities had ever been detected.

In recent years, the emergence of the Internet as an easily accessible, worldwide network for electronic communications has increased the potential for committing large-scale thefts and frauds by computer.

In 1997, a hacker living in Sweden jammed the 911 emergency system in west-central Florida, an incident that FBI Director Louis Freeh described as a "dress rehearsal for a national disaster." That same year, a hacker known as "Smak" was caught after 10,000 credit card numbers were stolen from the files of an Internet service provider in California; he had attempted to sell them to an undercover FBI agent for $260,000. A hacker in St. Petersburg, Russia, was arrested at London's Heathrow Airport after using a laptop computer to transfer at least $5.4 million from Citibank in New York to accounts in banks around the world.

Many experts have characterized the Internet as the electronic equivalent of the Wild West—a vast new frontier offering enormous opportunities to those who travel its roads and pathways, but lacking a sufficient number of sheriffs to maintain order.

II. Types of Computer Crime

A. *Fraud*

1. Definitions:

   a. Creation of nonexistent companies to receive payments, obtain credit, etc.

   b. Billing for nonexistent goods or services

   c. Manipulation of data to create a false picture of an individual's or a corporation's financial assets

   d. Other forms of misrepresentation involving computer-generated records or payments, e.g., documents, identification cards, accounting statements, invoices, etc.

EXAMPLE: A 27-year-old technician was charged with rigging the Los Angeles Dodgers' computerized ticket system in order to steal 7000 tickets.

The Dodgers had discovered a mail order for an unusually large number of tickets placed through an account that had been opened three weeks earlier. Team officials, however, knew that the computer was not operating on that date.

Police officers attended the game and asked spectators in the seats marked on the suspicious tickets where they had been purchased. Investigators traced the tickets to a ticket broker, who led them to the suspect—whom they described as a "computer genius." The suspect had helped to install the system, and had taught staff members how to operate it.

B.   *Embezzlement*

1.   Definition: Employee diversion of company funds for personal use

2.   Examples:

   a.   Bank clerk transfers funds from inactive accounts to personal accounts or for the purchase of negotiable instruments

   b.   Employee enters false payroll data into the computer in order to obtain unjustified overtime payments or higher wages

   c.   Employee instructs computer to pay a nonexistent supplier who is, in reality, the offender

   d.   Employee creation of phantom staff members who are paid with cheques that are later double-endorsed and cashed by the offender

NOTE: You don't have to be a genius to commit computer-related crimes. Computer operators often receive little more than a week's training. This training will, however, provide them with sufficient knowledge of the system's passwords and other security measures to gain access to vital data.

The majority of computer frauds are committed through the modification of computer input source documents such as vouchers, inventory transmittals, shipping slips, and bank deposit slips.

C.   *Misappropriation of Computer Time*

1.   Definition: The unauthorized use of a company's computer facilities for private amusement or gain

2.   Examples:

   a.   Employee prints out a confidential mailing list for sale to a competitor

   b.   Employee establishes a private computer consulting business that uses company-owned computer resources

   c.   An outsider uses telephone links to a company's computers in order to:

      (1)   Perform calculations

(2) Obtain information for personal research needs

(3) Browse through confidential company records for amusement or profit

(4) Test his skills by challenging the computer's internal security defences

(5) Alter programs to commit acts of high-tech vandalism

D. Theft of Programs

1. Through telecommunications or internal theft, unauthorized user steals valuable programs for his personal use or sale to others.

2. Types of programs susceptible to theft:

   a. Accounting programs

   b. Engineering programs

   c. Programs used for creating experimental models, e.g., wind resistance for airplanes, stress factors for building construction, etc.

E. Theft of Information

1. Programs and information such as mailing or customer lists are duplicated and sold surreptitiously to competitors or other persons who value them.

2. Illegal acquisition of valuable confidential information, such as:

   a. Marketing plans

   b. Secret processes

   c. Product design

   d. Copyrighted material

   e. Electronically distributed internal communications

   f. Technical data

   g. Passwords

   h. Personnel information

F. Sabotage

1. Vandalism against employer

2. Attempted disruption of company operations

3. Political protests

G. Espionage

1. The theft of secrets, personal information, intellectual property, etc., from confidential computer sites

H. Money Laundering

1. The use of computers by organized crime groups to launder drug money and other illegally obtained funds

2. Through electronically encrypted messages communicated to different geographical regions, crime syndicates arrange to transfer the proceeds of their crimes through illegitimate company bank accounts.

III. Warning Signs of Computer Crime

A. *Suspicious Circumstances*

1. Numbered control forms such as purchase orders, invoices, and cheques not recorded or filed in sequential order
2. Customer complaints about:

   a. Funds not being credited to their accounts or else credited inaccurately

   b. "Zero-dunning"

      (1) Customers receive bills showing a balance of "$0.00."

      (2) This may indicate that the customer actually has a credit balance that has been diverted to an employee's account.

3. Low business income despite the fact that computer-generated information indicates a high sales volume
4. An unusually high number of employee complaints about:

   a. Inaccurate earnings statements

   b. Excessive withholding of deductions

5. Computer reports or printout carbons found in a garbage can outside of the business premises

B. *Poor Security*

1. Insecure storage of continuous-form cheques
2. Easy access to computer area:

   a. No restrictions on employee movement

   b. After-hours work not supervised, logged, or controlled

   c. Passwords posted on the wall or kept in an easily obtained operations manual

   d. Employees who work extremely long or unusual hours

   e. Employees who take no vacation

   f. Employees who leak confidential information, such as network topology, backup procedures, etc.

IV. Examples of Computer Crime Techniques

A. *The "Salami" Technique*

1. Definition: "Slicing off" a small portion of funds generated by an existing computer account record and diverting it to an account created by the offender

2. Mortgage payments, biweekly payroll cheques, and other forms of disbursements usually involve a gross figure that has been divided by the appropriate number of weeks or months to arrive at a rounded-off figure that is paid at specific time intervals.

   a. The offender will divert for his personal use the extra pennies or dollars that remain after rounding off.

   b. If the offender applies this tactic to a computer program involving thousands of payments, he will in a very short period of time amass a considerable amount of money in his own account.

   c. Because the payment amounts are essentially correct, his accounts will appear to balance.

B. The "Logic Bomb"

1. Purpose: Extortion or revenge

2. The offender programs the computer to self-destruct some or all of its existing programs if certain criteria are met.

3. Examples:

   a. An operator who believes he is about to be discharged instructs the computer to delete all its records and programs if a command is received to remove his name from the payroll.

   b. An operator drops into a corporation's computer a "logic bomb" that destroys a significant amount of nonessential information and then threatens to destroy the entire system if a ransom is not paid.

C. Electronic Eavesdropping

1. Computers and peripherals may generate signals that can be intercepted through electronic surveillance.

2. Types of offenders:

   a. Industrial or enemy spies

   b. Radical groups

   c. Extortionists

   d. Blackmailers

   e. Crackers and hackers

D. Viruses and Worms

1. Definitions:

   a. Virus: A computer program that interferes with the computer hardware, data files, or operating system. A virus has to be physically copied from one computer system to another. Viruses are designed to avoid detection.

   b. Worm: A stand-alone program. It operates independently of any other programs and tries to infect other network computers.

2. Consequences:

    a.   Some viruses and worms create only minor inconveniences and do not damage any data, while others are extremely destructive.

    b.   Certain viruses can crash entire systems and destroy data permanently.

    c.   The willful placement of a virus or worm on a computer system is a criminal offence.

V. Methods of Access

A. *Browsing and Scavenging*

This activity can be performed electronically through online browsing, or it may be done directly by gaining access to a secure area where backup tapes or manuals are stored.

1. An unauthorized person with some familiarity with the computer experiments until he develops the correct codes.
2. An unauthorized person reads the access codes by looking over the shoulder of an authorized programmer or computer operator.
3. An unauthorized person searches wastebaskets for discarded printouts, tapes, or disks that indicate access codes. This activity is known as "dumpster diving." It is extremely popular with crackers and hackers, who often attempt to gain access to telecommunication sites for the purpose of committing telecommunication and toll frauds.

EXAMPLE: An amateur computer enthusiast in California made a habit of poking around in garbage cans outside the offices of a local telephone company. He gradually built up a library of discarded computer manuals. With this information, he realized that he could manipulate the company's computer to follow his commands.

He discovered a method of instructing the computer to order equipment deliveries from its computerized warehouse. He soon went into business.

The enthusiast started a highly profitable company that sold telephone equipment at prices that always seemed to be below the local telephone company's bids. His success was understandable: low overhead, a reliable supplier, a quality product line, and prompt service. Poor employee relations, however, were his downfall.

A disgruntled employee, upset about his refusal to grant him a pay raise, called police. The would-be entrepreneur was arrested and sentenced to 60 days in jail. He served 40 days.

B. *"Trapdoor"*

1. Definition: An electronic route through computer software that bypasses normal security controls
2. The programmer may have created the trapdoor to make the design of the program easier, but intentionally or unintentionally failed to remove it after the program became operational.
3. The offender uses the trapdoor password to gain unauthorized entry for any of the following purposes:
   a. To gain access to privileged information
   b. To introduce viruses
   c. To use other unauthorized programs in the system
   d. To create additional trapdoor passwords so that the system can be accessed at a later time

EXAMPLE: An offender may use a pen-register, a device that records and analyzes dialling pulses, to learn the password. This device will also send out combinations of dialling pulses until some computer responds, then lock onto the signal and record the computer's access number.

C. *Personation*

1. An offender uses a legitimate user's facilities to gain entry into the computer system.
2. By using a second user's identification codes, he is able to access the second user's computer records.

D. *Masquerading*

1. The offender uses an authorized user's identity (user name and password) to gain access to the computer system.
2. With his own computer or other equipment, he intercepts messages between a user and a central system.
3. By performing what is called "piggyback entry," the offender can also substitute his own messages for the bona fide data being exchanged, e.g., change the amount of, or redirect, funds being transferred between banks, approve credit applications that have been denied by head office, etc.

E. *Session Hijacking*

1. When an authorized user temporarily moves away from his terminal without properly logging off, the offender uses that terminal to read or change files to which he would not normally have had access.
2. Using a covert terminal, the offender connects to a communication line between the authorized terminal and the computer.

a. The offender waits until the authorized terminal is online but not in use, and then switches control to the covert terminal.

b. The computer thinks it is still connected to the authorized user, thereby giving the offender access to the same files and data as the authorized user.

F. *IP Spoofing*

1. Certain UNIX programs used in networks grant automatic access based on IP addresses.

2. Users on systems running the trusted IP address are not required to identify themselves by providing an account number and password, as is normally required.

G. *Password Sniffing*

1. Password sniffers are programs that collect data about users when they type in their user names and passwords to access another computer through a network.

2. These programs are particularly effective at gathering such information when users connect to the Internet via an Internet service provider.

H. *Scanning or "War Dialling"*

1. Scanning or "war dialling" involves programming a computer to dial hundreds of telephone numbers sequentially until it finds a phone line connected to a modem.

2. Once connected, the scanning software runs through a dictionary of user names and passwords in sequence until it receives a positive response from the target's computer system and gains access.

VI. Profile of the Computer Criminal

A. *Motivations*

1. Financial commitments:
   a. Living beyond his means
   b. Gambling
   c. Drug addiction
   d. Medical expenses

2. Rationalization:
   a. The company, his managers, or his peers are dishonest.
   b. The money involved isn't "real"—just figures on a printout sheet.
   c. He needs the money more than the company does.
   d. He has been unfairly treated by the company.
   e. He is committing a "victimless" crime.

3. Challenge:
   a. To test his wits against the computer's security protection
   b. To create a more glamorous, exciting self-image
   c. To achieve wealth and fame

B. *Personal Characteristics*

1. The personal characteristics of an offender usually depend on his motivation for committing the crime.

   a. In cases involving computer crime committed for economic gain, offenders are often well educated and in their late 20s and early 30s.

   b. In cases in which the motivation is not economic gain, offenders tend to be much younger—sometimes even in their early teens. Known as crackers or hackers, they are motivated by the intellectual challenge of breaking into a computer system to which their peers have been unable to gain access.

2. Because computer crime offenders can be motivated by everything from pure economic gain to personal amusement, it is extremely difficult to develop a profile that applies to most cases.

3. Anyone with a limited amount of training and a basic computer with a modem has the wherewithal to commit serious computer crimes.

4. A computer crime offender frequently exhibits the following characteristics:
   a. Male
   b. No criminal record or prior criminal activity
   c. Married with children
   d. Middle-class lifestyle—professional/managerial status
   e. Income among top 40 percent of the population
   f. Works alone to commit the crime (probably the most common trait because computer crimes can be committed from home on a stand-alone computer connected to the Internet or some other network)
   g. Crimes are work-related and carefully planned
   h. Highly knowledgeable about computers and law enforcement procedures

VII. Countermeasures

A. *Audit Trails*

1. Computers can be programmed to identify and record:

    a. Terminal used to gain access
    b. When accessed
    c. Identification number of the operator
    d. Files accessed by the operator
    e. How they were used

2. A computer-generated journal or log that produces this information is a key element of audit control.
3. All magnetic tapes, disks, cartridges, and other media must be inventoried and carefully accounted for at all times.
4. Security control should be considered an important element in all aspects of system design.

NOTE: Electronic information output devices should be screened from the casual observation of passersby whenever critical material is being programmed or processed.

B. *Shared Responsibility*

1. A computer system is extremely vulnerable if certain key programs, jobs, or files are the exclusive knowledge of one person.
2. Every critical function should be assigned to a backup person whose presence and knowledge will act as a check against illegal activity by the primary operator or programmer.
3. All managerial, technical, and office employees who work with, or around, the computer system should be:

    a. Alerted to the vital importance of security in protecting the company and preserving their jobs
    b. Instructed in security control procedures
    c. Specifically warned against revealing their passwords to anyone, including co-workers

C. *Outside Testing*

1. Computer systems should be regularly examined by external auditors for their integrity and security.
2. Programs involving cheque writing and cheque reconciliation require special attention.

D. *Hiring Practices*

1. Companies and organizations should apply rigorous standards to verifying the character and employment history of persons working in their computer operations.
2. Polygraph tests can be useful in screening employees who are required to work in highly sensitive, computer-related areas.

VIII. Computer Crime Investigation

TIP: Focusing on the motivations of computer crime offenders (see above) is a helpful tool in keeping an investigation productive and on track.

A. *Officer Preparation*

1. Have a basic understanding of computer operations and terminology.
2. Develop the technical skills to direct an investigation that may draw upon the expertise of private consultants.
3. Be aware of the various schemes used to penetrate computer systems.
4. Be able to identify the source documents that can be important evidence in proving your case.

NOTE: A law enforcement officer who lacks proper training should not attempt to conduct a computer crime investigation. In unskilled hands, evidence may be compromised, missed, or destroyed. A misstep such as improperly shutting down a server could result in important evidence being lost.

B. *Documentary Evidence*

1. Documentary evidence is the most important element in computer crime investigation.
2. Documents will account for approximately 80 percent of the physical evidence you will recover.
3. Forensic science analysis can be used to analyze magnetic tapes, disks, cassettes, input documents, and other relevant material for:
   a. Fingerprints
   b. Hairs
   c. Indented writing
   d. Erasures and alterations
   e. Handwriting analysis
   f. Printer identification
   g. Trace evidence
4. To identify the author of a questioned document, consider the following:
   a. Origin of document
   b. Contents
   c. Circumstances of preparation
   d. Nature of deletions, additions, or other alterations
   e. Age of document
   f. Paper source

     g. Handwriting
     h. Typewriting

C. *Search Checklist*

1. Diskettes —if used for gathering evidence—must be formatted prior to the search using the correct operating system, e.g., DOS, NT, Macintosh, etc.
2. Backup media—large-capacity recording media such as Jazz Drives capable of retrieving data from computer systems that cannot be removed from the premises
3. Adhesive labels and tape for labelling diskettes, cabling, and computer components—facilitates reassembly of a computer system
4. Utility programs—helpful in accessing, searching, and retrieving information in the target computer system
5. Clean bootable operating system diskettes—a precaution against offenders who load on their computer systems programs that will cause all data to be deleted.
6. Camera equipment—use a video camera as well as a Polaroid to record the scene, screen displays, suspects, etc.
7. Virus-detection software
8. Thermometer
9. Flashlight
10. Toolkit—assorted screwdrivers and pliers used for computer adjustments and disassembly

D. *Search and Seizure Procedures*

NOTE: In planning your search, consider carefully whether the location will be hostile or friendly. If you anticipate that the suspect will be on the scene when you enter, you will need to adopt prevention strategies that would be unnecessary if you were entering an office in which staff were uninvolved in the crime and likely to cooperate in your investigation.

1. Make notes of everything you do.
2. *Never* shut down the on-site systems immediately, *especially in a network environment.* Valuable evidence could be lost.
3. Move users away from their keyboards immediately.
4. If the system is running, photograph the screen.
5. Remove diskettes from the drives.
6. Disconnect modems.
7. Photograph documents still on the printer.
8. Check the area around the system to get a sense of the technical sophistication of the users.

9. Seize all manuals, diskettes, and scratch pads.
10. Watch for unique equipment (DVD drives, CD-ROM drives, etc.).
11. Complete an orderly shutdown of the computer equipment.
    a.   This is extremely important when working with a server.
    b.   Do not search the server without the assistance of a qualified technical expert who is familiar with the system.
12. During your search, if you run the computer program or even merely touch the keyboard without using the proper procedure, you could contaminate the evidence collected.
13. Some programs cause file dates to change, while others prevent the recovery of deleted or hidden data.

NOTE: There is no requirement that you conduct your analysis of the computer system at the site where the search warrant was executed. As a result, you should be prepared to seize and immediately transport the following:

1. **All hardware, including any peripheral devices such as printers, modems, CD-ROMs, cables, etc.**
2. **All computer software**
3. **All computer diskettes, tapes, and other backup media**
4. **All computer manuals and related documentation, including discarded printouts**

17. IN THE WITNESS BOX

I. Preparing for Court

A. Reports, Statements, and Physical Evidence

1. Collect all reports relating to your case in one accordion-style file folder. This file should include, as appropriate:
    a. Original occurrence report
    b. Follow-up investigation reports
    c. Written statements by police officers
    d. Reports by forensic science experts
    e. Reports of your department's identification branch
    f. Photographs
    g. Evidence receipts
    h. Sketches
    i. Witness statements
    j. Letters and memorandums relating to the case
    k. Autopsy reports
    l. Comprehensive list of all physical evidence, indicating:
        (1) Name or description of object
        (2) Where recovered
        (3) Who recovered it
        (4) Relevance to the case, e.g., "murder weapon," "torn from assailant's jacket," etc.
        (5) How marked
        (6) Where marked
        (7) Who marked it
    m. Psychiatric reports
    n. Criminal and penitentiary records
    o. Copy of disclosure
    p. Copy of brief
    q. Copy of search warrants, etc.

B. Prosecution Witnesses

1. Notify all prosecution witnesses as to when and where they will be required to appear, including:
    a. Investigating officers

b. Police officers or persons in authority who came into contact with the accused after his arrest

c. Coroner or medical examiner

d. Pathologist

e. Forensic science experts

f. Ambulance drivers

g. Physicians

h. Civilian witnesses

NOTE: In some cases, it may be a good idea to interview the witness closely before the trial to determine his background. This will help to avoid surprises if the defence counsel seeks to discredit your witness during cross-examination.

You should also advise civilian witnesses that they will be notified to attend court by subpoena, so they do not become shocked or upset when they are served. In most major cases, the prosecutor will have you set up a series of meetings with witnesses prior to the trial date. He will go over their anticipated evidence, and may have the witnesses give "mock" testimony.

To avoid needless frustration and wasted time, you may wish to put doctors and off-duty police officers on call for the day when their case is expected to come up in court. You can then contact them an hour or so before they are to appear to request that they come to the courthouse.

2. In the interests of good public relations, at the conclusion of the trial you should inform all witnesses of the outcome and thank them for their cooperation.

C. *The Complex Brief*

1. Although minor offences can usually be dealt with on the basis of occurrence reports and other supporting documents, major jury trials will require the preparation of a brief that offers a comprehensive review of all the evidence.

2. The complex brief should be:

a. Typed on legal-size paper (21.6 cm x 35.6 cm.; 8½ in. x 14 in.)

b. Bound in hard covers

c. Affixed with a label indicating:

(1) Plaintiff, e.g., governmental authority in whose name the charge was laid

(2) Accused's name

(3) Charge

(4) Relevant section number of the Criminal Code

D. *Contents of the Complex Brief*

1. An introductory page with the police force crest, and the names of the

    a. Prosecuting attorney
    b. Defence counsel
    c. Investigating officers

2. A table of contents indicating the page numbers for each section of the brief

3. Copies of information or other court documents sworn out in relation to the charges, e.g., search warrants, Feeney warrants, etc.

4. An identifying page that includes the accused's:

    a. Photograph
    b. Name
    c. Date of birth
    d. Height
    e. Weight
    f. Hair colour
    g. Colour of eyes
    h. Occupation
    i. Marital status
    j. Date and time of arrest
    k. Personal history

        (1) Place of birth
        (2) Social insurance number
        (3) Driver's licence number
        (4) Correctional services number
        (5) Next-of-kin address
        (6) Spouse or girlfriend/boyfriend
        (7) Previous addresses
        (8) Known employers
        (9) Criminal record
        (10) Police contacts

5. Case history:

    a. Outline of all events leading up to the occurrence
    b. Full description of the offence
    c. Short synopsis of the investigation
    d. Occasions when disclosure given, including pretrial dates

6. Continuity—a brief chronological history of custody of the major exhibits and the body (if appropriate) to establish a chain of custody between initial police seizure of the evidence and its final disposition

7. Exhibits:

   a. List of all exhibits that will be offered in evidence, e.g., photographs, weapons, clothing, etc.

   b. The names of the witnesses who will introduce them

8. Voir dire documents:

   a. Chronological list of all persons in authority who spoke with the accused

   b. Copies of all written statements made by the accused

   c. Summary of videotaped interviews of the accused (with transcripts in major cases)

9. Outline of wiretap evidence, which covers:

   a. Witness involvement

   b. Authorization

   c. Installation

   d. Monitoring

   e. Transcribing

   f. Typing of transcripts

NOTE: The actual transcripts of wiretap evidence should be contained in separate briefs to keep the trial brief to a manageable size.

10. Witnesses' synopses, arranged in alphabetical order, each of which contains:

    a. The name of the witness

    b. An introduction indicating qualifications, police experience, etc.

    c. A brief outline of the witness's expected testimony

    d. Copies of any reports or written statements the witness may have prepared, e.g., pathology report, identification report, signed statements to investigating officers, etc.

11. Psychiatric evaluations of the accused

E. *Personal Appearance*

1. If you are not appearing in uniform, dress conservatively for court.

   a. For male officers, a dark business suit (grey, brown, or blue) is preferable, but a blazer-and-slacks combination is also appropriate. Avoid sports jackets, especially those with colourful plaid patterns. They are out of place in a dignified courtroom setting.

    b.   For female officers, suits, tailored slacks, blouses, sweaters, and dresses with subdued colours are all acceptable.

    c.   *Never* mix uniform and civilian clothing.

    d.   Ensure that your handgun is not visible.

2.   If you are appearing in uniform, be sure that it is neat, clean, and well pressed, and conforms with departmental dress regulations for court appearances.

3.   Although undercover officers often wear unconventional dress in the performance of their regular duties, this practice should not be carried into the courtroom. Beards and long hair should be neatly trimmed for court appearances.

4.   In cases where the identity of the undercover officer cannot be disclosed, he may be disguised during his testimony or give evidence from another room using a video camera linked to the courtroom.

F.   *Conduct Outside the Courtroom*

1.   Arrange to arrive at court at least 60 minutes prior to opening, so that you will be available to discuss the case with the prosecutor or court officer.

2.   Maintain a mature, serious, and professional demeanour in and around the courtroom. If the victim or witnesses see you joking or bantering with fellow officers or courtroom staff, they will be unfavourably impressed with your attitude toward the case.

3.   Do not discuss the case in public areas with other police officers or civilian witnesses.

    a.   Avoid speaking with the accused or his counsel. You may find comments made during an apparently informal conversation will resurface during cross-examination, often with embarrassing consequences.

    b.   If the defence lawyer wishes to speak to you, do so only in the presence of your partner or another officer. *Never* speak about a case to the defence lawyer alone.

4.   Do not read your notes in corridors or other public areas.

    a.   Your notes are intended to refresh your memory *during* your testimony, not to be memorized.

    b.   Upon request, the presiding judge may permit you to refer to your notes in court.

II. In Court

A. Taking the Oath

1. When taking the oath, maintain an attitude of maturity and seriousness.

    a. Do not hold the Bible or any other religious symbol in an offhand, casual manner. Hold it firmly in your right hand, and with respect.

    b. Face the clerk of the court and swear the oath in a calm and deliberate manner.

    c. A smiling, lighthearted attitude may suggest to the jury that you take your role as a witness equally lightly, and may affect your credibility.

B. Giving Evidence

1. Although with experience you will develop your own style of giving evidence effectively, consider these suggestions:

    a. Testify in your own words, using simple vocabulary that is easily understood.

    b. Follow a logical, chronological sequence.

    c. Avoid using police jargon or legalistic terminology. Do not use "street talk" unless you are quoting the accused.

    d. Speak clearly, deliberately, and at a slow, measured pace. The judge is making notes of your evidence; your pace of speech should allow him to make notes without rushing or demanding frequent repetition of your evidence.

2. Testify only to facts that you personally know to be true.

    a. Do not offer hearsay or other forms of excluded evidence unless directed to do so by the court.

    b. Do not exaggerate your evidence by incorporating unnecessary description into your factual statements.

    c. During cross-examination, answer all questions that the judge has permitted, even if your replies may appear favourable to the accused.

NOTE: Never hesitate to tell the truth. Although an act of perjury may be tempting when testifying against a particularly repugnant accused, your role is simply to offer evidence to the court. It is for the judge and jury to determine guilt or innocence; your role in court is confined to providing them with truthful, objective information that assists them in making that decision.

3. Never hesitate to acknowledge an error during your testimony.

    a. Apologize immediately for the mistake and offer a correction.

    b. Do not attempt to cover up an error.

       (1) Your error could result in contradictory evidence being presented to the court.

       (2) You could become liable to a charge of perjury.

4. Act in a respectful manner toward all parties involved in the proceedings, including the defence counsel and the accused.

    a. Keep your temper in check during cross-examination, regardless of the provocation.

    b. Under our adversary system, the defence lawyer has a legitimate right to test the accuracy and credibility of the evidence that you present.

    c. An outburst or scathing remark could damage your credibility as an objective witness.

C. *Responding to Questions*

1. Wait until the entire question has been asked before responding.

2. Consider each question carefully before beginning your response.

    a. Although a pause of a few seconds may seem like an eternity to you, it will probably go unnoticed in court, except to impress the judge and jury with your desire to formulate an accurate response.

    b. During this pause, keep your eyes on your questioner so that the delay is correctly interpreted as caused by thoughtful contemplation, not hesitancy or insecurity.

    c. If you are unsure of the meaning of certain words or phrases, do not be embarrassed to ask for a repetition or a clarification of the question.

3. Confine your answer to the specific information demanded by the question.

    a. If the question can be satisfied with a "yes" or "no" answer, give it.

    b. If the question requires an explanation, be as brief and direct as you can.

    c. You may sometimes be asked to give *only* a "yes" or "no" answer.

       (1) In this situation, ask the judge for permission to qualify or expand your answer. Your request will usually be granted.

       (2) If not, the prosecutor can ask for a clarification during re-examination.

    d. Do not volunteer more than the question asks, but do not attempt to withhold information that should logically be included in your response. You will appear to have been evasive when the information is revealed through further questioning.

4. Answer all questions that are asked of you.

    a. If you prefer not to respond for fear of revealing the identity of an informant, or for some other legitimate reason, pause briefly before replying.

    b. The prosecutor will object if the question is improper. If not, make the court aware of the difficulty before answering.

5. Be alert to misleading questions that are intended to confuse you or obscure an important issue.

EXAMPLE: A favourite tactic of defence lawyers is to ask, "Officer, have you discussed your evidence in this case with anyone?" The questioner's tone may suggest that such discussions were improper. In fact, you may have justifiably discussed your evidence with many persons, including, for example, senior officers and the prosecutor, before deciding to lay charges.

Respond to this type of question by indicating to whom you spoke, their relation to the case, and your reason for speaking with them.

Prior to your testimony, there is nothing wrong with reviewing your notes with your partner, other involved police officers, the prosecutor, or even material witnesses. If questioned about this in court, be forthright: "Yes, I did review my notes with ..."

Another tactic to watch out for is the question that begins, "I suggest to you that ..." A favourite of older, more experienced defence lawyers, this question usually involves a simple statement that you are invited to agree with by responding "yes" or "no."

A skillful defence lawyer will build upon his initial, apparently innocuous statement with further questions that, through clever semantics, may lead you into agreeing with suggestions that are far from your true perception of the facts.

If you suspect that this tactic is being used, your best defence is to listen carefully to the exact wording of the question and to respond with a full statement of the relevant facts. This will break the rhythm of the questioning, and provide the court with a more accurate explanation of the evidence.

6. Do not allow yourself to be confused by rapid-fire or multiple questions.

   a.   Your questioner may be attempting to lure you into giving ill-considered answers.

   b.   This tactic is as obvious as it is common; simply slow down your pace of speech and think before responding.

   c.   If you are asked a multiple-part question, ask to have each segment repeated or rephrased so that each can be answered independently of the other.

7. If you are asked to identify an exhibit, examine it carefully. Be sure you see your mark or identifying tag before confirming that it is the exhibit that you handled during your investigation.

8. Describe in detail all distances so that they will be clear to anyone who reads the transcript.

9. Refer to yourself in your testimony as "I," never "we." You can testify only to what you experienced personally.

10. Always face the jurors when giving your response. You are speaking to them, not the examining counsel.

PART THREE
PERSONAL CHALLENGES

18. ETHICS

I. Introduction

Because of the special trust and authority bestowed upon them by society, police officers must meet a standard of professional and ethical conduct that exceeds that of most other professions and occupations. At the same time, police work presents officers with numerous opportunities to receive unethical or illegal personal benefits: drug dealers are normally arrested with large amounts of cash on their persons; criminal investigators routinely acquire highly personal and sensitive information that could be sold to private individuals or organizations for large amounts of money; even routine traffic stops can present opportunities for petty bribery.

In the vast majority of these cases, police officers respond in a manner that does credit to both themselves and the policing profession. However, the cases of police corruption that have come to light across North America in recent years suggest that constant, strenuous reinforcement of ethical standards is required in every police service.

For many officers, problems arise when they are presented with a situation in which they are forced to choose between opposing standards, both of which they feel they must uphold. For example, if an officer witnesses his partner using excessive force on a suspect, that officer's personal loyalty comes into immediate conflict with his duty to enforce the law and comply with departmental policy. A different kind of conflict confronts the officer who encounters a sympathetic individual who has committed a petty act of theft or trespass in order to survive the night; even though the law has clearly been broken, the officer may decide that it is in no one's best interest that the case be prosecuted.

Complicating matters further is the fact that not all police officers share the same set of ethical standards. Some tend to view the law itself as a maze of complicated and misguided rules that prevent them from doing their job the way they feel it should be done. Such officers may create a world of "shadow rules," an unwritten code of police conduct that prevails over official department procedures and the law itself. They may also come to believe that the pressure to improve performance with respect to numbers of arrests, traffic tickets, and other measurable activities requires them to "bend the rules" in order to win recognition and promotion.

In these difficult circumstances, there is no easy solution to ensuring that police officers perform appropriately. But acceptance of a realistic and broadly supported set of ethical standards can go a long way toward ensuring that honest police officers are recognized, rewarded, and promoted to positions of leadership within their organizations.

II. Personal Factors Underlying Ethical Decisions

A. *Sense of Duty*

1. How you resolve conflicts between your sense of duty as a police officer and your personal sense of responsibility to others as a humane, caring person

2. Examples: "If I follow departmental policy and make an arrest in this situation, will anyone really be better off?" "Now that I've determined that this homeless person should be released, do I have an obligation to help him find shelter?"

B. *Sense of Loyalty*

1. How you resolve conflicts between your loyalties to different groups and individuals

2. Example: "Is my primary obligation to protect a fellow officer who used excessive force in subduing a suspect, or to report his actions to my supervisor in order to protect the reputation of the service as a whole?"

C. *Honesty*

1. How far you are prepared to go in order to ensure that the truth, as you understand it, prevails

2. Examples: "To be an effective police officer, do I have to violate my personal standards of honesty and trustworthiness?" "Am I prepared to fabricate the circumstances of an arrest in order to prevent valuable evidence from being ruled inadmissible in court?"

D. *Sense of Justice*

1. How you define what is morally right and wrong, without regard for legal or other standards imposed by others

2. Example: "Is what I'm being asked to do by my fellow officers or supervisors in accordance with my own natural sense of justice in this situation?"

III. Resolving Ethical Dilemmas

In a society in which strict enforcement of every law is neither desirable nor expected, it would be impossible to establish a code of conduct or set of guidelines broad enough to encompass every situation that a police officer might face while on duty. However, considering the following questions may assist you in working through an ethical dilemma.

1. What were the circumstances that gave rise to the dilemma?
2. What written instructions or guidelines can you consult? (e.g., departmental code of ethics or directives, Judges' Rules, Criminal Code of Canada, Canadian Charter of Rights and Freedoms (see Appendix), other relevant documents and publications)
3. Which individuals should you consult? Your partner? Your supervisor? The Crown Attorney's office?
4. What are your options, and what are the pros and cons of each?
5. Who would be hurt and who would be helped by each option, and to what extent?
6. Which option would have the most/least effect in resolving the problem?
7. Is there a decision you can make that (a) fully respects the rights and needs of everyone involved, and (b) is consistent with both your personal standards of integrity and your duties as a police officer?
8. Are you confident that the decision you make today will seem to have been the right one a year from now? Five years from now?
9. Would you feel comfortable telling your fellow officers, your supervisor, and your chief about your decision? What about family and friends?
10. Could you testify truthfully about your intended actions in court without exposing yourself or your police service to criticism or legal liability?
11. Would you feel ashamed if your actions were recorded on videotape, without your knowledge, and reported in the news media?

Illustration 16
EDMONTON POLICE SERVICE:
THE POLICE OFFICER'S CODE OF ETHICS

As a police officer, I recognize my primary obligation is to serve the public effectively and efficiently by protecting lives and property, preventing and detecting offences, and preserving peace and order.

I will faithfully administer the law in a just, impartial, and reasonable manner, preserving the equality, rights, and privileges of citizens as afforded by law.

I accept that all persons, rich or poor, old or young, learned or illiterate, are equally entitled to courtesy, understanding, and compassion. I will not be disparaging of any race, creed, or class of people.

In the performance of my duties I acknowledge the limits of my authority and promise not to use it for my personal advantage. I vow never to accept gratuities or favours or compromise myself or the department in any way. I will conduct my public and private life as an example of stability, fidelity, and morality, and without equivocation adhere to the same standards of conduct which I am bound by duty to enforce.

I will exercise self-discipline at all times. I will act with propriety toward my associates in law enforcement and the criminal justice system. With self-confidence, decisiveness, and courage, I will accept all the challenges, hardships, and vicissitudes of my profession. In relationships with my colleagues I will endeavour to develop an esprit de corps.

I will preserve the dignity of all persons and subordinate my own self-interest for the common good. I will be faithful in my allegiance to Queen and country. I will honour the obligations of my office and strive to attain excellence in the performance of my duties.

19. JOB STRESS
I. Introduction

Although law enforcement is often considered to be a physically dangerous profession, its emotional dangers are far greater. By nature, police officers tend to mask their emotional responses to their frequent encounters with violence, tragedy, and death. They are usually idealistic and believe strongly in such values as courage and inner strength.

Although many officers are extremely successful in masking their emotional responses to stressful situations, this does not mean that these encounters have no effect. After several years of service, many police officers lose enthusiasm for their work, find difficulty in relating to their friends and family, and develop other symptoms of "optorectalitis"—a term sometimes used in police circles to describe "a crappy outlook on life." These officers are not emotionally weak; they are simply human beings who, like all human beings, must eventually react to the powerful effects of stress. And they are not alone; some authorities believe that as much as 60 to 80 percent of all human disease is stress-related.

Stress is not necessarily either good or evil in itself; it is simply a response to external stimuli. The circumstances in which it arises and the way you deal with it determine whether stress has a positive or negative effect. In a dangerous situation, for example, stress causes the "fight or flight" reaction—heightened senses, faster heartbeat, higher adrenaline levels—which helps you to deal with the danger more effectively.

If you are passed over for a promotion you feel you deserve, you are also placed in a stressful situation. If you brood about it, become resentful and insubordinate, and eventually assault a prisoner or an innocent civilian to vent your frustration, the stress has a negative effect. On the other hand, if the missed promotion causes you to re-examine your life, to take further educational programs, and to resolve to become a more effective officer, the stress effect has been highly positive.

Stress is an inevitable factor in human existence; how you cope with it will determine its effect on your police career—and your life.

II. The Causes and Effects of Stress

A. Definition

Stress—Nervous tension that results from internal conflicts evolving from a wide range of external situations

B. Major Stress Factors in Police Work

1. Routine and boring tasks:

 a. Excessive paperwork
 b. Dull or unnecessary meetings
 c. Patrol of the same area for long periods of time
 d. Continually investigating the same type of offences
 e. Continually encountering negative criminal personalities

2. Communications breakdown:

 a. A belief that you are not appreciated or supported by superiors, subordinates, peers, or the courts
 b. An inability to make others understand or accept your point of view
 c. Difficulty in understanding the opinions of persons outside police work, e.g., family, friends, social acquaintances, etc.

3. Shift work
4. Work overload:

 a. Unpredictable, fluctuating work pattern
 b. A sense of being weighed down by the burden of your responsibilities
 c. Excessive overtime that disrupts sleep, family, and social life

5. Role conflict:

 a. Frustration at the public and legal perception of a police officer as a cool, impartial agent of the law who is not entitled to make mistakes or feel emotions. This perception conflicts with your belief in yourself as a normal, fallible human being who is entitled to have feelings, express opinions, and occasionally commit a minor error or transgression.
 b. Conflict between your self-image as a protector and servant of the public, and the hostility that you often experience from its members in carrying out your duties

6. Threat response:

 a. Frequent exposure to potentially fatal or injurious incidents, e.g., gun calls, violent domestics, fires, bomb searches, etc.
 b. Your duty to risk your life or well-being in situations for which you are not personally responsible, e.g., robberies in

progress, high-speed chases, hostage situations, violent domestics, etc.

7. Frequent encounters with death and suffering
8. Cultural conflict—Dealing with individuals or groups whose customs and moral values differ from, or are in conflict with, your own
9. Decision-making responsibility:

   a.   Being required to make instant decisions that may have life-or-death consequences for yourself and others

   b.   Awareness that your decisions will be closely scrutinized and criticized by your fellow officers, your superiors, and the courts

10. Lack of advancement:

    a.   A perception that there are few opportunities for promotion in your organization

    b.   A belief that less effective or less qualified officers are being promoted above you

11. Empathy—A sharing of the pain of others who have been victimized or brutalized
12. Social restrictions—Subtle or overt rejection by others at social occasions, such as dances and parties, because you are a police officer

III. Symptoms of Negative Stress Reaction (Burnout)

A. Psychological Reactions

1. Poor attitude
2. Alcohol or drug abuse
3. Excessive smoking
4. Lack of motivation
5. Constant fatigue
6. Loss of self-esteem
7. Poor or lackadaisical job performance
8. Cynical, uncaring attitude toward others
9. Constant irritability
10. Frequent insomnia
11. Use of tranquillizers
12. Sense of persecution
13. Anxiety attacks
14. Depression
15. Marital discord
16. Aggressive behaviour

17. Inflexible attitudes
18. Hardening of emotions

B. *Physical Reactions*

1. Headaches
2. Ulcers
3. Diabetes
4. Asthma or other respiratory problems
5. Psychosomatic illnesses
6. High blood pressure
7. Cholesterol or heart problems
8. Allergic respiratory response (frequent colds, rash on legs, etc.)
9. Twitching eyes or facial muscles
10. Dry throat
11. Tension aches or pains in stomach, back, neck, and forehead

IV. **Preventative Action**

A. *Regular Self-Assessment*

1. Undertake periodic, constructive reviews of your personal achievements, goals, and difficulties.
2. Avoid dwelling on past mistakes or disappointments. They cannot be changed; their only value to you in the present is to teach you ways to deal with the future.

B. *Personal Improvement*

1. The best defence against negative stress is personal growth.
2. Actively work to increase your interest in your career by reading, attending courses, and discussing police-related issues.
3. Take all available courses, not only in police subjects, but in such areas as psychology, business management, history, and English that can be of indirect benefit in your work.
4. If circumstances prevent you from advancing in your career at the moment, remember that there is horizontal as well as vertical growth.

   a. Learn about fingerprinting, forensic science, criminal law, administration, hostage negotiations, and other police-related subjects that will expand your professional knowledge.
   b. When an opening does appear, you will be ready.
5. Enhance your sense of long-term security by developing a financial plan to manage your investments and prepare for your retirement.
6. Attend stress management workshops.

C. *Physical Fitness*

1. Participate in a regular program of aerobic exercise.

    a. Physical activities that develop heart and lung capacity, such as running, walking, and swimming, have been proven to reduce stress, disease, and fatigue.

    b. Achieving a high degree of physical fitness will dramatically increase your ability to deal with violent or emergency situations.

2. Follow sound nutritional practices.

    a. Make your lunch hour a rest break from police work if department policy permits. Avoid eating in the cruiser or at the station.

    b. Cut down on your consumption of salt and sugar (potato chips and soft drinks), caffeine (tea, coffee, and chocolate), and nicotine (cigarettes).

    c. Include generous portions of fresh fruit, vegetables, and whole grain cereals in your diet.

3. Learn to practise deep-relaxation techniques in times of extreme stress.

D. *Time Management*

1. Many psychologists believe that the practice of delaying tasks that you know must be done creates a high degree of stress.

2. To avoid procrastinating:

    a. Try to complete your most unpleasant duties first each day, saving your most pleasant jobs as a kind of personal reward.

    b. Realize that most jobs do not have to be perfect. Don't waste time attempting to achieve perfection on tasks that aren't worth the trouble.

    c. When undertaking a massive project, do not be discouraged by the sheer size of the job to be done.

    (1) Divide the job into smaller tasks that can be completed comfortably on a daily basis.

    (2) Limit your span of concentration to the easily manageable task at hand; avoid thinking about the project as a whole.

    (3) Once all the small tasks have been completed, review the entire job to ensure consistency of approach, lack of duplication, etc.

3. Create a list of short- and long-term career and personal goals.

4. Work out a personal action plan to achieve these goals.

5. Plan your activities on a daily, weekly, monthly, and annual basis to achieve the same goals.

6. Assign a priority number to each task on your daily activity list.

   a. Endeavour to complete at least two or three of your top-priority items each day, and move the remaining items to the next day's list.

   b. Revise your priorities frequently to ensure that the level you have assigned remains realistic. For example, if you have a job to do with a deadline six months away, which you know you can complete in six weeks, you may assign it a priority 6 today; 30 weeks from now, if it has not been started, you will probably want to make it a 1 or 2 priority.

E. *Social Relationships*

1. Fellow police officers can share an understanding and concern that you may not experience in the "outside world." These relationships can be extremely supportive and helpful.

2. Outside friends can, however, give you a broader perspective with which to deal with internal conflicts and problems. They can also remind you that the world isn't as bad as it sometimes seems, thus helping you to avoid developing an "us versus them" attitude.

3. Avoid lengthy gripe sessions with fellow officers. They may deepen your sense of frustration and depression by feeding a problem until it has grown out of all proportion to its true dimensions.

4. Do not allow yourself to become a passive victim of circumstance. Plan your daily activities to achieve a balance between your responsibilities to your job, your family, and yourself.

   a. Schedule at least one activity each day that gives you something to look forward to.

   b. Avoid doing boring or repetitive tasks just to fill time. Decide what you want to do with your time and do it.

   c. Take things one at a time. Many persons become involved in doing too many things at once. The result? They never accomplish anything.

5. Plan your days off in advance so that you always have something enjoyable or worthwhile to do, even if shift work prevents you from being joined by friends or family. Wasting your days off will cause you to develop a sense of frustration about police work that, combined with other factors, can be extremely stressful.

6. Get enough rest.

    a. Experiment with your sleeping habits to determine how many hours of sleep you need each night to avoid fatigue.

    b. Take this result into account in drawing up your daily activity plan.

7. Learn to accept situations that are beyond your power to change.

8. Draw a clear separation in your mind between your professional and your personal life.

EXAMPLE: I knew of a police chief who took this separation principle very seriously. He arrived at work each morning in civilian clothes and changed into his uniform before going into his office. At the end of his working day, he showered and changed back into civilian clothes before leaving the building. The act of changing back and forth was a symbolic gesture that drew a clear dividing line between his personal and his professional lives.

9. Find a "third place" where you can be alone with yourself, outside the home and police environments.

    a. Your third place might be your den, a jogging track, a library, or the act of going for a nightly walk—any place or activity where your family and professional lives can't intrude.

    b. Use your third place to read, meditate, paint, play a musical instrument, enjoy a hobby, or undertake any other pleasurable activity that you want to do.

10. Learn to say "no."

    a. In your personal life you will often be called upon to undertake tasks that are beyond your expertise, your interests, or your responsibility.

    b. These tasks can create stress through frustration and should be avoided if possible.

11. Schedule controllable stressful events so that they are spread out and can be dealt with comfortably.

    a. Any change in your life (e.g., a promotion, transfer, marriage, divorce, moving, etc.) will cause stress to varying degrees.

    b. A combination of stressful events could lead to an overload that results in physical as well as emotional illness.

EXAMPLE: Don't plan to move the day after your wedding, which also happens to be two days before your scheduled promotion and transfer to a new station.

F. *Attitude*

1. Although a suspicious nature is an asset to an effective police officer, don't carry that attitude into your personal relationships. Your spouse and children will not be pleased if you use field interrogation techniques around the home to deal with family problems.

2. Counteract the negative impact of frequent encounters with criminal behaviour, citizen hostility, and human suffering by sharing your feelings and concerns with family members and close friends.

3. Consider life's problems to be challenges, not tragedies.

   a. Some psychologists believe that personal attitude makes the difference between individuals who "crack" under pressure and those who don't.

   b. Strong persons view their emotional response to personal tragedies as hurdles to be overcome, not catastrophes to be endured.

3. Commit yourself fully to your job and your family.

   a. Never allow yourself to think that "nobody cares" or that what you do doesn't matter.

   b. If you have any doubts about your importance in the scheme of things, consider the tragedies that have occurred when police services have been withdrawn during labour actions.

   c. You have qualified for admission to one of the most worthwhile, interesting, and demanding jobs in the world. You have every reason to be proud of what you do, and what you have achieved.

APPENDIX

CANADIAN CHARTER OF RIGHTS AND FREEDOMS

Whereas Canada is founded upon principles that recognize the supremacy of God and the rule of law:

Guarantee of Rights and Freedoms

Rights and freedoms in Canada

1. *The Canadian Charter of Rights and Freedoms* guarantees the rights and freedoms set out in it subject only to such reasonable limits prescribed by law as can be demonstrably justified in a free and democratic society.

Fundamental Freedoms

Fundamental freedoms

2. Everyone has the following fundamental freedoms:
(a) freedom of conscience and religion;
(b) freedom of thought, belief, opinion and expression, including freedom of the press and other media of communication;
(c) freedom of peaceful assembly; and
(d) freedom of association

Democratic Rights

Democratic rights of citizens

3. Every citizen of Canada has the right to vote in an election of members of the House of Commons or of a legislative assembly and to be qualified for membership therein.

Maximum duration of legislative bodies

4. (1) No House of Commons and no legislative assembly shall continue for longer than five years from the date fixed for the return of the writs at a general election of its members.

Continuation in special circumstances

(2) In time of real or apprehended war, invasion or insurrection, a House of Commons may be continued by Parliament and a legislative assembly may be continued by the legislature beyond five years if such continuation is not opposed by the votes of more than one-third of the members of the House of Commons or the legislative assembly, as the case may be.

Annual sitting of legislative bodies

5. There shall be a sitting of Parliament and of each legislature at least once every twelve months.

Mobility Rights

Mobility of citizens

6. (1) Every citizen of Canada has the right to enter, remain in and leave Canada.

Rights to move and gain livelihood

(2) Every citizen of Canada and every person who has the status of a permanent resident of Canada has the right
   (a) to move and take up residence in any province; and
   (b) to pursue the gaining of livelihood in any province.

Limitation

(3) The rights specified in subsection (2) are subject to
   (a) any laws or practices of general application in force in a province other than those that discriminate among persons primarily on the basis of province of present or previous residence; and
   (b) any laws providing for reasonable residency requirements as a qualification for the receipt of publicly provided social services.

Affirmative action programs

(4) Subsections (2) and (3) do not preclude any law, program or activity that has as its object the amelioration in a province of conditions of individuals in that province who are socially or economically disadvantaged if the rate of employment in that province is below the rate of employment in Canada.

Legal Rights

Life, liberty and security of person

7. Everyone has the right to life, liberty and security of the person and the right not to be deprived thereof except in accordance with the principles of fundamental justice.

Search or seizure

8. Everyone has the right to be secure against unreasonable search or seizure.

Detention of imprisonment

9. Everyone has the right not to be arbitrarily detained or imprisoned.

Arrest or detention

10. Everyone has the right on arrest or detention

(a) to be informed promptly of the reasons therefor;

(b) to retain and instruct counsel without delay and to be informed of that right; and

(c) to have the validity of the detention determined by way of *habeas corpus* and to be released if the detention is not lawful.

Proceedings in criminal and penal matters

11. Any person charged with an offence has the right

(a) to be informed without reasonable delay of the specific offence;

(b) to be tried within a reasonable time;

(c) not to be compelled to be a witness in proceedings against that person in respect of the offence;

(d) to be presumed innocent until proven guilty according to law in a fair and public hearing by an independent and impartial tribunal;

(e) not to be denied reasonable bail without just cause;

(f) except in the case of an offence under military law tried before a military tribunal, to the benefit of trial by jury where the maximum punishment for the offence is imprisonment for five years or a more severe punishment;

(g) not to be found guilty on account of any act or omission unless, at the time of the act or omission, it constituted an offence under Canadian or international law or was criminal according to

the general principles of law recognized by the community of nations;

(h) if finally acquitted of the offence, not to be tried for it again and, if finally found guilty and punished for the offence, not to be tried or punished for it again; and

(i) if found guilty of the offence and if the punishment for the offence has been varied between the time of commission and the time of sentencing, to the benefit of the lesser punishment.

Treatment or punishment

12. Everyone has the right not to be subjected to any cruel and unusual treatment or punishment.

Self-incrimination

13. A witness who testifies in any proceedings has the right not to have any incriminating evidence so given used to incriminate that witness in any other proceedings, except in a prosecution for perjury or for the giving of contradictory evidence.

Interpreter

14. A party or witness in any proceedings who does not understand or speak the language in which the proceedings are conducted or who is deaf has the right to the assistance of an interpreter.

Equality Rights

Equality before and under law and equal protection and benefit of law

15. (1) Every individual is equal before and under the law and has the right to the equal protection and equal benefit of the law without discrimination and, in particular, without discrimination based on race, national or ethnic origin, colour, religion, sex, age or mental or physical disability.

Affirmative action programs

(2) Subsection (1) does not preclude any law, program or activity that has as its object the amelioration of conditions of disadvantaged individuals or groups including those that are disadvantaged because of race, national or ethnic origin, colour, religion, sex, age or mental or physical disability.

Official Languages of Canada

Official languages of Canada

16. (1) English and French are the official languages of Canada and have equality of status and

equal rights and privileges as to their use in all institutions of the Parliament and government of Canada.

Official languages of New Brunswick

(2) English and French are the official languages of New Brunswick and have equality of status and equal rights and privileges as to their use in all institutions of the legislature and government of New Brunswick.

Advancement of status and use

(3) Nothing in this charter limits the authority of Parliament or a legislature to advance the equality of status or use of English and French.

Proceedings of Parliament

17. (1) Everyone has the right to use English or French in any debates and other proceedings of Parliament.

Proceedings of New Brunswick legislature

(2) Everyone has the right to use English or French in any debates and other proceedings of the legislature of New Brunswick.

Parliamentary statutes and records

18. (1) The statutes, records and journals of Parliament shall be printed and published in English and French and both language versions are equally authoritative.

New Brunswick statutes and records

(2) The statutes, records and journals of the legislature of New Brunswick shall be printed and published in English and French and both language versions are equally authoritative.

Proceedings in courts established by Parliament

19. (1) Either English or French may be used by any person in, or in any pleading in or process issuing from, any court established by Parliament.

Proceedings in New Brunswick courts

(2) Either English or French may be used by any person in, or in any pleading in or process issuing from, any court of New Brunswick.

Communications by public with federal institutions

20. (1) Any member of the public in Canada has the right to communicate with, and to receive available services from, any head or central office of an institution of the Parliament or government of Canada in English or French, and has the same right with respect to any other office of any such institution where

(a) there is a significant demand for communications with and services from that office in such language; or

(b) due to the nature of the office, it is reasonable that communications with and services from that office be available in both English and French.

Communications by public with New Brunswick institutions

(2) Any member of the public in New Brunswick has the right to communicate with, and to receive available services from, any office of an institution of the legislature or government of New Brunswick in English or French.

Continuation of existing constitutional provisions

21. Nothing in sections 16 to 20 abrogates or derogates from any right, privilege or obligation with respect to the English and French languages, or either of them, that exists or is continued by virtue of any other provision of the Constitution of Canada.

Rights and privileges preserved

22. Nothing in sections 16 to 20 abrogates or derogates from any legal or customary right or privilege acquired or enjoyed either before or after the coming into force of this Charter with respect to any language that is not English or French.

Minority Language Education Rights

Language of instruction

23. (1) Citizens of Canada

(a) whose first language learned and still understood is that of the English or French linguistic minority population of the province in which they reside, or

(b) who have received their primary school instruction in Canada in English or French and reside in a province where the language in which they received that instruction is the language of the English or French linguistic minority population of that province,

have the right to have their children receive primary and secondary school instruction in that language in that province.

Continuity of language instruction

(2) Citizens of Canada of whom any child has received or is receiving primary or secondary

school instruction in English or French in Canada, have the right to have their children receive primary and secondary school instruction in the same language.

Application where numbers warrant

(3) The right of citizens of Canada under subsections (1) and (2) to have their children receive primary and secondary school instruction in the language of the English or French linguistic minority population of a province

(a) applies wherever in the province the number of children of citizens who have such a right is sufficient to warrant the provision to them out of public funds of minority language instruction; and

(b) includes, where the number of those children so warrants, the right to have them receive that instruction in minority language educational facilities provided out of public funds.

Enforcement

Enforcement of guaranteed rights and freedoms

24. (1) Anyone whose rights or freedoms, as guaranteed by this Charter, have been infringed or denied may apply to a court of competent jurisdiction to obtain such remedy as the court considers appropriate and just in the circumstances.

Exclusion of evidence bringing administration of justice into disrepute

(2) Where, in proceedings under subsection (1), a court concludes that evidence was obtained in a manner that infringed or denied any rights or freedoms guaranteed by this Charter, the evidence shall be excluded if it is established that, having regard to all the circumstances, the admission of it in the proceedings would bring the administration of justice into disrepute.

General

Aboriginal rights and freedoms not affected by Charter

25. The guarantee of this Charter of certain rights and freedoms shall not be construed so as to abrogate or derogate from any aboriginal, treaty or other rights or freedoms that pertain to the aboriginal peoples of Canada including

(a) any rights or freedoms that have been recognized by the Royal Proclamation of October 7, 1763, and

(b) any rights or freedoms that may be acquired by the aboriginal peoples of Canada by way of land claims settlement.

Other rights and freedoms not affected by Charter

26. The guarantee in this Charter of certain rights and freedoms shall not be construed as denying the existence of any other rights or freedoms that exist in Canada.

Multicultural heritage

27. This Charter shall be interpreted in a manner consistent with the preservation and enhancement of the multicultural heritage of Canadians.

Rights guaranteed equally to both sexes

28. Notwithstanding anything in this Charter, the rights and freedoms referred to in it are guaranteed equally to male and female persons.

Rights respecting certain schools preserved

29. Nothing in this Charter abrogates or derogates from any rights or privileges guaranteed by or under the Constitution of Canada in respect of denominational, separate or dissentient schools.

Application to territories and territorial authorities

30. A reference in this Charter to a province or to the legislative assembly or legislature of a province shall be deemed to include a reference to the Yukon Territory and the Northwest Territories, or to the appropriate legislative authority thereof, as the case may be.

Legislative powers not extended

31. Nothing in this Charter extends the legislative powers of any body or authority.

Application of Charter

Application of Charter

32. (1) This Charter applies

(a) to the Parliament and government of Canada in respect of all matters within the authority of Parliament including all matters relating to the Yukon Territory and Northwest Territories; and

(b) to the legislature and government of each province in respect of all matters within the authority of the legislature of each province.

Exception

(2) Notwithstanding subsection (1), section 15 shall not have effect until three years after this section comes into force.

Exception where express declaration

33. (1) Parliament or the legislature of a province may expressly declare in an Act of Parliament or of the legislature, as the case may be, that the Act or a provision thereof shall operate notwithstanding a provision included in section 2 or sections 7 to 15 of this Charter.

Operation of exception

(2) An Act or a provision of an Act in respect of which a declaration made under this section is in effect shall have such operation as it would have but for the provision of this Charter referred to in the declaration.

Five year limitation

(3) A declaration made under subsection (1) shall cease to have effect five years after it comes into force or on such earlier date as may be specified in the declaration.

Re-enactment

(4) Parliament or a legislature of a province may re-enact a declaration made under subsection (1).

Citation

Citation

34. This Part may be cited as the *Canadian Charter of Rights and Freedoms.*

INDEX